Approaches to Teaching
English Renaissance Drama

Approaches to Teaching
World Literature

Joseph Gibaldi, series editor

For a complete listing of titles,
see the last pages of this book.

Approaches to Teaching English Renaissance Drama

Edited by

Karen Bamford

and

Alexander Leggatt

The Modern Language Association of America
New York   2002

For information about obtaining permission to reprint material from
MLA book publications, send your request by mail (see address below),
e-mail (permissions@mla.org), or fax (646 458-0030).

Library of Congress Cataloging-in-Publication Data

Approaches to teaching English Renaissance drama / edited by Karen
Bamford and Alexander Leggatt.
p. cm. — (Approaches to teaching world literature ; 75)
Includes bibliographical references and index.
ISBN 0–87352–773–9—ISBN 0–87352–774–7 (pbk.)
1. English drama—Early modern and Elizabethan, 1500–1600—Study and
teaching.   2. English drama—17th century—Study and teaching.   3.
Renaissance—England—Study and teaching.   I. Bamford, Karen.   II.
Leggatt, Alexander.   III. Series.
PR653 .A67 2002
822'.309—dc21   2002014761
ISSN 1059-1133

Cover illustration of the paperback edition: Title page from a 1658 edition of *A Witch of
Edmonton: A Known True Story*, by William Rowley, Thomas Dekker, John Ford & Co.
Courtesy of the Huntington Library

Set in Caledonia and Bauer Bodoni. Printed on acid-free, recycled paper

Published by The Modern Language Association of America
26 Broadway, New York, New York 10004-1789
www.mla.org

CONTENTS

PREFACE TO THE SERIES

In *The Art of Teaching* Gilbert Highet wrote, "Bad teaching wastes a great deal of effort, and spoils many lives which might have been full of energy and happiness." All too many teachers have failed in their work, Highet argued, simply "because they have not thought about it." We hope that the Approaches to Teaching World Literature series, sponsored by the Modern Language Association's Publications Committee, will not only improve the craft—as well as the art—of teaching but also encourage serious and continuing discussion of the aims and methods of teaching literature.

The principal objective of the series is to collect within each volume different points of view on teaching a specific literary work, a literary tradition, or a writer widely taught at the undergraduate level. The preparation of each volume begins with a wide-ranging survey of instructors, thus enabling us to include in the volume the philosophies and approaches, thoughts and methods of scores of experienced teachers. The result is a sourcebook of material, information, and ideas on teaching the subject of the volume to undergraduates. The series is intended to serve nonspecialists as well as specialists, inexperienced as well as experienced teachers, graduate students who wish to learn effective ways of teaching as well as senior professors who wish to compare their own approaches with the approaches of colleagues in other schools. Of course, no volume in the series can ever substitute for erudition, intelligence, creativity, and sensitivity in teaching. We hope merely that each book will point readers in useful directions; at most each will offer only a first step in the long journey to successful teaching.

Joseph Gibaldi
Series Editor

PREFACE TO THE VOLUME

The teaching of non-Shakespearean English Renaissance drama presents many challenges, not the least of which is that it is non-Shakespearean. While versions of Shakespeare's work are a constant presence in our culture, including our popular culture, his contemporaries seem more rooted in their own time and their own theater. Yet while this means an extra historical effort to gain access to them, that very effort is one of the rewards of teaching them. Getting in touch with a culture radically different from ours and with a theater whose conventions seem stylized, even at times bizarre, allows those moments of discovery that make a classroom come alive. In the process our students may learn that Shakespeare himself belongs to that lost world and requires the same effort; but they will also learn that his contemporaries are writers with their own distinctive voices, often very unlike his, demanding and rewarding attention in their own right, and that for all their initial strangeness, there is much that we can recognize in the images of life they offer. Finally, having got to know them, we return to our own world, able to look at it with fresh eyes, as one looks at one's own country with fresh eyes after having been away from it for a while. This interplay of the strange and the familiar runs through our teaching of Renaissance drama and through the essays in this collection.

In line with the general aims of this series, the essays gathered here are written by professionals in the field and based on their classroom experience. Accordingly, they are not so much conventional critical essays (though the issues that concern contemporary criticism are certainly present here) as they are practical advice, offered by teachers to other teachers, about methods they have found helpful in bringing these plays to life in the classroom. The central focus is on approaches. A collection of conventional criticism might have tried to ensure coverage author by author and play by play to make sure that major texts were dealt with, thereby establishing (for its own purposes at least) a kind of canon. We have thought it more important, and more consistent with the aims of the volume and the series, to ensure that major approaches are covered. This kind of coverage in fact extends the usefulness of the essays. Using the principle stated by Sherlock Holmes ("You know my methods, Watson; apply them"), a reader about to teach *Volpone* can apply to that play the advice in Joseph Candido's essay on teaching Jonson's language in *The Alchemist*. Thomas Akstens's essay on the demonic in *Doctor Faustus* can be applied to Robert Greene's *Friar Bacon and Friar Bungay*, Lori Schroeder Haslem's essay on the female body in *A Woman Killed with Kindness* and *The Duchess of Malfi* to *'Tis Pity She's a Whore*—and so on.

At the same time, though we are not concerned to establish a canon of plays, the authors generally recognized as most important, such as Marlowe,

Jonson, Webster, and Middleton, figure prominently here, and the essays range widely over different genres and styles. A reader in search of a particular play that does not appear in the essay titles may well find a substantial discussion of it by consulting the index of titles. Nor are the texts discussed here always the most familiar ones. *The Tragedy of Mariam* is just starting to find its way into the canon, propelled by a new interest in women writers. *The Witch of Edmonton* has not yet found the prominence it arguably deserves, though it can be a rich discovery for those who encounter it. Lesser-known works can be the growing edge of the canon, and it is appropriate that some of them should find a place here. The question of how the canon changes is itself a fascinating one and will be dealt with later in the volume in the second half of my essay, "The Strangeness of Renaissance Drama." But it should be noted here that changes in the popularity of plays are bound up with changes in critical approach, and decisions about approach have largely determined the plays discussed here. As an early reader of this volume remarked, "The plays we ask our students to read are by and large those which serve our own purposes and preoccupations." They are the plays that concern us now. If we were to go with the plays most popular with the original audiences, this collection might have been dominated by essays on *Mucedorus*.

The first stage in the preparation of this volume was a survey of teachers to get a sense of their approaches, their concerns, the methods and resources they use. The result can be seen as a rough preliminary discussion, a kind of transcontinental brainstorming session, out of which, refined and selected through second thoughts, came the essays (some volunteered, some commissioned) in this volume. We begin by summarizing the results of the questionnaires: first, a survey of classroom practice, then a summary of information on the resources instructors use. A resource now widely used in the teaching of Shakespeare is filmed performance; Philippa Sheppard's filmography lists what is available for the work of Shakespeare's contemporaries, a list that will surprise those who assume there is virtually nothing.

The remainder of the volume deals with approaches to teaching, beginning with an introductory essay that comments on some of the main concerns of the collection and deals with the changing canon. The essays then fall into three sections. The first concerns texts and resources, beginning with texts. Leah S. Marcus alerts us to the problems in our most basic resource by raising the question, what is a text? A. R. Braunmuller surveys available resources on original performance conditions, and Philippa Sheppard shows how the use of visual material can give students a sense of the world in which these plays were written.

We have called the remaining two sections "Strategies" and "Contexts," recognizing a difference in emphasis between essays concerning practical, hands-on classroom methods and essays concerning the shaping of cultural and historical context for classroom use—essays, in other words, focusing on method and essays focusing on material. Since method and material are of course bound up with each other, the division will seem a little arbitrary at times. Discussions of method rightly touch on material and vice versa. The division is not intended to be a sealed border, but we have found it useful as a way of shaping the overall discussion.

The surveys place great emphasis on language as a challenge in teaching Renaissance drama, and the section on strategies begins with an essay on this basic starting point, Joseph Candido's account of how he teaches the language of *The Alchemist*. Equally basic is the question of authorship, and the collaborative essay by Jayson B. Brown, William W. E. Slights, and Reta Terry describes appropriately collaborative methods to alert students to the issues involved in multiauthor plays. Frances Teague describes a method for dealing with basic reading problems students may have on a first encounter, and James Hirsh and Theodore B. Leinwand show how they apply specific reading strategies to particular plays. The collection then turns from reading the text to performing it. Helen Ostovich provides a wide-ranging essay on teaching through performance, while Laurie Maguire focuses on a particular play, *The Tragedy of Mariam*, and Ric Knowles ends the group by questioning the assumptions involved in teaching through performance. C. E. McGee ends the section with a strategy for using the new, still developing resource of the Internet.

A focus on text, whether read or performed, has long been with us in teaching. In the criticism of Renaissance drama, context is now equally prominent. Arthur F. Kinney begins the section on context by showing how archival documents can alert students to questions of class and power. The same questions figure in Jan Stirm's essay, and her final turn to questions of race leads into Rebecca Ann Bach's essay on racial and religious difference. The linked questions of gender, the body, and sex are the subjects of essays by Christina Luckyj, Lori Schroeder Haslem, and Mario DiGangi, while Phebe Jensen's essay on festivity deals with social and material concerns of another kind. As Knowles ends the group of performance essays by questioning the assumptions involved, John Hunter ends the group of historical essays by questioning the ways we use history. The context of drama includes not just historical forces but the other arts, and Judith Weil's essay on *Bartholomew Fair* shows how to bring a play and a painting together. A sister art to drama is the masque, and a number of survey respondents include it in drama courses; Randall Ingram's essay discusses the issues involved in teaching this form. Context includes not just the time in which the plays were written but the time in which they now appear, and Thomas Akstens's essay on the demonic in *Doctor Faustus* bridges Marlowe's world and that of his students. In a parallel to C. E. McGee's essay ending the previous section, Paul Budra ends this one by putting us right into the world of the contemporary student, describing the use of popular film as a teaching resource.

The section on strategies begins with the close reading of language and ends with the Internet; the section on contexts begins with archival documents and ends with Quentin Tarantino. That in itself should indicate the wide range of opportunities, the play of past and present, involved in the teaching of English Renaissance drama.

A. L.

ACKNOWLEDGMENTS

We would like to thank all those colleagues who responded to the survey on teaching English Renaissance drama. Their generosity provided the basis for this volume. We are also grateful to the anonymous readers whose comments helped to strengthen the manuscript and to the series editor, Joseph Gibaldi, for his help throughout its development. We owe a special debt to Amanda Hathaway Jernigan for her timely assistance in preparing the list of works cited and the indexes.

Part One

PRACTICES AND MATERIALS

Classroom Practice

Alexander Leggatt

In the survey conducted in preparation for this volume, instructors were asked to report on the courses in which they teach Renaissance drama, the challenges and opportunities it presents, and the critical approaches they have found useful. Asked to describe the courses in which they taught Renaissance drama, nearly all respondents (forty out of forty-seven) wrote that it had a course to itself, for mostly mid- to upper-level students, from which Shakespeare was excluded. Nearly half reported teaching graduate courses in the subject. Respondents also listed around forty survey courses using from one to three Renaissance plays. Some courses on special topics (such as London, sexuality and gender, feminism and literature) use plays from this period. In short, the attention given to Renaissance drama is divided in roughly equal measure between treating it as a topic in its own right and seeing it in the context of a larger field of literature. The characteristic pace is to read one or two plays a week and to spend two or three hours of instruction time on each play.

In the lists of plays taught, there are two clear leaders, *Doctor Faustus* and *The Duchess of Malfi*; the former is particularly favored in survey courses; both plays figure in this collection. Other plays frequently mentioned include *The Alchemist, Arden of Faversham, Bartholomew Fair, The Changeling, A Chaste Maid in Cheapside, Edward II, Epicoene, The Jew of Malta, The Knight of the Burning Pestle, The Revenger's Tragedy, The Roaring Girl, The Shoemakers' Holiday, The Spanish Tragedy, Tamburlaine the Great* (both parts, though part 1 is sometimes taught alone), *'Tis Pity She's a Whore, The Tragedy of Mariam, Volpone, The White Devil,* and *A Woman Killed with Kindness.* The list indicates the range and variety of offerings, though it also shows that, Marlowe aside, in classroom practice Renaissance drama is usually Jacobean drama. Most of these plays are represented here, though inevitably not all of them. And long though the list is, it is not exhaustive. Some seventy other plays appear less frequently, and some masques, mostly by Jonson, are also mentioned.

The choice of plays is governed by both practical and philosophical reasons. Availability through inexpensive single editions or affordable anthologies is a key factor. Some instructors use anthologies, not always enthusiastically; others reject them altogether. Besides being guided by personal interest, instructors pick plays for their representativeness, their place in English drama's development, and their illustration of cultural themes. Though a few like to concentrate on a small number of writers, most prefer a wide and varied range.

A sample of reasons for the choice of particular plays includes *The Jew of Malta* for "the cultural presentation of race"; *Doctor Faustus* for the transition from "medieval to early modern culture"; *The Knight of the Burning Pestle* for "issues of class and audience participation"; and *The Duchess of Malfi* for "Jacobean darkness, issues of women's position." In a course called Women in Literature, *A Woman Killed with Kindness* figures in "a unit on anorexia."

Asked to say what aspects of Renaissance drama their students find most engaging, many respondents list issues of race, gender, sexuality, and politics; variations on this list appear in eighteen of the forty-seven surveys. A smaller number find their students enjoy the sensationalism: outrageous plots and characters, sex and violence, spectacle and "trendy cynicism." A few report an interest in considerations of genre and dramatic technique, in alternative staging possibilities, and in particular devices such as trial scenes and eavesdropping scenes.

According to over half the respondents the most difficult or challenging aspect of the subject is language. The problems include obscure jokes and classical allusions; Jonson and Webster are listed among the troublemakers. The most commonly reported solution is close reading, including reading aloud. Other difficulties include features listed elsewhere as engaging: the extravagance that leads to complex plotting and "bizarre last acts"; the difficulty of cracking the social codes involved in questions like race, class, and gender and the temptation to simplify the beliefs of this period into a single worldview. When instructors identify the most important features of this drama for their students to understand, the social issues listed above figure in roughly half the answers. So do theatrical considerations such as structure, genre, and performance possibilities. There is a good deal of overlap: "That these plays are products of the culture—and also why they are successful theater" is a characteristic response. Language is listed as a key issue in seven replies. Some instructors want their students to appreciate the sheer quality of the work, gaining "a new sense of respect for the accomplishments of the past."

On the question of what critical approaches or methodologies are most useful, one instructor speaks for many in declaring, "I'm a pluralist." Approaches that gain frequent mention include new historicism, feminism, performance-based criticism from scene work to stage history, close reading, and materialism including cultural materialism. Other topics range from queer theory to Aristotle's *Poetics* ("still"). Reflecting the general eclecticism, one respondent traces what seems to be a characteristic pattern: to begin with close reading, then go on to a wide range of topics (power, feminism, textual transmission) as appropriate for the play. (A similar progression can be traced in the structure of this volume.) Several respondents caution against getting too fixed in one approach or applying any approach too narrowly.

Most respondents stress the importance of historical context; among those who describe their methods of getting it into the classroom, eleven refer to lectures, ten to handouts (lists of secondary readings and samples of primary material), and three to student research projects. One combines extracts from contemporary documents, in-class critique of "a contentious essay," and scene work: "I choose an issue-laden scene, get the students to read it aloud, notice when they snicker or stumble, ask leading questions."

As to the parallels between the Renaissance and our own time, ten reported that they draw such parallels, "otherwise it all becomes isolated and aesthetic." The methods vary from making passing, spontaneous remarks in lectures to showing video clips suggesting "parallels between pop culture and Renaissance drama." A couple of respondents referred to themes of permanent interest: "things have not changed that much in five hundred years." Others stress a play of similarity and difference, and three stress difference, insisting that students should not confuse Renaissance attitudes with their own.

Asked how they dealt with the relations between Shakespeare and his fellow dramatists and whether he should be included with his contemporaries or excluded, fifteen reply that they prefer to include him (one adds, "warily"), and thirteen that they exclude him (not always willingly). Even when he is excluded, instructors make passing references to him. A few see his tendency to overshadow his contemporaries as a problem: "Lots of wonderful theater gets short shrift because of him." The majority view, however, is that he should be included, so that he can appear not as a "titanic genius" but as "one among many." This allows pairings like *Richard II* and *Edward II* or *Measure for Measure* and John Marston's *The Malcontent*. (This kind of pairing can be seen in modified form in Theodore B. Leinwand's essay, which approaches Middleton and Massinger through a brief discussion of *The Merchant of Venice*.) If there is one salient feature that emerges from these questionnaires, it is the importance of context; and Shakespeare and his contemporaries are seen as creating contexts for each other.

Editions, Recommended Reading, Performance, the Internet

Karen Bamford

Editions: Anthologies and Alternatives

Instructors surveyed in 1997 were almost unanimous in their dissatisfaction with available anthologies of Renaissance drama: "There is no good student text of Renaissance drama with an extensive and sophisticated apparatus"; "*I wish there were a good, reasonably priced text!!*" Russell Fraser and Norman Rabkin's two-volume *Drama of the English Renaissance* (1976)—with forty-one plays, the only major anthology in print at the time—is by common agreement prohibitively expensive. Respondents also complained about the quality of the text and minimal notes. "I find Fraser's editing irritating and patchy, both in the rather flashy introductions and the annotations"; "its introductions to the individual plays are undersized, underinformative, understimulating; and it is out of date textually." Other complaints included the lack of plays by women; the failure of the introductions to the plays to address historical context or current critical debates; the poor binding, narrow margins, and physical bulk of the volumes. Since the survey was taken, however, Blackwell has published a new anthology, *Renaissance Drama*, edited by Arthur F. Kinney, and Norton will publish one in 2002, edited by David Bevington, that will include twenty-seven plays: *The Spanish Tragedy; Endymion; Friar Bacon and Friar Bungay; Tamburlaine the Great, Part One; Doctor Faustus; The Jew of Malta; Edward II; Arden of Faversham; The Shoemakers' Holiday; The Malcontent; The Tragedy of Mariam; Volpone; Epicoene; The Alchemist; Bartholomew Fair; The Knight of the Burning Pestle; The Maid's Tragedy; The Woman's Prize; The Revenger's Tragedy; The Roaring Girl; A Chaste Maid in Cheapside; Women Beware Women; The Changeling; The White Devil; The Duchess of Malfi; A New Way to Pay Old Debts; and 'Tis Pity She's a Whore.* Blackwell's anthology includes twelve plays (*The Spanish Tragedy, Arden of Faversham, Doctor Faustus, Edward II, The Shoemakers' Holiday, A Woman Killed with Kindness, The Knight of the Burning Pestle, A Chaste Maid in Cheapside, Bartholomew Fair, The Duchess of Malfi, The Changeling,* and *'Tis Pity She's a Whore*); five entertainments (Mulcaster's *The Queen's Majesty's Passage*; Sidney's *The Lady of May*; *The Honorable Entertainment Given to the Queen's Majesty in Progress, at Elvetham in Hampshire* [anon]; Jonson's *The Masque of Blackness*; and Munday's *The Triumphs of Re-United Britannia*); introductory essays and bibliographies for each dramatic text; and an appendix of "cultural documents" (source texts and music).

Many instructors, as an alternative to Fraser and Rabkin, assemble course packs, distribute photocopies, and use Internet texts and a variety of paperback editions of individual plays and minor anthologies. *Elizabethan Drama*, edited by John Gassner and William Green, includes eight plays: *Arden of Faversham*, *The Spanish Tragedy*, *Friar Bacon and Friar Bungay*, *Doctor Faustus* [B-text], *Edward II*, *Everyman in His Humour*, *The Shoemakers' Holiday*, and *A Woman Killed with Kindness*. *Drama of the English Renaissance*, edited by Martin L. Wine, includes nine plays: *Doctor Faustus*, *The Shoemakers' Holiday*, *Volpone*, *The Knight of the Burning Pestle*, *The Masque of Blackness*, *Philaster*, *The Duchess of Malfi*, *The Changeling*, and *The Broken Heart*. Like Gassner and Green's anthology, Wine's is inexpensive but lacks substantial apparatus.

For many instructors price is the most crucial factor in selecting texts. One respondent wished that "Dover Thrift sort of editions; very cheap" existed for more plays; another called for the reappearance of the Regents Renaissance series of inexpensive, scholarly paperback editions. Many use the Penguin collections of plays by Marlowe, Jonson, Middleton, Webster, and Ford: "the price is right, texts are mainly adequate." The Revels single-text editions, though praised as "outstanding," are considered by most too expensive for undergraduates. By far the most popular single text editions are the New Mermaids. Relatively inexpensive, they win praise for their scholarly introductory material and notes and their attention to theatrical history. As single texts, they also have the considerable virtue of portability: "Not being hefty volumes, students usually bring them to class, and they can get up and move around with a book in hand"; the volumes "fit the profile of a separate playscript. Bulky anthologies are either outdated or counterproductive in achieving performance effect."

The range of texts available in the New Mermaids series is, however, limited. One respondent regretted that "there are no cheap single-volume editions of plays like *Gallathea* and *The Roaring Girl*." As an individual text, Elizabeth Cary's *The Tragedy of Mariam* was at the time of the survey available only in Barry Weller and Margaret W. Ferguson's excellent but relatively expensive California edition (1994). Broadview Press published in 2001 *The Tragedy of Mariam*, edited by Stephanie Hodgson-Wright, as a less expensive paperback in its Literary Texts series. Cary's play is also available, along with three others, in *Renaissance Drama by Women: Texts and Documents* (Cerasano and Wynne-Davies). Making a virtue of necessity, one respondent reported teaching *Mariam* in a feminism seminar with photocopies of the Malone Society reprint. "As an assignment I asked the students to edit fifteen lines with a deliberate attempt at feminist glossing and to write a feminist introduction in the same kind of detail as the New Mermaids series. (The students responded to the challenge and performed brilliantly and originally.)" For a third-year Stuart drama course, the same instructor collected out-of-copyright New Mermaids texts, hired a research assistant to help scan them onto disk, and divided the class into units to edit the texts. "The aim is not to turn out fully fledged textual scholars but to give students a proprietorial interest in the texts they are studying, an insight into the ways in which textual (supposedly 'factual,' neutral) decisions are interpretive and subjective—and to provide inexpensive texts for classroom use and discussion. So far the students are loving the course, and the first lot of edited acts is fresh and innovative."

Recommended Reading

Although several respondents declared that they don't usually assign critical reading to undergraduates—"students have a hard enough time with the texts themselves"—most instructors recommend, if not require, some secondary reading, and the most frequently cited title in this category was *The Cambridge Companion to English Renaissance Drama*, edited by A. R. Braunmuller and Michael Hattaway. "The best one-volume support for undergraduate study of the drama of this period"; "This book provides the best prolegomena to the course of any study I've encountered. It also includes extensive bibliographies and a helpful chronological table." Introductory essays on "playhouses and players," "the arts of the dramatist," and "drama and society" survey material and dramaturgical and social contexts; six subsequent chapters survey the drama by genre (private and occasional drama; political drama; romance and the heroic play; pastiche, burlesque, tragicomedy; comedy; and tragedy); a final essay looks at Caroline drama. Each chapter concludes with an annotated bibliography of its subject, and an appendix offers forty additional pages of bibliographies with biographical notes on individual authors. The chronological table that concludes the volume provides "a full but not complete list of plays of the period 1497–1642" with the author and acting company when known (Braunmuller and Hattaway 419). *The Bedford Companion to Shakespeare*, edited by Russ McDonald, "gives a brief, document-based overview of social and political history, as well as bibliographical leads for more specialized topics"; it offers "a convenient source of primary documents on performance spaces, antitheatricality, gender, and ideology." Also recommended was *The Age of Shakespeare*, edited by Boris Ford, volume 2 in *The New Pelican Guide to English Literature*. In addition to general essays on Elizabethan literature and society, it includes chapters on Marlowe, Jonson, Chapman, Tourneur, and Middleton, as well as substantial bibliographies. Other handbooks cited include *A New History of Early English Drama*, edited by John D. Cox and David Scott Kastan (described below), and *The Revels History of the Drama in English*, volumes 3 (1576–1613) and 4 (1613–1660).

Staging the Renaissance, an anthology of criticism edited by Kastan and Peter Stallybrass, rivals *The Cambridge Companion* in popularity with instructors of Renaissance drama. Designed to replace Ralph James Kaufman's *Elizabethan Drama* and Max Bluestone and Norman Rabkin's *Shakespeare's Contemporaries*, *Staging the Renaissance* gathers twenty-four critical essays reprinted from journals or excerpted from books originally appearing between 1979 and 1989. Its regular appearance on lists of recommended reading suggests that its essays—primarily new historicist and feminist—form a core of currently canonical criticism. Part 1, "The Conditions of Playing," includes excerpts from Steven Mullaney's *The Place of the Stage*, Leonard Tennenhouse's *Power on Display*, Annabel Patterson's *Censorship and Interpretation*, and Lisa Jardine's *Still Harping on Daughters*, as well as essays by Jonathan Crewe on antitheatrical discourse, Jean Howard on women as spectators, Jonathan Goldberg on sodomy, and Stephen Orgel and Randall McLeod on texts. Part 2, "The Plays," includes Stephen Greenblatt on *The Jew of Malta*, Catherine Belsey on *Arden of Faversham*, Kastan on *The Shoemakers' Holiday*, and Frank Whigham on *The Duchess of Malfi*, as well as essays by James Shapiro, Jonathan Dollimore, Peggy A. Knapp, Karen Newman, Leah Marcus, Stallybrass, Marjorie Garber, Ann Rosalind Jones, and Sara Eaton on plays by Kyd, Jonson, Middleton, Cary, and Webster. Other anthologies of criticism recommended by respondents were *Rewriting the Renaissance*, edited by Margaret W. Ferguson, Maureen Quilligan, and Nancy J. Vickers ("a merger of feminist and new historicist initiatives," with a "very interesting and useful bibliography"), and *Women in the Middle Ages and the Renaissance*, edited by Mary Beth Rose.

The most frequently named critical work by a single author was Stephen Greenblatt's influential *Renaissance Self-Fashioning*; and the first chapter of Greenblatt's *Shakespearean Negotiations*, "The Circulation of Social Energy," was recommended as "an effective introduction to the new historicist approach to Tudor-Stuart theater." Other critical works cited by several respondents were Joel Altman's *The Tudor Play of Mind*, Michael Bristol's *Carnival and Theatre*, Jonathan Dollimore's *Radical Tragedy*, Michael Hattaway's *Elizabethan Popular Theatre*, and Steven Mullaney's *The Place of the Stage*. Frequently cited works of feminist criticism include Catherine Belsey's *The Subject of Tragedy*, Karen Newman's *Fashioning Femininity and English Renaissance Drama*, Mary Beth Rose's *The Expense of Spirit* and Lisa Jardine's *Still Harping on Daughters*. Older critical works cited include David Bevington's *From Mankind to Marlowe*, Alexander Leggatt's *Citizen Comedy in the Age of Shakespeare*, Brian Gibbons's *Jacobean City Comedy*, and Richard Levin's *The Multiple Plot in English Renaissance Drama*. Even earlier works still current include Fredson Bowers's *Elizabethan Revenge Tragedy*, Muriel Bradbrook's *Themes and Conventions of Elizabethan Tragedy* and *The Growth and Structure of Elizabethan Comedy*, Madeline Doran's *Endeavors of Art*, and L. C. Knights's *Drama and Society in the Age of Jonson*.

Andrew Gurr's *The Shakespearean Stage* and *Playgoing in Shakespeare's London*, along with Alan Dessen's *Elizabethan Stage Conventions and Modern Interpreters*, were the most frequently mentioned studies of playing conditions, conventions, and audiences. Cited as useful sources of history for undergraduates were Keith Wrightson's *English Society*, John Guy's *Tudor*

England, Lawrence Stone's *Family, Sex, and Marriage*, and Barbara Rosen's *Witchcraft in England*.

Most respondents were reluctant to distinguish between works they would recommend for students and those they would recommend to other instructors, and the same clear favorites emerged in both categories: Braunmuller and Hattaway's *Cambridge Companion*, Kastan and Stallybrass's *Staging the Renaissance*, and Greenblatt's *Renaissance Self-Fashioning*. In the one exception to this pattern, Cox and Kastan's *A New History of Early English Drama* (1997) was one of books most frequently cited as an important text for instructors but not for students. Given its publication in the same year the survey was conducted, its preeminence here is remarkable. (If we took a second poll in 2002, it would probably have assumed a leading place among works recommended or required for students as well as for instructors.) In contrast to *The Cambridge Companion to English Renaissance Drama*, with its focus on dramatic texts and genres, *A New History* dislodges "authors and scripts" from the "center of dramatic history" and relocates them from "within the social and material circumstances in which early English drama was enabled and inhibited" (5). Its twenty-five substantial chapters treat drama in relation to physical space (churches, households, the universities, streets and markets, theaters, and libraries), social space (religious, civic, domestic, courtly, literary, and popular cultures), and its conditions of performance and publication (touring, costumes, censorship, acting, personnel, "playwrighting," publication, patronage, revision, repertory, and manuscripts).

Performance

Most respondents commented on the importance of teaching the Renaissance plays as scripts for performance. "We talk about different venues and different audiences; the consequences of provincial playing." Many emphasize acting choices in their teaching, alluding to productions they've seen, interpretive stage traditions, and audience response. Some use the board to sketch possible staging or critique a clip from a video when available. One instructor finds it "very valuable to take an hour and go outside with a class to map out the dimensions of medieval and Renaissance stages. It also helps to show how badly the sound travels in an outdoor setting and how this restricted the amount of 'action' on an early modern stage. Getting students to stand in the position of audiences and players alike is quite illuminating."

Over half the respondents involve students in some kind of performance exercise in class. "It helps enormously with basic comprehension and with helping them grasp the dynamics between characters"; "I very much favor some in-class performance of crucial scenes—for the verve, for the sense of dramaturgy, the dramatic immediacy." Performance exercises range from impromptu reading aloud of key speeches—"This not only gives the class a break from my voice but often helps the reader (and listeners) to understand the passage in a new light"—to highly organized group presentations worth a percentage of the course grade. An informal approach involves "oral reading interactions with minimal blocking and no rehearsals. We may do a number of takes and discuss differences. Mostly it's a matter of liberating the words from the page, hearing them and what they create." "My classes stage many readings during the semester, a few students performing and the rest directing. These impromptu performances can help students realize how many decisions even the simplest of performances require." Another respondent has adapted exercises from the Folger Library's *Shakespeare Set Free* series on teaching, edited by Peggy O'Brien: these "help students discover the meanings of speeches and the dramatic interactions implicit in the text. I have distributed parts of specific scenes, cast students in the various roles, and read through the script. Following discussion of questions, observations, reactions, etc., another group of students would be cast in the same roles and we would go through the piece again. More discussion, then a third group of students, and so on. Large roles might have three or four actors (one per page) so that we could get through the thirty or forty students in the class during one lecture period."

Helen Ostovich's essay in this collection ("'Our Sport Shall Be to Take What They Mistake': Classroom Performance and Learning") provides a more detailed account of performance exercises. Interested instructors should also consult *Teaching Shakespeare through Performance*, edited by Milla Cozart Riggio.

The Internet

In contrast to the enthusiasm with which many respondents commented on performance in the classroom, the survey revealed only tepid interest in the Internet as a teaching tool. Instructors expressed concerns about the quality of material on the Web ("I find most Web sites self-proclaiming wastes of time"), students' inability to evaluate that material appropriately, and the problem of unequal access to the Internet's resources. A few respondents, however, have begun to use the Internet extensively: as a source of both primary texts and scholarly and critical comment. Valuable points of entry to the Web for instructors of Renaissance drama include the *Mr. William Shakespeare and the Internet* page, maintained by Terry A. Gray at Palomar College (shakespeare.palomar.edu/); Jack Lynch's list of literary resources (andromeda.rutgers.edu/~jlynch/Lit); the University of Victoria's *Internet Shakespeare Editions* site, maintained by Michael Best (web.UVic.CA/ shakespeare/index.html); and the *Records of Early English Drama* Web site, maintained by Abigail Ann Young (www.chass.utoronto.ca/~reed/reed.html). *The On-line Books Page* (//onlinebooks.library.upenn.edu/) provides links to thousands of online texts, hundreds of them from the English Renaissance. A subject search reveals over seventy-five Renaissance play texts available online, including the complete works of Marlowe, Middleton, and Shakespeare. C. E. McGee's essay in this volume, "Webbing Webster," offers one teaching model for instructors interested in exploiting the pedagogical potential of the Web for Renaissance drama.

NOTE

Unless otherwise indicated, quotations of Shakespeare are from the Riverside edition.

A Renaissance Filmography

Philippa Sheppard

This select, descriptive filmography of adaptations of Renaissance plays excluding Shakespeare is offered as a practical tool to instructors wishing to infuse their lectures with some examples of performance. Since non-Shakespearean Renaissance plays are rarely produced in North America, particularly outside urban centers, these films may represent the only chance many students have to see versions of the plays in performance. Viewing modern interpretations reminds students that these plays are not just artifacts to be studied in the classroom and opens students to the range of dramaturgical possibilities in these rich scripts.

I think directed viewing is often the best way to integrate sections of film into a lecture. I usually select a crucial scene in the play and ask the students to prepare answers to questions about interpretation of character, language, and theme. If there is time, we also consider the ways in which aesthetic decisions (costume, set, lighting, cinematography) affect the viewer's understanding of the scene.

I often choose the scenes in *The Changeling* in which Beatrice-Joanna commissions De Flores to kill Alonzo de Piraquo (2.2) and in which she and De Flores renegotiate the reward (3.4). I lecture on these scenes in the class before the screening. At the end of the class, I write some questions on the board for the students to think about; some examples: Can you define the characteristics of Beatrice-Joanna's rhetoric that lead to the misunderstanding about the reward? What does her language in both scenes tell us about her character? Why does De Flores misinterpret her?

Before the screening, we discuss the questions from the last class, and then I write some more, related questions on the board that focus the students' viewing: Does the actress's body language reinforce any characteristics in her spoken language? What aspects of Beatrice-Joanna's character does the actress seem to be emphasizing? How does the actor playing De Flores convey his motivations? Even students who are not caught up with their reading can participate in the postfilm discussion.

For adaptations of Shakespeare plays, readers should consult Kenneth Sprague Rothwell and Annabelle Henkin Melzer's invaluable Shakespeare filmography, *Shakespeare on Screen*. I loosely follow their format here, but include only chief members of cast and crew. Readers should also see Harry Keyishian's "Checklist of Medieval and Renaissance Plays (Excluding Shakespeare) on Film, Tape, and Recording" for brief accounts of other versions. The narrow range of non-Shakespearean adaptations of plays from the period 1552–1642 necessarily restricts the scope of this list to the better-known plays. I have included some modern analogues to the plays in addition to faithful interpretations.

Selected Films

The Changeling (an adaptation of Middleton and Rowley's play; Great Britain, 1993. Color, 90 min.). The text is heavily cut, including the entire subplot, but what remains is engaging and well acted. It is useful to discuss the consequences of excising the subplot. Certainly, a modern audience may find the playwrights' treatment of the mentally ill offensive. The production conforms to television's demands for naturalism with period costumes and setting, voice-overs, and close-ups. If the instructor has the leisure to show the whole film, a question about the way in which the director makes clear the transformation of Beatrice-Joanna from the spoiled young lady of the opening scenes to "the deed's creature" (3.4.139) might be in order.

   Credits: producer-director: Simon Curtis; Alsemero: Hugh Grant; Beatrice-Joanna: Elizabeth McGovern; De Flores: Bob Hoskins; Vermandero: Leslie Phillips.

   Distribution and availability: in Canada: Intern. Tele-film, 1-800-561-4300; in the United States: Films for the Humanities and Sciences, 1-800-257-5126.

Doctor Faustus (an adaptation of Marlowe's play; Great Britain, 1967. Color, 93 min.). In adapting their stage production for the screen, Richard Burton and Nevill Coghill made cuts (including the comic subplot) to accommodate Burton's lingering over every syllable, especially in Faustus's opening speech, and to leave time for the precious sound and visual effects, which will earn guffaws from students.

   However, the theological conversations between Mephistophilis and Faustus and the concluding scenes make effective excerpts to show in the classroom. The theatrical history of the production can be used to spur a discussion of the exigencies imposed on a text by different media (page to stage to screen).

   Credits: producers: Richard Burton and Richard McWhorter; directors: Burton and Nevill Coghill; Doctor Faustus: Burton; Mephistophilis: Andrew Taylor; Helen of Troy, fantasy women: Elizabeth Taylor; and the Oxford University Dramatic Society.

   Distribution and availability: Columbia Pictures Corp.; Oxford Univ. Screen Productions; Nassau Films; Venfilms; on video.

The Duchess of Malfi (an adaptation of Webster's play; Great Britain, 1972. Color, 125 min.). This production anticipates some of the more conservative but successful BBC Shakespeares: the sets and costumes are authentic, even lavish, and the acting is formal and somewhat stagy for the small screen. Some sizable but unobtrusive cuts are made to the text (Bosola, in particular, loses quite a few lines).

   A possible approach to this production is to ask students about casting decisions. How is our response affected by watching an older Duchess, a boyish Antonio, and an open-faced Bosola? Does the director intend us to sympathize with the malcontent all the way through? The most successful scenes in this production feature Ferdinand, well realized by Charles Kay. Although a useful teaching tool, this production may confirm some students' negative expectations of period drama—a little stuffy and middle-aged.

Credits: producer: Cedric Messina; director: James McTaggart; script editor: Rosemary Hill; Duchess: Eileen Atkins; Bosola: Michael Bryant; Ferdinand: Charles Kay; Cardinal: T. P. McKenna; Antonio: Gary Bond.

Distribution and availability: BBC; in Canada: Internat. Tele-film; in the United States: Films for the Humanities and Sciences.

The Duchess of Malfi (an adaptation of Webster's play; Canada, 1962, Monochrome, 90 min.). This radically abridged version is well acted by a young, attractive cast that appeals to student audiences. The most effective scenes in this production are the romantic encounters between Antonio and the Duchess, which achieve a real sense of intimacy and passion.

The cuts to the text are so extensive that the result is somewhat choppy. A good exercise might be to ask students to trace the cuts and formulate arguments both in favor of and against them. For example, the excision of the wax figures seems a dramatic opportunity thrown away, whereas the choice not to dramatize the flights from Malfi and Ancona (staged in the BBC) magnifies the claustrophobic atmosphere and highlights the images of entrapment.

Credits: director-producer: Mario Prizek; Duchess: Frances Hyland; Antonio: John Vernon; Bosola: Douglas Rain; Ferdinand: Lloyd Bochner; Cardinal: Powys Thomas.

Distribution and availability: a very few copies are available to North American university audiovisual libraries as a loan from the Canadian Broadcasting Corp., Toronto (contact Roy Harris at 416 205-7608). As a result of my inquiry, the financial viability of educational sales is being considered.

Edward II (based on Marlowe's play; Great Britain, 1991. Color, 90 min.). Although director Derek Jarman cuts quite a bit of the text and alters the order of scenes and speeches, this imaginative modern-dress adaptation can still make an effective teaching tool. However, some students may find offensive the graphic sex, nudity, a sadomasochistic Mortimer, and a cross-dressing, violent young Prince Edward.

One approach that works well here is to ask the students to focus on the thematic effect of directorial changes to the script. For instance, Jarman imposes a gay protest element onto the play; in fact, the film culminates with a march. Jarman views Gaveston's sexual orientation as the reason for his persecution at the hands of the nobles, whereas Marlowe suggests Gaveston's social climbing enrages the courtiers. By throwing all the emphasis on the sexual rather than on the political, Jarman narrows the play's scope. Edward is seen only as lover, not as ruler, and therefore his culpable neglect of his realm is obscured.

Jarman also changes the ending of the play. The horrific murder of Edward by Lightborn (who, in this version, is commissioned by Isabella) becomes a dream sequence. This not only alters history but breaks up the pattern of political retribution set up by Marlowe.

Credits: producers: Sarah Radclyffe and Simon Curtis; director: Derek Jarman; screenplay: Jarman, Stephen McBride, Ken Butler; Edward II: Steven Waddington; Lightborn: Kevin Collins; Gaveston: Andrew Tiernan; Isabella: Tilda Swinton; Kent: Jerome Flynn; Mortimer: Nigel Terry.

Distribution and availability: Alliance / Fine Line Features / British Screen & BBC films / Working Title. Produced in association with Uplink Japan. On video.

Related reading: Horger; Jarman; Davenport; and Evans.

Faust (includes excerpts from Marlowe's play; Czechoslovakia, 1994. Color, 90 min.). The Czech animator Jan Svankmajer (*Alice*) uses an enchanting combination of live action, Claymation, stop-motion animation, and traditional Czech puppetry to reinterpret the Faust legend for a modern audience. Petr Cepek plays an ordinary man who, finding himself in a decrepit theater, idly dresses himself in a Faust costume and then is coerced into maintaining the role, both on stage and in real life. There is not much dialogue, but what there is is a wonderful medley of Goethe, Grabbe, Marlowe, and the Czech Folk Puppeteers' original writing. The Marlowe excerpts are taken from some of the best sections of the play: from the dramatic first entrance of Mephistophilis after Faustus has summoned him (sc. 3) and from his reentrance after convening with Lucifer—the scene in which Faustus signs over his soul (sc. 5). This film provides a vivid introduction to the whole Faust legend and can galvanize classroom discussion about the reasons for the legend's appeal to audiences of different nationalities and time periods, leading to an identification of its archetypal or mythological qualities.

Credits: writer-director: Jan Svankmajer; producer: Jaromi Kallista; BBC producer: Colin Rose; text adviser: Jiri Strach; Faust: Petr Cepek; English version, dubbing: VideoLondon Sound Studios: all voices: Andrew Sachs; director: Matt McCarthy.

Distribution and availability: Athanor / Heart of Europe Prague K Production / Lumen Films, BBC Bristol, Kino Intl. On video.

Oberon, the Faery Prince (a student performance of Jonson's masque; the United States, 1993. Color, 9 min. introd., 1 hr. production, 30 min. afterword). This video is invaluable in providing students with a reasonably authentic experience of a Jacobean masque. Thomas Bishop, a professor at Case Western Reserve, introduces the masque, especially as a political device—

propaganda to inspire viewers with the magnificence of James I. Bishop also provides a succinct historical and performance background, referring to Alfonso Ferrabosco, Robert Johnson, and Inigo Jones. The introduction includes the reading of an eyewitness account of the performance at court.

In the masque itself, the students' acting is somewhat hammy, but the music is of a high calibre. It might be useful to remind viewers that masques were performed in part by amateurs too—the courtiers themselves. Great efforts have been made to reconstruct the set, costumes, and even choreography in the spirit of Inigo Jones. The troupe has even managed to simulate something of the court atmosphere, with the president of Case Western standing in for James I. The video concludes with an extremely useful section in which contemporary engravings of dance steps are intercut with clips from the performance.

Credits: musical reconstruction: Peter Holman, Ross W. Duffin; producers: Duffin, Bishop, David Evett; stage direction: Barrie Rutter; choreography and dance director: Ken Pierce; musical direction: David Douglass; Oberon, the Faery Prince: Pierce.

Distribution and availability: from the Dept. of Music, Case Western Reserve Univ., Cleveland, OH 44106-7105; 216 368-2400.

Related reading: Slights.

Robin Hood and the Friar: *A 16th Century Folk Play* (a student production; Canada, 1983. Color, 20 min.). This work opens with an educational introduction to the folk play that includes a Staffordshire stained glass (the Betley window) depicting Robin Hood characters, and a voice-over of the English religious reformer Hugh Latimer's complaint that people went to folk plays instead of sermons. It is a lively performance by University of Toronto students, featuring good fight choreography and costumes and a stylized use of blue fabric to represent the brook under the bridge where the Friar challenges Robin Hood. There is some improvised dialogue that does not altogether fit. The dance at the end captures an authentic flavor of late medieval England. This video would provide a good illustration of the folk play in the initial, prolegomena lectures of a Renaissance drama course.

Credits: producer-director: Michael Edmunds; Robin Hood: John B. Mayberry; Friar: David Parry; Little John: Allan Park; Maid Marion: Jackie Gelineau.

Distribution and availability: produced by the Poculi Ludique Societas and the Media Centre, Univ. of Toronto. Video available from Univ. of Toronto, Information Commons.

Volpone (an adaptation of Jonson's play; Canada, 1969. Color, 90 min.). This radically cut version is great fun and usually appeals to students. It boasts lavish sets and some inventive, yet subtle, imitation of the animals suggested by the roles in the play in the costumes, gestures, and sounds of the actors:

Volpone has bushy ginger whiskers and eyebrows, and Corbaccio, garbed in black, has a long, beaklike nose.

It would be worth asking students about the production's interpretation of Celia. She seems momentarily tempted by Volpone. Does her vacillation have the effect of reducing Volpone's perfidy, which Jonson's conclusion seems to judge severely?

Another approach would be to ask students about the nature and effect of the cuts. Metatheatrical elements such as the playlet performed by Volpone's zanies and much of Scoto of Mantua's spiel, in addition to the entire Lady Politic Would-Be subplot, end up on the editing-room floor.

Credits: director-producer: Mario Prizek; adaptor: Ian Thorne; Volpone: Jack Creley; Mosca: Brian Petchey; Corbaccio: Chris Wiggins; Corvino: Leo Leyden; Voltore: Joseph Shaw.

Distribution and availability: A very few copies are available to North American university audiovisual libraries as a loan from the Canadian Broadcasting Corp., in Toronto (contact Roy Harris at 416 205-7608). As a result of my inquiry, the financial viability of educational sales is being considered.

Other Films of Interest

Comus (Canada, 1972, Univ. of Toronto. Monochrome, 56 min. Directed by Bill Somerville, with Elias Zarou, Mary Mulholland, and Wendy Thatcher). This student production of Milton's masque is available on loan to university libraries. While the set and costumes are inexpensive, the student performances are full of verve and humor.

Faust (Germany, 1926. Monochrome, silent, 100 mins. Directed by F. W. Murnau, with Emil Jannings, Gosta Ekman, and Camilla Horn). Many silent films were made based on the Faust legend, but this is probably the best. The German expressionist style does not date.

The Honey Pot (loosely based on Jonson's *Volpone*; United States, 1966. Color, 150 min. Directed by Joseph L. Mankiewicz, with Rex Harrison, Cliff Robertson, and Maggie Smith). The Volpone duping plot metamorphoses halfway through into an Agatha Christie-like whodunnit. It is still worth showing clips of the film to students if only because the script, written in 1960s Hollywood, assumes that *Volpone* is a household word.

Mephisto (loosely based on the Faust legend with excerpts from Goethe; Germany, Hungary, 1981. Color, 144 min. Directed by Istvan Szabo, with Klaus Maria Brandauer, Karin Boyd, and Rolf Hoppe). This production is based on a novel by Klaus Mann about an unscrupulous actor who gradually allows himself to become an aesthetic prop of the Nazi government just so that he can keep acting. The part with which he becomes most closely associated is Goethe's Mephistophilis. A useful addition to a lecture on the way in which each generation uses the Faust legend to comment on its society's ills, from Marlowe onward.

Volpone (France, 1940. Monochrome, 95 min. Directed by Maurice Tourneur, with Harry Bauer and Louis Jouvet). This film was based on the Stefan Zweig adaptation of Jonson's play in which the subplot, the zany retainers, and the poetry are removed.

(See also the films *Seven* and *Devil's Advocate* for Faustian parallels and *Queen Margot* for illustrations of events in Marlowe's play *The Massacre at Paris*).

Part Two

APPROACHES

Introduction:
The Strangeness of
Renaissance Drama

Alexander Leggatt

Let me begin, as I often do in teaching, with the opening sentence of L. P. Hartley's novel *The Go-Between*: "The past is a foreign country; they do things differently there" (7). The essays that appear in this volume and the surveys conducted in preparation for it bear out the impression that when we teach Renaissance drama we are guiding our students into a foreign country. This volume deliberately excludes Shakespeare to concentrate on his contemporaries, whose strangeness we feel more acutely. Yet Shakespeare is part of the challenge: his familiarity and his reputation as the universal genius who speaks to every time and culture make it all the more urgent for us to see what is historically particular, even foreign, about him. The strangeness we find in his contemporaries may help break down our sense of Shakespeare's familiarity so that we may see him more clearly.

In our historical moment, to see a writer clearly is to see that writer as part of a historical moment, as not so much an individual talent as an intersection of social and cultural forces. No one familiar with the current state of criticism will be surprised at the prominence in this volume of essays concerned with questions about gender, class, race, and property or at the general insistence that the values at stake are not universal but local and constructed. Because apparent modern parallels can so easily be found, it is important to keep a sense of strangeness. One contributor, Christina Luckyj, reports that some of her students express their sense of the subordinate position of Renaissance women by imagining them "in the kitchen." But that (she suggests, though not in quite these terms) is to confuse *A Woman Killed with Kindness* with 1950s suburbia and to forget that there were servants. Jan Stirm's essay, in turn, points out that we have to be historically alert when we imagine servants. Both Luckyj and Stirm describe their use of evidence from the Renaissance to put their students more securely into the past, and Luckyj stresses that a clear sense of a past culture needs to include an awareness of its contradictions. If anachronism is one danger, overconfident generalization—natural when there is so much to say in so little time—is another.

These texts are not just social documents but plays, and as plays they have their own historical strangeness. Frances Teague's paper begins by describing the difficult border crossing her students encounter when they come to Renaissance drama from courses in the novel, even from courses in Shakespeare, and their discovery that stock methods like looking for motivation or finding the turning point have no currency here. Many of the surveys point out that students find the extravagant plotting and characterization of Renaissance drama a source of both delight and bewilderment. The language of this foreign country—the past—appears in the surveys as the principal difficulty, yet Joseph Candido's essay shows how to tackle the problem not by getting around the language but by working through it; and one survey respondent lists among the most important features of this drama "the menace and seductiveness of splendid language."

Many of the essays on social issues describe the use of nondramatic texts from the period to recover a lost culture, and A. R. Braunmuller describes the material available to help us recover a lost theater. We can see the two enterprises working together if we remember that theater is part of culture and culture is a kind of theater. Gender, we are regularly reminded, is a role, a performance. This perception makes theater the natural medium for a critical exploration of gender, especially when we recall that the women of Renaissance drama were constructed mostly by male writers and performed entirely by male actors. While stock characterizations and plots with a determined end speak for a culture whose values may have seemed natural at the time but now look formulaic, experiments with dramatic convention such as unconventional endings and challenges to stereotype (Vittoria's "This character scapes me" [*The White Devil* 3.2.102])[1] show a society, and a theater, creative enough to think beyond stock expectations—or at least anxiously aware that the eternal truths may not be eternal after all. Theater reflected society through a medium in which everyone was an actor, everyone was performing, and every performance (onstage and off) was provisional and open to judgment.

We may take one scene as typical of the forces at play and the issues that require attention. Near the end of act 1 of *The Duchess of Malfi* the Duchess draws her steward Antonio into marriage with her. She is working against the grain of her society. There is a class barrier to overcome: it is worth remembering that Antonio's relation to the Duchess is the same as Malvolio's relation to Olivia and that while Antonio has a proper name the Duchess is simply the Duchess. Yet class is paradoxically an enabling force: it is natural (or rather "natural") for her to give him orders, and this time the order is to marry her. However, in marriage negotiations it is "natural" for the man to take the initiative, and it is expected, especially at this level of society, that he will approach the bride's family for approval. The Duchess takes the lead, working in private, defying her brothers' insistence that as a widow she should not marry again. Early in the sequence Antonio plays into her hands by urging her to find a new husband, without naming himself as the candidate. Which attitude, we are trained to ask, was typical of Webster's society—that a widow should marry again or that she should not? A little research gives us the answer: what was typical was the contradiction.

As well as reading socially, we need to read theatrically, and the two processes work together. The scene is less private than it looks. If we simply read the speeches of the two characters, we may forget that Cariola is hiding behind the arras, hearing every word. The theater audience will be aware of this, and this awareness turns what appears to be a private scene into a public one. It cannot be private in any case, since the Duchess and Antonio cannot simply be alone with each other. Their society, with its demands and assumptions, is always with them and in the auditorium, in the same light, several hundred people are watching them. Finally, the unseen Cariola has a legal function: her presence as witness turns the lovers' exchange of vows into a binding marriage. In that way too the unseen witness embodies the presence of society.

The scene is theatrical in other ways. It makes use of a significant prop, the Duchess's ring, which she vowed never to give away except to her second husband. She gives it to Antonio. As she puts it on his finger, he kneels, and she raises him. As so often, we have to be alert to the visual language as well as to the spoken words. The words themselves are resonant, demonstrating what our respondent calls the "menace and seductiveness" of Jacobean language. When Antonio says of the ring, "There is a saucy and ambitious devil / Is dancing in this circle" (1.2.329–30), we see how much can be compressed into two lines: Antonio's alertness to the Duchess's sexual feeling and his own; his fear of his own political ambition, with our sense that this marriage is more than just a matter of consenting adults in private; and the image of the dancing devil, an image that (as Thomas Akstens's essay shows) is not just a stock reference but a way of evoking a living fear.

This is a scene, in short, in which verbal and visual language work together and social anxieties inform a private moment. But that is not all. There is a quality in this scene that does not need footnotes or class handouts and that such aids could not help us with. To teach Renaissance drama is to experience a constant play of the strange and the familiar. Some of the essays in this volume, and many of the responses to the survey, suggest that a way of dealing with the strangeness of Renaissance drama is to point to features in the lost world that can be paralleled in our own. Paul Budra's essay draws analogies between Renaissance theater and contemporary movies (the conditions of production, the self-referentiality of the texts); a survey respondent noted, "Asking students about summer jobs often prompts them to recognize early modern deference." The first part of the scene is built on a tension between caution and desire, as both characters mean more than they say directly. They are playing with fire, and they know it; as the Duchess's boldness gets more direct, so does Antonio's fear. She gives him their first kiss: "here upon your lips / I sign your *Quietus est*" (1.2.379–80). *Quietus est* needs a footnote; the kiss does not. Desire may be differently constructed in our time, and our reasons for fearing it may be different, but we can recognize the tension itself without being guilty of anachronism. Some students (and teachers) may feel, though they may not want to talk about it, that in their own lives they have acted versions of this scene.

I have just risked two critical heresies, as critical heresy is defined in our time. One is the insistence that there is something personal in this scene, something that is not just socially constructed. (And, yes, I can imagine an argument that even the kiss needs a footnote.) Lashed to the stake and feeling the heat of the flames, we still have the right to ask, Is there something in the Duchess's boldness and Antonio's fear that is a matter not just of class and gender positions but of character and personality? The other, related heresy is the claim that beneath the differences of language we can glimpse in other cultures a human reality that transcends time. That both claims are open to abuse and can blind us to other realities is obvious, but not to risk heresy is to be not just a creature of one's historical moment but a prisoner of it.

Our moment will pass. That the critical preoccupations of our era, and of this volume, have now been current for about twenty years suggests that, perhaps sooner than we think, what our authors have done here may come to look like a consolidation of the beliefs of an era just as that era was drawing to a close. To risk the personal again: for one who has been around for a while, there is a special fascination in reading the surveys and imagining what a time-traveling academic from, say, 1960, would make of them. Beginning with the list of plays taught, he (this academic probably would be male) would recognize old favorites at the center of the repertoire—*Doctor Faustus, The Duchess of Malfi, The Alchemist, The Changeling*—but would find that some (to him) essential texts had slipped surprisingly far down the list. In a field of forty-seven, why only nine references to *The Malcontent*, four to *Endymion*, and three each to *The Old Wives' Tale* and *Ralph Roister Doister*? (Given that our survey was not universally distributed, these figures have a greater claim to dramatic effect than to scientific accuracy; but they are revealing enough to be worth quoting.) And why do so many instructors teach *The Roaring Girl*—and what on earth is *The Tragedy of Mariam*? One answer is that we are creatures of the marketplace (the canon is what you can get in paperback) and that some of the old favorites, including *The Old Wives' Tale* and *The Malcontent*, were in the once standard Brooke and Paradise, *English Drama 1580–1642*, but not in its main successor, Fraser and Rabkin's *Drama of the English Renaissance*. The playwrights as well as the plays have suffered: Fraser and Rabkin replaces those two plays with *David and Bethsabe* and *The Dutch Courtesan* respectively, but the replacements have not caught on. This means that as *The Old Wives' Tale* and *The Malcontent* have faded, Peele and Marston have faded along with them.

Changes in critical interest are another factor. *The Tragedy of Mariam* has benefited from an effort throughout the discipline to recover the work of neglected women writers. A new interest in gender roles accounts for the emergence of *The Roaring Girl*. A woman dressed as a man interests our time as a ruler dressed as a malcontent interested an earlier generation. The same interest may explain why Fraser and Rabkin's substitution of Lyly's *Gallathea* for his *Endymion* has been more successful than some of its other substitutions, though that play's survey figure (eight) is more modest than *Endymion*'s would have been a couple of generations ago. In our time as in his own, Lyly's stylized, romantic mode has gone out of fashion. Changing taste as well as changing anthologies may account for the declining interest in the romance of Greene and the coterie fantasies of Beaumont and Fletcher. That there is more to these writers than such labels can account for is a growing discovery in criticism that still awaits full translation into the classroom.

A more pragmatic answer to the question why certain plays are taught is that time is limited, and picking plays for a course is an exercise in filling a lifeboat. To make room for a new play like *The Roaring Girl*, an old play like *Philaster* may have to go. By the same token, as new emphases emerge, old ones become exhausted. Our time traveler would probably insist you cannot teach Renaissance drama without a background lecture on melancholy, through which you would trace the figure of the stage malcontent. *The Malcontent* survives in a modest way, but more as a political play than as a study of Elizabethan psychology.

The answers to the survey question about critical approaches instructors found most useful put new historicism in the lead. There was only one reference to "post-New Historicist critics," but it came from one of the younger respondents. We need to stay tuned. Predicting the future is a notoriously futile exercise, and whatever replaces our historical moment, it will not be a simple return to the past. The river flows one way, and it is unlikely that our successors will find themselves lecturing on the great chain of being. What we can do to stay alert to the future is to use the strangeness, the constructedness of Renaissance drama and Renaissance society to keep us alert to our own strangeness, our own constructedness. Just as Bertolt Brecht claimed he used historical settings to make his audiences critically aware of their own time, we can let these plays interrogate us even as we interrogate them. We see how this can work in Frances Teague's claim that she lives for the moment when her students challenge the formulaic assumptions in the questions she asks, having realized the plays do not work the way her questions imply they do; and in Ric Knowles's interest in questioning the hierarchies of gender and authority in the very rehearsal process by which he examines those features of a Renaissance play.

It would be agreed, I suspect, by most of our authors and survey respondents that old-style character criticism is dead. Yet when Knowles cites W. B. Worthen to the effect that interviews with actors are "the last outpost of character criticism," it may be worth taking a small pause for thought. Actors do not just confront these plays; they take them into their own voices and bodies, and those voices and bodies are the medium through which the plays come to us in performance. It is a matter of widespread regret that our students have so few chances (in some cases, none at all) to see Renaissance drama in performance and that Philippa Sheppard's filmography, though longer than many readers would have expected, is still shorter than one would like. What we see (or have to imagine) on the stage is not just a play of social forces but a collection of—we may not like the word "characters," given how the term has been abused, but "people" or "personalities" may make us equally nervous, and while "bodies" will take us some of the way, we still have to distinguish between a theater and a morgue. Let us say, then, that there are characters on the stage, though we are still sorting out what that word means, and that the Duchess and Antonio are as alert to each other personally as the actors playing them have to be technically. History has taught us to read beyond the personal; theater may teach us to read beyond the social.

A reader in 2040 may find our disinclination to talk about character as strange as the refusal of New Criticism (in its purest form; the ordinance was regularly violated) to bring the writer and his times into the consideration of a work of art. More likely, such a reader may think I have picked a bad example and what is really strange about us is something I have not even thought to mention. We are in any case as strange to the Renaissance as the Renaissance is to us, and being critically alert to what they took for granted should help us question our own assumptions. The essays in this volume show the alertness of instructors, and of students, in a wide variety of ways; I have had space here to cite only a few. This is clearly a vital and challenging subject; what I have tried to suggest here is that its vitality gives it a growing edge, and if we are not to let our own critical discoveries lapse into unexamined routines, we need to be alert to the direction of that growth.

NOTE

[1]Quotations of *The White Devil* are from Christina Luckyj's edition; those of *The Duchess of Malfi* are from Elizabeth M. Brennan's edition.

Texts That Won't Stand Still

Leah S. Marcus

The texts of Shakespeare's plays have in the last century or so stabilized at least to the extent that most modern editions share a strong family resemblance. If I am teaching Hamlet's "To be or not to be," I can be confident that, with the exception of two or three words and minor variations in punctuation, my students and I will be able to discuss the speech intelligently and productively even if we are using different texts of *Hamlet*. Different editions of Shakespeare vary occasionally in language and more frequently in act and scene divisions, notes, and stage directions, but modern editions are similar enough that students who already possess a good modern text of Shakespeare need not purchase another simply because I have ordered it for the course. The same is by no means true of non-Shakespearean drama. Although the range of available texts suitable for use in the classroom is shrinking alarmingly, there is still a vast lack of consensus about what constitutes the best text of many of the most frequently taught plays. I take as my example Marlowe's *Doctor Faustus*, which exists in a number of modern editions but is still notably unstable in terms of what each edition posits as the language and action of the play. I discuss *Doctor Faustus* as a way of engaging a larger question: how, if at all, should we incorporate our knowledge of textual differences into our teaching of non-Shakespearean plays?

What follows is a nightmare scenario that almost (but not quite) happened to me last spring and may actually have happened to someone else. After a gap of fifteen years, I find myself once again teaching a sophomore survey of British literature, and I opt to use *The Norton Anthology of English Literature*, volume 1, as my major text for the course, just as I had in the past. The day before we are to begin discussion of *Doctor Faustus*, I have a publisher's deadline and read proofs far into the night. It is late and I am exhausted. I have taught the play many times and written about it as well—surely just this once I can get away without rereading it before I teach it. Little do I know that between the Norton fourth edition (1979) I previously used and the sixth edition (1993) I have ordered for my present students, *Doctor Faustus* has undergone a sea change. The Norton fourth edition text of the play had been based on the 1616 published version, with generous additions from the 1604 published version. The Norton sixth edition text I use now is based, instead, on Roma Gill's edition of the play (1990), which uses as its copy-text the 1604 published version of the play.

I enter the classroom cheerily the next morning at nine o'clock sharp. My first difficulty comes almost as soon as I have walked in the door, for one of my students states in puzzlement, "I wasn't sure I read the right assignment because you assigned acts 1 to 3 and the book only has scenes 1 to 3." My first premonition of disaster: Norton fourth divides the play into acts and scenes; Norton sixth does not. What that means is that this student and others who adopted the same expedient solution to the discrepancy between my assignment and their text have read only the first three scenes—a fraction of the material I had hoped to discuss. But I plunge on, hopeful that others may have read further. The discussion proceeds fairly well through the first three scenes, but in discussing scene 4, one of the students asks me what is so funny about the Clown's mistaking of "guilders" for "gridirons" (Norton, 6th ed., 778). I am considerably nonplused because the joke does not exist in my mental (a.k.a. Norton fourth) version of the scene. As we make our way into act 3, the situation becomes worse. Bearing in mind G. K. Hunter's argument about the structure of *Doctor Faustus*—that the protagonist's gradual descent into demeaning hijinks instead of high-minded pursuits of knowledge serves to register his moral decay—I ask the students to speculate about why Marlowe would want to show Doctor Faustus embroiling himself in the conflict between Bruno and the Pope. But this foray meets with total incomprehension because in my students' edition of the play, no such episode exists. By this point, I have entered fully into my textual nightmare. Class discussion falters and I retreat in defeat.

Because of my feeble mnemonic powers, I would never in reality teach a play without re-reading it first, but my handling of *Doctor Faustus* last spring was nonetheless affected by the fact that my mental map of the play was so different from the version the students had before them. And a similar experience would likely repeat itself no matter which edition I chose, because the available editions vary so profoundly. Most editors of the play have been content to adopt either 1604 or 1616 as their copy-text. But since both early printed versions are hopelessly "corrupt," editors take considerable freedom in combining the two to create the most unified and artistically satisfying version of the play. There has, however, been little consensus about what language and structure the ideal text should include. To what extent and in what ways should we allow the textual instability of the play to become the deliberate focus of consideration in the classroom?

One option, particularly attractive for graduate courses or advanced and honors undergraduate courses, is to teach the play in both its early versions, using, perhaps, David Bevington and Eric Rasmussen's Revels paperback edition of the two texts of *Doctor Faustus* (1993). Although even this edition occasionally normalizes one version of the play by adopting readings from the other, it can give students an excellent sense of the differences between the two early texts and serve as a springboard for discussion of how Marlowe's (or his company's) intentions might have changed over time and how the different versions of *Doctor Faustus* might have resonated differently with early audiences in disparate times and places. There can be few better ways to convince students of the historically contingent nature of Renaissance play texts in general than to discuss the alterations between the 1604 and 1616 versions of *Doctor Faustus*. While such an endeavor can prove confusing even for advanced students, it usually fascinates them and gives them a feeling of interpretive empowerment. If they can be made to see that a given play text, considered in the aggregate of its early versions, may well differ even within itself in terms of the kinds of material it presents and the range of interpretations it thereby licenses, students lose their seemingly inbred assumption that the play has a single, unique meaning that their professor already knows and that they are required to discover.

For example, students interested in considering the question of free will versus fate or predestination in the play (and who among them is not?) are able, if they consult Bevington and Rasmussen's two-text edition, to recognize key points at which the two versions diverge on the issue of Faustus's ability to repent. The mysterious Old Man's speech in the 1604 text, with its talk of "vile and loathsome filthiness" whose "stench" pollutes the "inward soul" (Bevington and Rasmussen 187), is much more Calvinist in its emphasis on sin as innate corruption than his corresponding speech in the 1616 version, which promises, even at this late stage in the play, that Faustus's soul is still "amiable" and salvageable if "custom grow not into nature" (see Warren; Bevington and Rasmussen 274; Marcus 38–67). And there are other elements of the two versions that support the notion that Faustus's degree of freedom varies significantly from one to the other. If students see how the two texts differ in their interpretation of Faustus's degree of agency for his own salvation, then they are better able to understand the complexity of moral choice in the play and feel more confident in drawing their own conclusions about his "hellish fall" (Bevington and Rasmussen 286). Indeed, some of my graduate students who were studying both texts of the play once came to the alarming and interesting conclusion that the 1604 version, despite that text's greater emphasis on predestination, leaves open the possibility that Faustus may yet be

saved at the end since that version, unlike the 1616 version, does not leave
its audience with the horrific image of Faustus's mangled body all "torn asun-
der" (Bevington and Rasmussen 285) on stage. The line of speculation can be
pushed considerably further: is the image of the mangled body indeed em-
blematic of Faustus's spiritual destiny, and, if so, what is the relation between
dismemberment of body and perdition of soul? As we consider such issues,
class discussion moves away from the fixity of any given reading text and
toward a more speculative investigation of staging and its effect on interpretation. By considering different versions of the play as potential blueprints for
different performances, students become acquainted with the quicksilver art-
istry of the early modern theater and become receptive to the interpretive
possibilities opened up by different stagings even of a single, relatively stable
dramatic text.

Moreover, consideration of the textual complexities of *Doctor Faustus* can
serve as a segue into a broader discussion of the ways in which modern editing
shapes the early modern texts we use in the classroom. One enlightening
exercise for those interested in gender issues is to take the 1604 and 1616
versions of Faustus's second encounter with Helen of Troy in Bevington and
Rasmussen's edition and compare them with the composite text offered in the
Norton fourth. Students tend to assume that the early modern era was more
deeply misogynist than any more recent period of Western history, and they
may possibly be right, but consideration of the shaping that the Helen episode
undergoes in the older Norton version will show them how misogyny can also
be written into the text by its editors. In the Norton fourth, two speeches by
the Old Man frame Helen's second visit to Faustus, during which he greets
her with the play's most famous lines, "Was this the face that launched a
thousand ships / And burnt the topless towers of Ilium?" (Norton, 4th ed.,
789), and claims, when she allows him to kiss her, "Her lips sucks forth my
soul—see where it flies!" In the Norton fourth version of the Old Man's
speech, preceding Helen's amorous visit to Faustus, the Old Man clearly implies that Faustus can still be saved "if custom grow not into nature" (his
speech in the 1616 version). But after he witnesses Faustus's amorous entan-
glement with Helen, he concludes that the magician is lost: "Accursed Faustus,
miserable man, / That from thy soul exclud'st the grace of heaven [. . .]"
(Norton, 4th ed., 788–89). This speech—and indeed the Old Man's return to
the stage—does not exist in the 1616 version, and the clarity it offers about
Faustus's downfall is an editorial artifact that goes back at least as far as
Frederick S. Boas's edition of *Doctor Faustus* (1932). The scene is a reprise
of the old familiar story of Eve and of female temptation as the cause of male
perdition, but it exists in this decisive form in neither early version of the play,
and it is clearly an editorial construct. If students are made aware of the
radically different forms taken by *Doctor Faustus* in modern editions, they
will receive a valuable introduction to the interpretive nature of editorial practice and come to recognize subtle ways in which gender biases they are likely

to attribute to Marlowe may instead be partly the creation of nineteenth- or twentieth-century editors.

Exploration of issues discussed above is also possible online. The *Perseus Project* of Tufts University has developed a valuable hypertext edition of *Doctor Faustus* as part of its larger online *Works of Christopher Marlowe*.[1] In addition to a wealth of information about Marlowe's life and work, this site offers linked versions of both the 1604 and 1616 texts of *Doctor Faustus* that facilitate study of the relations between them by allowing students and scholars to move easily between the two early versions of the play in either modernized or original-spelling texts. Matches between the two versions are linked, according to the language of the Web site, "where they correspond to one another either exactly, approximately, or abstractly." In addition, the Perseus edition links both early texts with their common source in the *English Faust Book* (London, 1592). Eventually, the site will also include linked historical and textual notes to all the texts as well as linked versions of more recent (usually conflated) editions of *Doctor Faustus*, thereby facilitating the study of editorial interventions in the texts of the play over several centuries.

The *Perseus Marlowe* site, particularly once all its components are in place, could easily occupy students for weeks or even months, had we but world enough and time. But what if the necessary class time is simply not available? Let's return to my survey course of last spring and other courses at a similar level: how and to what degree is it possible or advisable to introduce students to the textual complexities of *Doctor Faustus* when they may be struggling to understand the play even in the single version offered by, say, the Norton sixth, which I happened to use? In my experience, imposing textual complexity on students who have displayed no interest in such matters only confuses them in a way that is pedagogically unproductive. However, students often ask questions about the play that can lead directly into a helpful discussion of the contrasting theology or any one of a number of other areas in which the two early texts differ. Even though the level of immersion is not as intensive, students still feel empowered to offer their own interpretations when they realize that the plays in their earliest printed versions varied profoundly. To take but one example that is limited in scope and therefore feasible in a survey situation, they are usually fascinated to discover the theological differences between the two versions of the Old Man's speech and their destabilizing consequences for the rest of the play. Indeed, it is often we the professors, rather than they the students, who resist the productive chaos produced by an inquiry into textual differences. *Doctor Faustus* may represent an extreme case in its instability, but it is more characteristic of the period than we usually care to admit. Not only known cases of revision, like the two texts of *The Spanish Tragedy* and the witches from Thomas Middleton that somehow wandered into *Macbeth*, but lesser-known examples, like the several different authorial versions of Middleton's *A Game at Chess*, offer fascinating conundrums for consideration in the classroom.[2] In the study of *Doctor Faustus*, as in the study of many other non-Shakespearean plays whose texts won't stand still, an exploration of the variant forms a given play has taken in the course of its history can lead directly into the most central interpretive issues confronting our profession today.

NOTES

[1]See Marlowe, *Doctor Faustus*, ed. Hilary Binda. Binda, who created the Perseus *Doctor Faustus*, offers an introduction to the site in an online article, "Hell and Hypertext Hath No Limits: Electronic Texts and the Crises in Criticism." My warmest thanks to Hilary Binda for sharing her work in progress.

[2]See Trevor Howard-Hill's speculation in "The Author as Scribe or Reviser? Middleton's Intentions in *A Game at Chess*."

Performance Conditions

A. R. Braunmuller

We who teach the plays of the period known variously as English Renaissance; early modern England; and the Elizabethan, Jacobean, and Caroline ages live in a wonderful moment. For the first time in many centuries, the foundations of early modern London's theater, or at least the manifest physical foundations of the Rose and the Globe Theatres, are no longer metaphors. Those foundations are now realizable, intermittently viewable facts. They are illustrated in A. R. Braunmuller and Michael Hattaway (10–11 [the Rose]) and fully analyzed by Simon Blatherwick (the Rose and esp. the Globe). Above all, students enjoy—and welcome—a sense of the material past and the past's materiality. Now they have the opportunity to enjoy that sense in a way their predecessors never did.

The students who enroll in my department's course English Drama 1567–1642, Excluding Shakespeare (or Liz-Jac non-Shak) are advanced ones, most of whom have at least two terms' experience with Shakespeare's plays in the university classroom, and they are likely to know some Shakespearean plays on film or video or, sadly less likely, on stage. (Lamentably, there are few films or videotaped performances of non-Shakespearean plays from our period; see the filmography by Philippa Sheppard in this volume.) The students' experience makes them sophisticated readers and imaginers of early modern theatrical texts, though not always very knowledgeable about the conditions under which these plays reached their earliest audiences. They need to be reminded of various framing circumstances: the names, dates of construction, and physical shapes and sizes of professional theater spaces (the large public amphitheater and the much smaller, more elite hall theater); the names and special talents of noted professional actors, their career patterns, class, and sex; the social and financial circumstances of actors in general along with the various ways the profession was structured economically; public, ecclesiastical, and governmental attitudes toward the theater (see Foakes; Nungezer; and Rutter; all provide ample quotation from early documents).

As knowledgeable Shakespeareans, the students also need to be reminded of moments when Shakespeare dramatized aspects of performance—the mechanicals' rehearsal in *A Midsummer Night's Dream*, Hal and Falstaff's rehearsal of Hal's meeting with his father in *Henry IV, Part 1* (2.4), Hamlet's discussion with the actors. Plays written by Shakespeare's contemporaries and successors are also rich in such episodes—for instance, Lord Letoy's company in Brome's *Antipodes*, Massinger's *The Roman Actor*, the induction to Marston's *Antonio and Mellida* (see Braunmuller and Hattaway 55–57) and his treatment of Oliver Owlet's Men in *Histriomastix*, and the preparations for the play "The Marriage of Wit and Wisdom" before Cardinal Morton in *Sir Thomas More*. Still more useful pedagogically are contemporary accounts of theatergoing, though they are few (see Braunmuller; Cunningham; Gurr [*Play-going*, esp. 105–14 and 205–51]; Platter; and Salgado). These eyewitness accounts provide useful starting points for discussing the experience of the theater—for example, what was recorded or omitted, since the accounts rarely include ordinary and therefore unremarked details that we would dearly like to know. Did indoor performances begin with three "soundings" (trumpet calls? backstage knockings?) that Jonson mentions at the beginning of *Cynthia's Revels*, *Poetaster*, and *Every Man Out*? Was there ever a movable curtain concealing some or all of the stage, and, if so, in what direction did it move? How many entrances for spectators were there at the Rose? the first Globe? the second Blackfriars?

As will become clear, I think giving students copies of original documents in facsimile if possible, with modern transcriptions as needed, stimulates their understanding of the past's pastness and intrigues, even inveigles, them to think more deeply. Much of this material past can also be conveyed, or at least memorably underpinned, with visual assistance—slides, handouts, overhead projections, class Web sites, and so on.

R. A. Foakes's volume of illustrations is a splendid source for maps and drawings of the theater district and images of individual actors, often in costume and sometimes even with their customary props. These identifiable actors are all comics: Richard Tarlton as himself, John Greene as Nobody, Robert Armin as John of the Hospital, Thomas Greene as Bubble. Foakes's volume also offers a rich collection of woodcuts from title pages. Photo reproductions of various title pages are useful, even all-text ones (like that for Marlowe's *Edward II* with its revealing comments about the Mortimer, Jr., plot or the elaborate one for Peele's *Edward I*), but especially ones with woodcuts (e.g., later quartos of *The Spanish Tragedy* and *Doctor Faustus*, or *Philaster* and *Maid's Tragedy*). A good early modern London map (such as the one in Braunmuller and Hattaway 4–5) is a useful starting point for discussing theatrical topography, patterns of settlement, and so forth. Much more detailed is Adrian Prockter and Robert Taylor's *The A to Z of Elizabethan London*; the place-name index allows students to locate the real London that Jonson mentions in *The Alchemist* and *Bartholomew Fair* and that Dekker, Heywood, and others never tire of citing. If audience size is significant, we should begin with the large south-of-the-Thames open-air public theaters, surrounded by London's principal red-light district. With the exception of the early Red Lion (1567) and a venue at Newington Butts (1577), these theaters—the Rose, Swan, and first Globe (constructed in that order, 1587–99) and later the Hope (1614)—are second-generation buildings that mark the public theater's decisive move from London's northern suburbs (where the Theatre and Curtain were built in 1576–77, but only the Curtain long remained in use, later joined by the Fortune [1600] and Red Bull [c 1606]) to the river's immediate southern bank. Various legal and especially ecclesiastical terms and conditions made this area of London more congenial to the theater's noisy, disruptive, and very public activities than the northern areas that were longer settled, more densely built up, and better surveilled by city and court authorities, though the Fortune and Red Bull survived outside the northern limits of Guildhall's jurisdiction.

As both industry and experience, theater changed over a seventy-five year span. One consequence was that many, even most, scripts sooner or later seem to have been revised for revival; for example, Philip Henslowe paid Ben Jonson on 25 September 1601 and 22 June 1602 (Henslowe, *Diary* 182 and 203) for "new adicyons for Jeronymo" (203) apparently Kyd's long-popular *Spanish Tragedy*. Teachers can make these events and many others more vivid for students by circulating copies from the Dulwich College manuscripts reproduced in Henslowe, *Papers* (which includes the *Diary*). They then incidentally have the opportunity to note how everyday Elizabethan handwriting differs from ours and more generally to stress how haphazardly information about the early modern London theater comes to us and how it is always mediated, whether in the form of *Henslowe's Diary*, printed stage directions, manuscript letters, or dramatic dialogue.

Theatrical changes responded to less recoverable changes in public mood; to the quality, quantity, and temperament of a moment's dominant playwrights; to the changing genres and changing native and Continental sources those playwrights used; to foreign affairs and domestic tranquility or upset; and to many still subtler or now indefinable circumstances. Immersed in their commercial warfare, the playwrights were as aware as Horace in the *Ars Poetica* was of how words and plays and fashion changed over time. Plays shifted their forms as readily as clothes, that most derided of fashions:

> The fashion of play-making I can properly compare to nothing so naturally as the alteration in apparel: for in the time of the great-crop doublet, your huge bombastic plays, quilted with mighty words to lean purpose, was then only in fashion; and as the doublet fell, neater inventions began to set up. Now in the time of spruceness, our plays follow the niceness of our garments: single plots, quaint conceits, lecherous jests, dressed up in hanging sleeves; and those are fit for the times [. . .].   (Middleton, *Girl* 68; epistle)[1]

Examples to support these broad remarks include the flourishing of nativist, patriotic, usually anti-Spanish plays and English history plays that may slightly predate and then certainly follow the Armada's defeat in 1588 and the growing awareness of English exploration and imperial or colonial projects: Greene's *Alphonsus, King of Aragon*; Peele's *Battle of Alcazar*; Kyd's *Spanish Tragedy*; Lyly's *Gallathea* (deeply local, ostensibly classical) and *Mother Bombie* (more plainly English than *Gallathea*); or Peele's *Old Wives' Tale* and *Edward I*; Marlowe's *Edward II* and *The Massacre at Paris*; and the anonymous *Captain Thomas Stukeley*. At the turn of the century and around James VI and I's accession appeared a group of plays centered on Reformation events and per-sonalities: Rowley's *When You See Me, You Know Me*, Chettle's *Cardinal Wolsey*, Dekker's *Whore of Babylon*, or the anonymous *Thomas, Lord Crom-well*, for example. More than three decades after the Armada, the so-called Spanish Match of Prince Charles and the Infanta, popular with some courtiers, mostly unpopular with the broader populace, generated politically themed plays in the early 1620s, especially *A Game at Chess* (see Braunmuller; Ribner; Rackin; Cogswell; Braunmuller and Hattaway).

A particularly striking example of generational change in the dominant play-writing cadre occurs around 1599–1600. In the classroom, a chart or better yet a graph of play-performances and birth and death dates tells the tale. By 1599–1600, Marlowe, Kyd, Greene, and Peele were dead, and Lodge and Lyly were pursuing other careers; only Shakespeare persisted to become more fully himself, or more fully his works and eventually an anachronism. The newcom-ers who replaced this generation during the late 1590s and early 1600s in-cluded Chapman, Dekker, Heywood, Jonson, Marston, and Middleton. A less sharply defined change occurred when Fletcher, Massinger, and Shirley suc-cessively rose to dominate playwriting in the second through fourth decades of the seventeenth century, a period when fewer and fewer new plays entered the public stage (see Salingar, Harrison, and Cochrane).

How did it feel to attend one of these plays as first performed? Out of direct sight of the authorities, though not often out of mind, the Southbank theaters literally trumpeted their wares—the Swan Theatre's trumpeter ap-pears in an implausible perspective in the de Witt-van Buchell drawing (Foakes no. 26; Braunmuller and Hattaway 14)—and could draw huge crowds. Middleton's *A Game at Chess* (at the second Globe, August 1624) occasioned a large volume of surviving commentary (gathered in Howard-Hill's edition of the play and analyzed there and in Braunmuller). This ma-terial, along with copies of the first and third quartos' title pages and the title page of one of Middleton's sources, Thomas Scot's *Second Part of Vox Populi* (see Foakes no. 54, for all three), provokes speculation about theater practice, especially the apparent use of the Spanish ambassador's sedan chair, as well as public response.

Consider one of the shorter accounts, John Chamberlain's letter, 21 August 1624, to Dudley Carleton. *A Game at Chess*, Chamberlain wrote,

> hath ben followed with extraordinarie concourse, and frequented by all sorts of people old and younge, rich and poore, masters and servants, papists and puritans, wise men *et ct.*, churchmen and statesmen as Sir Henry Wotton, Sir Albert Morton, Sir Benjamin Ruddier, Sir Thomas Lake, and a world besides; the Ladie Smith wold have gon yf she could have persuaded me to go with her. I am not so sowre nor severe but that I wold willingly have attended her, but I could not sit so long, for

we must have ben there before one a clocke at the farthest to find any
roome.   (2: 478)

Although Chamberlain seeks to impress his correspondent with the "extraor-
dinarie concourse" to the Globe and although none of the important persons
he names can be proved to have attended, much may be inferred. For such
a popular play the Thames filled with watermen conveying spectators who
packed the wooden benches so far in advance of the performance's start that
some fastidious folk regretfully refused to attend. At least some of the time,
we may guess, everyone went to the theater without distinction of sex, age,
social class, or occupation—men, women, youngsters, and teenagers (some of
the "servants" must be apprentices, the theatergoing group the city authorities
feared most). Persons of every social order attended, knights and ladies (like
the widowed Lady Smith), high officials (Lake was a secretary of state, Wotton
had just been named provost of Eton College, Rudyerd was member of Parliament for Portsmouth and surveyor of the Court of Wards), and even those
who condemned plays ethically or professionally ("papists and puritans"). To
object to playgoing was to risk being thought "sour or severe," a censorious
killjoy. Finally, at least sometimes, "to find any roome" one had to get to the
theater an hour or more before the performance began.

   Once inside the theater, visitors unfamiliar with the buildings were struck
by the convincingly rich-looking painted "marble," the carved wood, and the
gilding (Chambers 2: 358, 362); modern students will have to make do with
images of aristocratic interiors, many of which followed precisely the same
pattern of truly expensive and wholly fake. As with those impressive interiors,
so with costumes and props from the theater. All are gone. Only a mock
charter used in the 1591 Theobalds entertainment for Elizabeth, which is now
in the Elizabethan Club (Yale University) collection, survives from London's
pre-1660 theater. Other surviving documents, such as written descriptions of
wardrobe and Henslowe's financial accounts, make it certain that costumes
constituted a company's single largest investment (far more than playbooks,
for example) and were as grand and impressive as could be afforded (see
Platter 167; Rutter), not least because they competed with the notoriously
extravagant attire of many Londoners and some audience members (see Linthicum and esp. Newman 111–27). While the medieval aesthetic, which translated all times and places into the contemporary, largely prevailed, fidelity to
real-world garb sometimes caused offense and usually illicited criticism. As
Henry Wotton's letter to Edmund Bacon, 2 July 1613, memorably says:

   The King's players had a new play [. . .] representing some principal
   pieces of the reign of Henry VIII, which was set forth with many extraordinary circumstances of pomp and majesty, even to the matting of
   the stage; the Knights of the Order with their Georges and garters, the

Guards with their embroidered coats, and the like: sufficient in truth
within a while to make greatness very familiar if not ridiculous.

(L. P. Smith 2: 32–33)

Early modern printed plays sport some extraordinary stage directions (see
Dessen; Dessen and Thomson). Some may reflect wishes rather than practi-
cable effects, but stage dialogue and independent accounts show that many
were realized in more than symbolic ways. How the theater produced its most
spectacular effects—the multiple suns of *The Troublesome Reign of King
John*, for instance; the dragon of Greene's *Friar Bacon and Friar Bungay*; the
tree with diadems and crowns that rises and falls in Peele's *Arraignment of
Paris*; "the sinking of Queene *Elinor*, who suncke at Charing-crosse, and rose
againe at Potters-hith" (Peele, title page, *Edward I*); and many other stage
effects—we infer from Continental practice and printed discussions, especially Sebastiano Serlio's *Tutte l'opere d'architettura*, translated into English
in 1611, which includes some helpful illustrations of neoclassical sets, and
Sabbattini's later work (see Serlio; Hewitt). Rises and falls, sinkings and risings
required the (single? central?) trapdoor of the public stage. Burning resin,
mentioned in the induction to *A Warning for Fair Women*, made smoke and
fog (see Hattaway 112), and fireworks (an Italian specialty) produced other
effects. For sound effects, bells rang, "chambers" (cannons with blanks like
those that set fire to the first Globe in 1613) fired, thunder (cannon balls in
troughs) tolled. The open-air public theater employed a delicate semiotic system for lighting effects—candles, torches, lanterns, and lamps meant "darkness," and "Lo, where the sun [. . .] [or moon]" represented day and night,
for example (see Hellinga; for a detailed account, see Graves). In act 2, scene
1 of Marlowe's *Jew of Malta*, the nighttime scene in which Abigail steals back
her father's hidden fortune, the father below, she "above" on the stage's upper
level, illustrates the way dialogue and props (e.g., *"Enter Barabas with a light"*)
combine to make a scene something it manifestly is not in the audience's real-
world experience.

Just as the audience could tell day from night and imaginatively realize the
paradox that when lanterns and candles appeared on the stage it grew "dark,"
so they enjoyed the variety—and the implausibility—of dramatic disguises. I
mentioned above the performance of "The Marriage of Wit and Wisdom"
being prepared in *Sir Thomas More*. The scene, like several others in this
underrated and highly teachable play, assumes an audience sophisticated in
deceit: "We would desire your honour but to stay a little: one of my fellows
is but run to Ogle's for a long beard for young Wit, and he'll be here presently"
(Munday et al. 147). This Ogle, as some audience members must have known,
is the very John Ogle who (with his son) supplied actors with beards and wigs
from the 1570s to at least the end of the century. If beards could be risible
props, then the ubiquitous convention of impenetrable disguise did not escape

self-conscious ridicule, as Angelo's comprehensive demolition in Chapman's *May Day* makes clear:

> though it be the stale refuge of miserable Poets, by change of a hat or a cloake, to alter the whole state of a Comedie, so as the father must not know his owne child forsooth, nor the wife her husband, yet you must not thinke they doe in earnest to carry it away so [. . .].
>
> (*Plays* 338)

What may be disguise of another sort appears on one of the most pedagogically useful title pages from the period, the 1615 quarto of *The Spanish Tragedy* (Foakes no. 44; Hattaway illus. 12). Comparing the image with the play text makes it clear that the image conveys not a single moment but a sequence of actions (reading chronologically from right to left), from Bel-imperia's call for help to Hieronimo's discovery of his son's pendant body. On the supposition that it conveys at least something of one of the most famous and most parodied episodes of the early modern English theater, the image yields many tantalizing possibilities. One notices the torch in Hieronimo's hand (it is night); he approaches the structure where Horatio hangs, which is fictionally an arbor but recalls the "frame for the [be]heading" in an early theatrical inventory (Henslowe, *Diary* 321). According to the text, Hieronimo enters *in his shirt* and asks, "What outcries pluck me from my naked bed?" (2.5.1). Is he differently dressed from the other living male figure portrayed in the woodcut? Hanged Horatio is booted and spurred, as fits his martial role but not the love scene the murderers have just interrupted, while Bel-imperia wears an elegant court dress rather old-fashioned by 1615. Her assailant appears to have a black face. This last feature raises two questions: which character the figure represents and what the black face signifies. Is it Prince Lorenzo, Bel-imperia's brother, who says in both text and woodcut, "Stop her mouth" (2.4.63)? Or is it one of the servants, Pedrigano or Serberine? Relatedly, might the black face indicate race (i.e., a "blackamoor," not implausible in Spain)? If so, then the figure is more likely to be a servant than brother to the manifestly white-faced Bel-imperia figure, and the actor would be wearing makeup (see Drew-Bear). If, as the dialogue suggests, the figure is Lorenzo, then the black face probably represents a mask, conventionally black when worn by villains.

This woodcut does not help much on one controversial issue, how boy actors appeared when performing women's roles. The first quartos of Beaumont and Fletcher's *The Maid's Tragedy* and *Philaster* (Foakes nos. 50 and 52, respectively) are probably still more distant from performance than the *Spanish Tragedy* title page; they do illustrate, however, two female figures, Aspatia dressed as a male and being wounded by the male Amintor in the former, Princess Arethusa undisguised but bare-breasted and bleeding in the latter.

Comparison of the Aspatia and Amintor figures may suggest to students, as it sometimes does to me, that an effort has been made to portray cruder, more martial, facial features for Amintor and more delicate (boyish? feminine?) ones for Aspatia. Both appear to be dressed in what passes for fashionable male court garb in Jacobean woodcuts.

It is hard to doubt that someone's prurience, rather than an anxious fidelity to performance, helped create Arethusa's image. That probable distortion is a reminder of the mediating layers that lie between us and the images and between the images and the stage. Perhaps the main distortion, after all, is the crudity of English woodcut technique available in the period's printing houses. Related distortions and mediations, or at the very least omissions, also mean that contemporary letters and documents, even contemporary financial accounts of theater business like Henslowe's diary, can provide only uncertain glimpses of performance conditions. Just as it is important for students to sense the past's reality, so too they need to recognize our fallible means of knowing that past.

NOTE

¹Quotations of *The Roaring Girl* are from Paul Mulholland's edition; those of *The Spanish Tragedy* are from Philip Edwards's edition.

Fair Counterfeits:
A Bibliography of Visual Aids for Renaissance Drama

Philippa Sheppard

It is a hackneyed truth that our students have grown up in a world where information is increasingly presented in a visual form, and most are quicker at interpreting images than words. A judicious use of visual aids can therefore be invaluable for stimulating their interest in unfamiliar Renaissance plays and for expanding their understanding of the times in which the plays were written. This annotated bibliography highlights books with useful illustrations for the teaching of Renaissance drama.

In an age of technology, it may seem hopelessly old-fashioned to be showing students pictures from books. But illustrated books still have many advantages over more complicated aids. They require little planning (no need to have a VCR, TV, or tape recorder set up), and they can be flexibly integrated into the lecture. There is no threat of mechanical failure or licensing infringement. Yet the illustrations still provide a needed change from aural learning and are wonderful aide-mémoires. My students have reported that they are able to keep playwrights straight much more easily if they can associate a face with a name and play title. In a survey course that examines twenty or more playwrights, distinguishing every playwright can be quite a challenge. In addition to showing my students images of Elizabethan and Jacobean life from books, I bring in relevant articles from newspapers and magazines and programs from theater productions. These materials are important because they prove to students that these plays are alive in theaters still; they are not museum pieces only studied in the halls of academe.

Visual aids have to be well timed in the lecture to be effective. Some students find it distracting to flip through a book while the instructor is talking. I pass around marked books, programs, articles, and such during the first or last few minutes of class, while I am taking silent attendance or writing a class plan or a list of secondary sources on the board. If the illustration is large and clear, I hold it up for the class to view at an appropriate moment in the lecture.

What follows is a selective, personal list. Many of the books are old; some are not particularly scholarly: They are selected solely on the merit and quantity of their plates.

The State

Political Figures: Portraits

Sydney Anglo's *Images of Tudor Kingship* reveals political figures as they are represented on coins, seals, standards, and monuments. Radu Boureanu's

Holbein is useful when providing historical background and for history plays; two instances of the excellent color reproductions are *The Ambassadors* (displays early Tudor scientific instruments, a lute, and a memento mori) and a portrait of Henry VIII and several of his wives. Lionel Cust's *Notes on the Authentic Portraits of Mary Queen of Scots* reproduces in black and white portraits from all over Europe, including depictions of Mary's trial and execution.

The best single volume for providing visual aids for the important figures in the Renaissance is *The National Portrait Gallery Collection* (Foister, Gibson, and Simson). Especially valuable when teaching history plays, the sixty-five large color reproductions of sixteenth- and seventeenth-century portraits include Richard II; Edward IV; Richard III; Henry VII; Catherine of Aragon; Thomas Wolsey; Thomas Cromwell; Anne Boleyn; Sir Thomas More and family; Edward VI; Thomas Cranmer; Lady Jane Grey; William Cecil; Robert Devereux, earl of Essex; James I; Anne of Denmark; and Oliver Cromwell. If you are teaching Jonson's *Oberon, the Faery Prince* as an example of a masque, Lucy Gent and Nigel Llewellyn's *Renaissance Bodies: The Human Figure in English Culture c. 1540–1660* is a good source for black-and-white portraits of Henry, Prince of Wales. J. W. Goodison's *Catalogue of Cambridge Portraits: The University Collection* boasts only a few portraits, but they are clear, large, and easily reproducible. Elizabeth W. Pomeroy's *Reading the Portraits of Queen Elizabeth I* comprises the famous portraits of Elizabeth: as princess, in her coronation robes, playing a lute, with the three goddesses (in *The Judgement of Paris*—a good illustration to accompany Peele's *The Arraignment of Paris*), the Armada portrait, the Darnley portrait, the Siena portrait, the Ermine portrait, the Ditchley portrait, and the Rainbow portrait.

An interesting selection of large, colorful reproductions of portraits, maps, and photographs of places and household objects is featured in A. L. Rowse's *The Illustrated History of Britain*. Roy Strong's *The Cult of Elizabeth: Elizabethan Portraiture and Pageantry* is invaluable, especially for teaching the plays of the University Wits, particularly Lyly, in which overlooked knights solicit the attention of a queen portrayed as a goddess. Of particular interest are the following monochrome illustrations: Elizabeth going in a procession to Blackfriars; Elizabeth as Cynthia (vital for *Endymion*); and several of Inigo Jones's designs for pageants, including Oberon's palace for Jonson's *Oberon, the Faery Prince*.

Religion

Many black-and-white plates depicting devils, Faust, and others engaged in the dark arts appear in Neil Brough's *New Perspectives of Faust*. Maria Perry's *The Word of a Prince* includes a number of monochrome portraits of religious figures, including Nicholas Ridley, Hugh Latimer, and Reginald Pole. The best book for illustrations on the Reformation and the Saint Bartholomew's Day Massacre (particularly fruitful when lecturing on Marlowe's *The Massacre at Paris*) is Neville Williams's *Reform and Revolt*. It includes black-and-white plates depicting Luther nailing his ninety-five theses to Palast Church door; the sale of indulgences; John Calvin; William Tyndale; Anabaptists (useful for Jonson's *The Alchemist*); the seven deadly sins (advantageous when teaching Marlowe's *Doctor Faustus*); Henry IV of Navarre; and Henry of Lorraine, duke of Guise. It also features color plates of the Council of Trent, Luther preaching, the Saint Bartholomew's Massacre, Catherine of Medeci, Henry IV presented with the keys of Paris, and Charles IX. See also *A Selection of Emblems*, edited by William A. McQueen.

Military Life and War

Peter Kemp's *The Campaign of the Spanish Armada* is richly illustrated with color and black-and-white plates depicting every aspect of the campaign from its inception to its aftermath; some examples: the Armada under attack in the Channel, the attack on the Armada by fireships near Calais, and the battle of Gravelines.

The Folger produces excellent illustrated booklets on Tudor and Stuart civilization, including John R. Hale's *The Art of War and Renaissance England*. This booklet reproduces, in black and white, engravings of drills, army formations, and weapons.

Colonization

A succinct booklet, Wesley Frank Craven's *The Virginia Company of London, 1606–1624*, is illustrated with eleven clear, black-and-white medium-sized plates, including the heading for a broadside issued by the company and Captain John Smith. Lavishly illustrated, John Winton's *Sir Walter Ralegh* is especially useful for depicting seventeenth-century exploration and colonization (particularly Guiana). It includes black-and-white and color plates of Raleigh (all stages in his life), Sir John Hawkins, Martin Frobisher, John Dee, Thomas Hariot, various ships, Florida Indians and the Ewaipanema, and Guianese "men whose heads / [Do grow] beneath their shoulders" (*Othello* 1.3.143–44).

Maps

The National Geographic Society's Art Department produced a map, *Shakespeare's Britain*, for their May 1964 issue. This map by Lisa Biganzoli titled *Shakespeare's Britain* is based on John Speed's map from his 1611 atlas, available in an edition titled *The Counties of Britain: A Tudor Atlas*. Biganzoli's map is excellent for teaching plays set in Britain and for background information on playwrights. Valeria Bella and Piero Bella's *Cartografia rara* is a collection of facsimiles of early maps of the known world and comprises many from the sixteenth and seventeenth centuries. David B. Quinn and A. N. Ryan's *England's Sea Empire, 1550–1642* provides modern monochrome maps showing trade routes and the circumnavigations of Drake and Cavendish. Gunter Schilder, Bernard Aikema, and Oeter van der Krogt's *The Atlas Blaeu-*

Van Der Hem of the Austrian National Library in eight volumes presents and fully annotates all six hundred maps covering the known world from Joan Blaeu's well-known *Atlas Maior* (1662–72), also available in a modern edition titled *Blaue's the Grand Atlas of the Seventeenth Century*. P. D. A. Harvey, *Maps of Tudor England*, is full of color and black-and-white maps that are useful for study of the period.

Education

I use modern guidebooks on Oxford and Cambridge to show students color photographs of individual colleges associated with certain playwrights (e.g., *Oxford in Colour*, by Elizabeth Ingpen and A. N. Court). For a general prolegomena, the following histories of the two universities provide good illustrations: John Prest's *The Illustrated History of Oxford University* and Elisabeth Leedham-Green's *A Concise History of the University of Cambridge*, which has a chapter on Tudor Cambridge that includes a monochrome print of the frontispiece to *Ignoramus*, a play performed by students in front of James I.

John Howard Brown's *Elizabethan Schooldays* includes small black-and-white plates of period schools, masters, and students. A complete visual representation (in watercolors) of the Inns of Court can be found in Cecil Headlam's *The Inns of Court*. See also Nicholas Orme's *Education and Society in Medieval and Renaissance England*.

Arts and Sciences

Literary and Theatrical Figures: Portraits

One of the richest sources for visual aids is Anthony Burgess's *Shakespeare*. It is lavishly illustrated and includes plates both in black and white and color depicting many aspects of Renaissance life, as well as portraits of the artistic figures of the day such as John Florio, Michael Drayton, George Chapman, Robert Burton, John Donne, Beaumont and Fletcher, the earl of Surrey, Lord Strange, Ferdinando Stanley, Lord Hunsdon, Edward Alleyn as Tamburlaine, William Kemp, Robert Armin, Children of the Chapel, Richard Burbage, William Sly, John Lowin (these last three are characters in the induction to Marston's *The Malcontent*), Nathaniel Field, Edward Alleyn, Richard Tarleton, Christopher Marlowe, Sir Philip Sidney, Ben Jonson, Henry Wriothesley (earl of Southampton), William Somerset (earl of Worcester), Richard Sackville (earl of Dorset), and Inigo Jones. See also Ann Hoffman's *Lives of the Tudor Age, 1485–1603* and Alan Palmer and Veronica Palmer's *Who's Who in Shakespeare's England*.

Theatrical Life

Jonathan Bate and Russell Jackson's *Shakespeare: An Illustrated Stage History* provides clear small black-and-white illustrations including two details from

John Norden's panorama of the City of London, a bear-baiting bill, Peacham's sketch of *Titus Andronicus*, a detail from Visscher's panorama of London showing the Globe and the Beargarden, de Witt's drawing of the Swan Theatre, a reconstruction of the Rose Theatre, a ground plan of the Rose, Hollar's sketch of Southwark showing the second Globe Theatre, Inigo Jones's designs for the Cockpit-in-Court, and the frontispiece to *The Wits* depicting some popular stage characters.

Illustrated with small monochrome plates, A. R. Braunmuller and Michael Hattaway's *The Cambridge Companion to English Renaissance Drama* includes de Jongh's sketch of London Bridge, 1627; a photograph of the Rose Theatre's foundations from the excavations; John Green in the anonymous play *Nobody and Somebody;* Inigo Jones's designs for an antimasque; and two designs for *Oberon*—useful when teaching Jonson's masque (Slights). Paul Cox's four drawings in color of the Globe and the Inigo Jones Theatre are featured in Andrew Gurr and John Orrell's *Rebuilding Shakespeare's Globe.* It also provides small black-and-white plates showing the audience on the balcony of a hall playhouse, the stage hangings of another hall stage, a Thames ferry with passengers, and the designs for the recently completed new Globe Theatre in London. Peter Thomson's *Shakespeare's Theatre* comprises only a few monochrome plates such as a modern map of London showing the location of the theaters from 1576 to 1613; a photograph of Southwark today; a model of the Swan Theatre; a drawing (c. 1600) of a mountebank's stage (useful for Jonson's *Volpone*); and a photograph of the hall screen at Middle Temple, in front of which *Twelfth Night* was played in 1602.

Art and Architecture

Zillah Dovey's *An Elizabethan Progress* and June Osborne's *Entertaining Elizabeth I* present illustrations of the houses Elizabeth visited as queen. A seminal work on the subject, Frederick Hartt's *History of Italian Renaissance Art* is lavishly illustrated with both black-and-white and color plates, useful for presenting contemporary interpretations of classical and religious subjects that appear as allusions in the plays; instances include Titian's *Rape of Europa* (1159–60) and *Cain Killing Abel* (1542), Correggio's *Jupiter and Ganymede* (1530s), and Parmigianino's *Cupid Carving His Bow* (1535). A huge, lavishly illustrated volume, Doreen Yarwood's *The Architecture of England* provides monochrome examples of Tudor and Jacobean architecture, including plans of the great houses. It also defines architectural terms and includes clear drawings of different styles.

Music

David C. Price's *Patrons and Musicians of the English Renaissance* comprises black-and-white plates of paintings and murals that depict musicians (some aristocratic) with tenor violin, cittern, treble violin, bandora, virginals, and lute.

See also *The New Grove Dictionary of Musical Instruments* in three volumes, edited by Stanley Sadie, for illustrations of period instruments and Morrison Comegys Boyd's *Elizabethan Music and Musical Criticism*.

Science and Medicine

Denise Albanese's *New Science, New World* contains black-and-white plates illustrating aspects of scientific life and of travel to the New World, such as an anatomy lesson and recent technological advances (printing press; magnetic wind rose, which was an early compass; still; cannon; mechanical clock). In fifteen volumes, R. T. Gunther's *Early Science in Oxford* is richly illustrated with black-and-white plates that comprise portraits of scientists and photographs and drawings of instruments and inventions.

Social History

Family Life

David Mountfield's *Everyday Life in Elizabethan England* contains reproductions of details from the *Life and Death of Sir Henry Unton*, a painting that depicts many aspects of Renaissance life; in addition it includes pictures of the Cobham family, a woman doing housework, family pets, weavers, female merchants, a street in Smithfield, a jeweller's studio, a printing house, and shops selling hats and hose. Lena Cowen Orlin's *Elizabethan Households* is replete with black-and-white plates depicting domestic affairs, a brickmaker (useful when giving a biography of Jonson), a leather wallet containing maps, a bedroom (1637), a husband beating his wife, a laundress at work, a moneylender (valuable when teaching *Eastward Ho!*), Leaden Hall Market, tableware of all kinds, a silver bodkin, a birthing stool, a parlor scene, and others. See also Mary Abbott's *Life Cycles in England, 1560–1720*.

Sport and Games

Lilly C. Stone's *English Sports and Recreations* contains monochrome reproductions of sixteenth- and seventeenth-century woodcuts depicting bowling, balloon ball, wrestling, ice-skating, swimming, jousting, hunting deer and boar, hawking, fishing, cockfighting, cards, tennis, the Cotswold games, children's games (tops, stilts, hobby horse—useful for Jonson's *Bartholomew Fair*), shovelboard, billiards, tables, dicing, a fencing school, and, most interesting, Elizabeth I offering to cut the throat of a slain deer.

Clothing and Appearance

Divided by region, Cesare Vecellio's *Vecellio's Renaissance Costume Book* covers the known world. The ample Italian section includes examples of ancient Roman garb (useful for Jonson's *Sejanus*). All the regions are subdivided into towns and into representatives of various classes and professions, from men of the cloth and fakirs to prostitutes and pirates.

H. K. Morse's *Elizabethan Pageantry* provides portraits of significant Renaissance figures, English and foreign, and analyzes their apparel, using quotations from contemporary sources like Thomas Coryate's *Coryat's Crudities*. Most interesting are plates showing hair bleaching, attire for weddings, riding lessons, court sessions, church, and war. The book also contains a useful glossary of sixteenth- and seventeenth-century sartorial terms.

Food and Drink

With a chapter devoted to Shakespeare's gastronomic London, Annette Hope's *Londoner's Larder* features monochrome plates of sixteenth- and seventeenth-century diners, street sellers, water carriers, street markets, and fishwives. Paola Marini, Paolo Rigoli, and Aldo Dell'Igna's *Cucine, cibi, e vini* is enlivened by black-and-white plates depicting Italian culinary scenes, kitchens designed by Palladio, cooking equipment, and a banquet. C. Anne Wilson's *Food and Drink in Britain* is illustrated with black-and-white plates showing the catching and smoking of salmon, the hunting of harts, early seventeenth-century diners with squared trencher-bread, and an Elizabethan kitchen.

Beasts

Often Renaissance playwrights use a beast in a figure of speech for which students have no mental image unless the instructor provides one. Matthaus Merian's *1300 Real and Fanciful Animals from Seventeenth Century Engravings* is composed of black-and-white reproductions of griffins, unicorns, basilisks, harpies, and the like. John Vinycomb's *Fictitious and Symbolic Creatures in Art* includes black-and-white illustrations of a huge number of beasts, along with detailed descriptions of them. The reproducible illustrations are contemporary, not Renaissance. The author divides the book into sections: celestial beings (e.g., seraphs), chimerical creatures of the dragon and serpent kind (e.g., cockatrice), other chimerical creatures and heraldic beasts (e.g., manticora), and fictitious creatures of the sea (e.g., siren). The book also gives clear explanations of heraldry terms, especially valuable for tackling history plays. When teaching *Volpone*, *Reynard the Fox* by Kenneth Varty and *350 Aesop's Fables* translated by Geo Fyler Townsend are also useful.

Death

James M. Clark's *The Dance of Death in the Middle Ages and the Renaissance* offers photographs of church murals and stained glass windows around Europe depicting death. Hans Holbein's *The Dance of Death* depicts the skeletal figure of Death in medias res and is invaluable for discussing the theme of death and the visual sources for some of the playwrights' images of death and for conveying to students a sense of everyday life in this period. Most members of Renaissance society, from the emperor to the fool, are figured in the epic dance.

Teaching Texture in
Jonson's *The Alchemist*

Joseph Candido

So this is a play for study.

The learned counsel of J. B. Steane, quoted here from his fine introduction to *The Alchemist* (2), may offer faint comfort to the typical undergraduate pondering the rhetorical and structural complexities of Jonson's play. "OK," such a student might respond, "but just *how* do I study a play like this? Where do I begin?" Before attempting to answer such questions, we would do well to remember what the field of Renaissance drama—its contours so familiar and sharply defined to those of us who teach it—often looks like to a student approaching it for the first time.

For many of our students, perhaps even most, Renaissance drama consists of a largely undifferentiated mass of troublesome "old" English from which they struggle to extract meaning. In the case of particularly difficult writers like Jonson, Webster, or Chapman, students find themselves grappling with works that, at first blush, seem almost completely inaccessible to them at the level of language and, perhaps even worse, largely indistinguishable in texture and tone from the works of other dramatists. One way a teacher can address this problem is by stressing that the key to understanding various authors is to focus on the linguistic texture of their plays—that is, the complex of allusion, idiom, stylistic devices, patterns of speech, and so on that make up their individual poetic imaginations. Teachers need to give students a way to read these playwrights—and by way to read I don't necessarily mean a modus operandi or interpretive attitude (though these would certainly and happily result), so much as a familiarity with writers' very different poetic idioms and an awareness of how each of these idioms creates its own imaginative world. Along these lines, I think that it is extremely important for students to hear Renaissance drama not just in performance but as poetry or prose that is accessible in just the same way that any other poetic or narrative utterance is accessible. (One can draw comparisons here with opera, another art form students tend to dislike until they hear how its music creates character and an atmosphere of ideas.) Once students hear passages read aloud in class and pay attention to the passages' literary texture, they can feel more confident about discussing a play's ideas, structure, relation to the dramatic tradition, or any other critical concerns that interest them. It is also useful, where applicable, to stress individualizing habits of speech (a character's obsession with repetition, for example, or preference for a particular word or words) and ask students why an author might want to include such a feature. If a teacher can help demystify language by confronting it head-on, language can become the aspect of the play that students learn to enjoy. In my experience, students never seem to have trouble interpreting a play from any critical perspective once they feel comfortable with its language.

All this gets us back to the hypothetical question posed above: how does one go about achieving such ends with a play like *The Alchemist*, bedeviled as readers so often are by its notorious clash of jargons, abundance of remote topical references, and learned obscurities? Surely we cannot make sudden scholars of ourselves or our students overnight, but we can nonetheless attend to many important issues in the play simply by heeding its linguistic texture. I would like to begin with the first of Sir Epicure Mammon's remarkable speeches (2.1), a voluptuously ecstatic aria on the tangible pleasures that come with acquiring the philosophers' stone:

> Come on, sir. Now you set your foot on shore
> In *Novo Orbe*. Here's the rich Peru:
> And there within, sir, are the golden mines,
> Great Solomon's Ophir! He was sailing to't
> Three years, but we have reached it in ten months.
> This is the day wherein to all my friends
> I will pronounce the happy word 'Be rich!'
> This day you shall be *Spectatissimi*.
> You shall no more deal with the hollow die,
> Or the frail card. No more be at charge of keeping
> The livery-punk, for the young heir, that must
> Seal, at all hours, in his shirt. No more,
> If he deny, ha' him beaten to't, as he is
> That brings him the commodity. No more
> Shall thirst of satin or the covetous hunger

Of velvet entrails for a rude-spun cloak
To be displayed at Madam Augusta's, make
The sons of sword and hazard fall before
The golden calf and on their knees, whole nights,
Commit idolatry with wine and trumpets,
Or go a-feasting after drum and ensign.
No more of this. You shall start up young Viceroys,
And have your punks and punketees, my Surly.
And unto thee I speak it first: 'Be rich!'   (2.1.1–24)[1]

There is a relatively simple idea at work here—the basic tension between the base matter of a grossly realized world and a powerful human longing to transcend it—that is expressly realized in Mammon's speech at the level of language. Such expressions as *"Novo Orbe,"* "rich Peru," "Solomon's Ophir," and *"Spectatissimi"* not only imply elevation by their obvious sonority but also clash with such strikingly less grandiloquent expressions as "rude-spun cloak," "commodity," and the devastatingly pejorative trio "livery-punk," "punks," and "punketees." The point is clear. Mammon's passion for the stone, no matter how benevolent his intentions for its use, is hopelessly and ironically rooted in a sybaritic personality just as "frail" and "hollow" as the world it seeks to transcend. The "commodity" scheme to which he alludes (a swindle by which the "livery-punk" would convince her gullible lover to sign away his fortune for worthless commodities that he would later have to sell at greatly reduced cost) glances at the position in which Mammon places himself with Dol, Subtle, and Face as a result of his own greed. Just as the sublime "golden mines" of Solomon fuse ominously in the speech with the idolatrous "golden calf" worshiped by the Hebrews, so Mammon's desire to turn the world to gold contains at its core the debased elements of his own destruction.

Once students see this basic point about Jonson's handling of Mammon, they then have a critical perspective with which to approach numerous other speeches and incidents in the play. Take, for example, the extraordinary sequence in 2.2 where Mammon propels himself into a sort of material sublimity that is itself a verbal intimation of the obsessive folly of alchemical projection:

I will have all my beds blown up, not stuffed;
Down is too hard. And then, mine oval room
Filled with such pictures as Tiberius took
From Elephantis, and dull Aretine
But coldly imitated. Then my glasses,
Cut in more subtle angles, to disperse
And multiply the figures as I walk
Naked between my succubae. My mists
I'll have of perfume, vapoured 'bout the room,

> To lose ourselves in; and my baths like pits
> To fall into, from whence we will come forth
> And roll us dry in gossamer and roses.
> (Is it arrived at ruby?)—Where I spy
> A wealthy citizen or rich lawyer
> Have a sublimed pure wife, unto that fellow
> I'll send a thousand pound, to be my cuckold.
> (2.2.41–56)

Here again we see an imagination (like the deceptive mirrors in Mammon's room that "disperse / And multiply the figures") where "succubae" and the "sublimed pure wife," separate moral entities at first, somehow get transmuted into like instruments for the same (im)moral use. Mammon would have his purity and defile it too. Jonson's startling linguistic contrasts in the long passage that follows (2.2.65–106) everywhere make the point, but nowhere more sharply than just moments before Mammon's reverie reaches its most extravagant heights. Mammon insists that even his flatterers must be "pure" and his fools "eloquent"; his poets, however, must be creatures of a more specific sort: "The same that writ so subtly of the *fart*, / Whom I will entertain still for that subject" (2.2.60–64; my emphasis). With a single word, Jonson shows the base uses to which Mammon's "gossamer" imagination inevitably returns.

At this point it would be useful to stress to students that *The Alchemist* is a virtual echo chamber of the concerns raised in Mammon's speeches. Everywhere we look the language of the play emphasizes the ironies implicit in a desire for purity that is rooted in a world of coarse adulteration. One thinks immediately of Ananias and "Wholesome," the "sanctified elders," whose "pure zeal" is indistinguishable from Greed (3.1.4), or the wonderfully named "Abel" Drugger, "A miserable rogue, [who] lives with cheese, / And has the worms," who needs purifying medicines and who yearns for the social elevation that would allow him to pursue Dame Pliant (2.6.81–82). Especially revealing in this regard is the sequence during which Subtle and Mammon try, for obviously different reasons, to quiet Surly's outspoken contempt for their enterprise (2.3.1–210). The spurious sense of elevation and learning implied by Subtle's extravagant jargon ("*balneo vaporoso*," "*lac virginis*," "*Materia liquida*," "*propria materia*," etc.), as well as his vocabulary of refinement ("perfection," "glorified spirit," "triple soul," "virtue," etc.) gets remorselessly unmasked by the contemptuous blazon with which Surly parodies Subtle's deliberately obfuscating, pseudoscientific terminology. Surly's catalog, ticked off with an almost Baconian precision, coldly links Subtle's fraudulent jargon with the sounds, smells, and textures of the junk heap:

> What else are all your terms,
> Whereon no one o' your writers 'grees with other?
> Of your elixir, your *lac virginis*,

Your stone, your medicine, and your chrysosperm,
Your sal, your sulphur, and your mercury,
Your oil of height, your tree of life, your blood,
Your marchesite, your tutie, your magnesia,
Your toad, your crow, your dragon, and your panther,
Your sun, your moon, your firmament, your adrop,
Your lato, azoch, zernich, chibrit, heautarit,
And then your red man, and your white woman,
With all your broths, your menstrues, and materials
Of piss and egg-shells, women's terms, man's blood,
Hair o' the head, burnt clouts, chalk, merds and clay,
Powder of bones, scalings of iron, glass,
And worlds of other strange ingredients [. . .].
                            (2.3.182–97)

All that students have to do to appreciate the full effect of Jonson's satire here is to pause for a moment over this complex of allusion and try to picture standing amid it. What would one see? What would one smell? How would one feel? In other words, what would be the texture of the place? Again, much of Jonson's satiric point is realized at the level of language—and, more specifically, in the sound of language. The temptation would be strong for me to remark that Jonson in 1610, roughly ten years after the appearance of *Hamlet*, expresses a sentiment not unlike that of Shakespeare's Ghost as he expounds on the reasons for Gertrude's adultery: "So lust, though to a radiant angel link'd / Will sate itself in a celestial bed / And prey on garbage" (1.5.55–57). This is a sidelight, of course, but a teacher could help place Jonson as a playwright in relation to Shakespeare (and perhaps to other of his contemporaries) simply by comparing the similarities and differences in the context, tone, and texture of these two statements.

The repeated appearances of Dol Common too—whether in her transmuted identities as Queen of Fairy and lady of nobility or in her "authentic" identity as common bawd—work a series of variations on familiar themes that are explicitly realized in the language and action of the play. One could profitably examine the whole process of naming in *The Alchemist* (and the related theme of disguise) as revelatory of a morally feckless world where the self becomes little more than a commodity readily transmuted—and bartered—for gold. (Again, a comparison with Shakespeare's use of disguise in any of his comedies might prove instructive here.) In this context the instability of Dol's names and her repeated appearances in various guises reinforce each other: in other words, the linguistic preoccupations of the play become tangibly realized in stage action. One can trace this process easily enough for students by pointing to a few significant episodes. For example, just before Mammon first catches sight of Dol, he recounts for Subtle the zealousness with which he has defended the stone against Surly's objections: "I [. . .]

cleared to him that Sisyphus was damned / To roll the ceaseless stone only because / He would have made ours *common*." At this moment Mammon sees Dol ("Who is this?" he utters in surprise), and Subtle pretends to remove her from his sight: "God's precious! What do you mean? Go in, good *lady* [. . .]" (2.3.207–11; my emphasis). The point is a delicate one, delicately made; but in an instant, by virtue of Mammon's inadvertent pun on "common," the immediate appearance of Dol, and Subtle's reference to her as "lady," Jonson establishes Dol as a sort of walking oxymoron, a "common" "lady" who embodies in her names and in her behavior the moral tension between loftiness and baseness that we see everywhere in the play. Soon afterward, the love-struck Mammon, evoking the virgin heroine of Ariosto's *Orlando Furioso*, calls Dol "a Bradamante! A brave piece!"; but Surly at once fixes and relocates her identity yet again: "Heart, this is a bawdy-house!" (2.3.225–26). The ensuing series of indecent puns on "converse," "commander," "superintendent," "quainter," and "tire" all reinforce the point (2.3.295–306) and help prepare the rhetorical way for Dol's ensuing manifestations. Later she reappears as the Queen of Fairy—"her Highness" and "her Grace"—fixed again as "common" by her supposed kinship with Dapper, "a special gentle, / That is the heir to forty marks a year, / Consorts with the small poets of the time, / [and] Is the sole hope of his old grandmother" (1.2.51–54). Afterward, now in her disguise as the lady of nobility, Face places her once more: "Why, this is yet / A kind of modern happiness, to have / Dol *Common* for a great *lady*" (4.1.23–25; my emphasis). The moral irony of Mammon's exaltation of what is literally common here takes on allegorical proportions: "Daughter of honour. I have cast mine eye / Upon thy form, and I will rear this beauty / Above all styles" (4.1.116–18). Whether as Queen of Fairy or noble lady, Dol reminds us, by her simple presence—her "form," as Mammon puts it—and her name, of the unchangeable commonness of all falsely transmuted matter in the play. Such a point, so easily made to students by simply alerting them to the explicit or implicit allusions to Dol's name in certain contexts, would allow them to recognize each of Mammon's subsequent paeans to her nobility as Jonsonian satire at its most savage. Consider, for example, how easily the language and diction of the following passage (replete as it is both with sexual innuendo as well as the sort of implicit allusion I have been discussing) could serve such a critical purpose when students realize that it is addressed to a woman named Common (italics indicate words or phrases one might want students to comment on in class):

> But this *form*
> Was not intended to so *dark a use!*
> Had you been *crooked, foul, of some coarse mould,*
> A cloister had done well. But such a feature
> That might stand up *the glory of a kingdom,*
> To live recluse is a mere solecism,
> Though in a *nunnery!* It must not be.

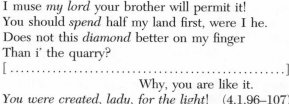

> I muse *my lord* your brother will permit it!
> You should *spend* half my land first, were I he.
> Does not this *diamond* better on my finger
> Than i' the quarry?
> [....]
>   Why, you are like it.
> *You were created, lady, for the light!* (4.1.96–107)

The same ironies could be pursued with reference to Mammon's remarkable speeches to Dol that follow (4.1.130–46 and 4.1.154–69) or to the parallel situation during which Surly pursues Dame Pliant, using an elevated Spanish that mocks her virtue as well as his feigned love (4.4.63–64, 76–77). Again, a single well-placed Jonsonian word in Surly's proposal to Pliant makes the point with stunning abruptness: "Lady, you see into what hands you are fallen, / 'Mongst what a nest of villains, And how near / Your honour was t'have catched a certain *clap*" (4.6.1–3; my emphasis). One could also mention in this context the function of sickness and disease in the play, particularly the fact that the presence of plague (the reason Lovewit leaves the house to Jeremy/Face in the first place) invests *The Alchemist* with a moral miasma explicitly realized throughout the play in its linguistic texture.

It is perhaps obvious by now that the approach I am suggesting for a difficult dramatist like Jonson is to begin with concrete and minute incidents and ask students how any particular event, individual utterance, or pattern of speech contains in its linguistic texture ideas that can shed light on the play as a whole. The metaphor I use with students to describe this process is hardly an elegant one, but I like to tell them that any single Jonson play is like a long salami: taste a small slice of it from anywhere, and you can taste the whole. I do not mean to pejorate or simplify important and challenging literature in saying this; on the contrary, I think that we can convey to our students the subtle and complex nuances of an imposing work like *The Alchemist* by first alerting them to facets of the play that they can see operating in little, and then allowing them to discover how ideas thus conveyed occur (often with revealing variations) throughout the play as a whole. I find that this approach gives students a greater sense of a play's intimate moments as well as of its larger thematic concerns. It also gives students a critical direction—a track to follow—without giving them a predetermined ideology to impose on a troublesomely resistant work of art. For example, students frequently disagree with my understanding of the passages quoted above (even my undergraduates occasionally dismiss me as naively moralistic or, even worse, formalistic); but when they do, I ask them for their understanding of the episodes in question and often receive startling, even stimulating, results. I suspect that the reason for this is that these students now feel comfortable reading the play; they are familiar with its linguistic texture, its literary terrain so to speak, and are confident expressing ideas about it.

I would like to close with one last illustration of how I think the process outlined above can lead to productive results in the classroom. When I teach *The Alchemist* I like to call students' attention to the episode near the play's end where Dol appears *"like the Queen of Fairy"* (5.4.20) and Dapper kneels before her to receive, at long last, her salutary advice regarding diet and gaming. The scene is blistering in its satire, replete with just the sort of linguistic tension and irony we have been discussing, particularly at the moment when Dapper leaves, obsequiously obeying Subtle's instruction to kiss Dol's "departing part" (5.4.57). I like to ask students where the humor resides in this episode and usually get the blunt but perfectly appropriate response that it is funny to see a shallow fool humiliate himself by kissing another's ass in the empty hope of gain. All well and good; this is Jonson's satiric point, made with typically Jonsonian gelidity. Now I ask them to put this scene beside two analogous scenes in *A Midsummer Night's Dream* (3.1.129–201 and 4.1.1–45) where another Fairy Queen (Titania) spends some quality time with another deluded creature (Bottom transformed into an ass), kissing him and actually falling in love with him. Both episodes are funny, yet each one evokes a completely different kind of laughter. I would argue (and here again students sometimes disagree) that the Jonsonian episode hasn't a trace of the warm charity implied by the magical (albeit momentary) union of human flesh and airy spirit contained in the Shakespearean scenes. Even Bottom realizes that he has mysteriously touched something higher than himself, had "a most rare vision," mind-bending and self-altering, "a dream past the wit of man to say what dream it was," despite its fleeting nature (4.1.205–06). Poor Dapper, however, who claims pathetically that "I cannot speak for joy" (5.4.33), is simply drained of an additional forty marks and sent off to abstain from "Woolsack pies" and "Dagger frumity" and to busy himself with such petty (and petty sounding) games as "mum-chance," "tray-trip," "primero," and "gleek" (5.4.41–47). (By the way, "gleek" also occurs in the Shakespearean sequence [3.1.146], but as a verb, and with the totally different meaning "to jest," and to totally different effect.) The revealing contrast here would give students an opportunity not only to compare the two dramatists' handling of a similar comic situation but also, once again, to place Jonson in relation to Shakespeare. In so doing, students could well find yet another way of seeing larger and more general matters reflected in smaller ones—or, to borrow a remarkably apt phrase from Jonson's subtle alchemist himself, an interpretive means to "open a vein with a pin" (5.4.37).

NOTE

[1]Quotations of *The Alchemist* are from J. B. Steane's edition.

The Witch of Edmonton:
A Model for Teaching Collaboration
in the Renaissance

Jayson B. Brown, William W. E. Slights, and Reta Terry

Think of teaching Renaissance plays with more than one author as a chance to introduce students to some of the best drama from the period and to the most pressing questions in early modern studies: the production of texts, the transmission of theatrical traditions, and the problem of authorship. Plays like *Eastward Ho!*, *The Roaring Girl*, *The Changeling*, and *The Witch of Edmonton* fit wonderfully well into the undergraduate classroom. The last of these is a particularly good choice, since one can capitalize on a kind of modern witchcraft craze, partly the legacy of high school study of *Macbeth*.

While the idea of individual genius—Shakespeare's, for instance—exerts a powerful attraction for most students, it's important for them to realize that an enormous percentage of plays in the period were jointly written (Carson 57–58) and all of them were collaborative productions of dramatists, censors, actors, costumers, and audiences (Bentley 198–99). Taking each of these contributions seriously opens a window of opportunity to rethink such staples of dramatic criticism as our notions of source, genre, textual reproduction, and authorship. Recently, Jeffrey Masten, building on the work of Roland Barthes and Michel Foucault, as well as on his own research into early modern textual production, has argued for the need to reconceive the entire business of playwrighting without the anachronistic conception of individual authorship (Masten 19; see also Chartier 25–59). As Masten points out, our understanding of the conditions of reading and playgoing have changed substantially in the wake of such poststructuralist reconceptions of the text as Foucault's "What Is an Author?", a piece that should probably be studied early in a course on Renaissance drama because it describes in relatively simple theoretical terms the type of non-author-oriented conditions that obtained in the late sixteenth- and early seventeenth-century theater. This situation, as Paul Budra points out in this volume, has been reproduced in Hollywood's committee-written filmscripts, which bear striking resemblances to the plays we are concerned with here. Once this theoretical ground has been broken, students can approach a play like *The Witch of Edmonton* not as the expression of three or more individual psyches but as an integrated piece of professional theater.

What follows is a model for teaching a 3–5 class unit on collaboration in either a drama survey or a more specialized course in Renaissance drama. It is based on the view that cooperative work in the classroom can increase students' understanding of collaborative playwrighting and performance in Renaissance repertory theaters. The point of the unit is to demonstrate to students that theatrical cooperation and integration, not authorial individuation and competition, are what drive a play like *The Witch of Edmonton*, attributed on its title page to "William Rowley, Thomas Dekker, John Ford, &c."

One way to begin the unit is to discuss with the class, on a relatively casual level, what an author is and how our modern notions of author stem from the relation this word has to concepts of authority that authors have over the texts they generate. This discussion can then be turned to how problematic such modern notions of "author" are in an early modern context. Students who have just managed to distinguish between poet and speaker often find this ingrained concept difficult to abandon. Offering some theater history at this point, stressing its various collaborative practices (cowriting, the company of actors and their representations of a given play text, censorial intrusion, and the revisions commonly undertaken at the moment of a play's revival, to name a few) can be an effective way of driving this point home. This historical survey would also provide a good opportunity to discuss what constitutes collaboration and to set boundaries for the definition of collaboration for the class. For example, a distinction between collaboratively written plays and plays that represent a collaborative product might be useful because such a distinction can be applied to other plays in the course where issues of collaboration seem less obvious (the folio *Macbeth*, for instance, is attributed solely to Shakespeare, even though the Hecate scenes were later added by an interpolator). Such class discussions establish that collaborative modes of producing meaning were the norm for the Renaissance stage.

From this point there are a number of ways to approach the integrative aspects of *The Witch of Edmonton*. One would be to draw attention to the character overlap that takes place between the plotlines. Cyrus Hoy contends that the authorial shares are "neatly contained" in *The Witch of Edmonton* and that the play "displays its own tripartite structure, with Dekker responsible for the areas of action dealing with Mother Sawyer, the witch; Rowley doing the comic scenes involving Cuddy Banks [. . .] and Ford composing the scenes of Frank Thorney and his romantic misfortunes" (6). Yet it becomes clear that these authorial shares are not neatly contained when one asks, who is responsible for the character of the devil dog Tom, who appears in all three plotlines? Who is responsible for writing Mother Sawyer and Cuddy Banks (or Sir Arthur Clarington) in scenes where they interact? What can then be indicated to the class is that the effect of this character overlap is not only structurally important, providing continuity and interchange between the plotlines, but also theatrically significant. On stage, such overlaps create not three individual narratives being played out alongside each other but rather a sense of community, where the lives of the characters intersect in the same microcosmic social structure.

A related way to approach the integrative qualities of *The Witch of Edmonton* is to indicate the thematic parallels between the plotlines, which can reveal the organizing principle shared among the play's contributors. For instance, the devil dog functions as an incarnation of social evils in all the play's plotlines, and the intricate wordplay on "dog" and "cur" in the text provides a thematic link between them. The black devil dog appears in the play just three lines after Mother Sawyer describes Old Banks as a "black cur" (2.1.116), drawing a connection between them by metaphorically assigning Old Banks demonic trappings as they are represented in the play. Cuddy Banks's description of the dog suggests the inward nature of the devil dog's evil but also its outward appearance: "A kind of cur where he takes, but where he takes not, a dogged rascal" (5.1.88–89). The dog who dogs is paralleled in the Frank Thorney and Susan Carter plot, where the devil dog appears and prompts Frank to murder; before Frank kills Susan, he tells her, "You have dogged your own death" (3.3.39). Drawing attention to the way the play blends generic categories shows how tragedy, comedy, and satire can be used as complementary approaches to offer social criticism through drama and to incorporate the individual talents of the play's contributors. The argument can be put to the class that instead of detracting from the play, this generic blending gives *The Witch of Edmonton* its dynamism and offers the play's audience a cohesive dramatic experience.

While these issues of collaboration can be developed in a lecture format, a number of alternative pedagogical techniques can emphasize for students the benefits and challenges of both textual and dramatic collaboration. The most obvious method is group work, which allows students to collaborate with one another to produce a (presumably) coherent presentation for the rest of the class. This technique can also serve as a time-saving device, offering self-directed instruction that addresses a wide range of topics simultaneously, each group sharing its insight on a particular aspect of the play with the whole class. To address both the thematic and collaborative aspects of the play, discussion topics can be chosen that are applicable to all three of its plotlines, such as issues of abuse and victimization (Who are the abusers? the abused? Can a single character be both? What is the nature of abuse in the play? Does victimization in turn beget abuse?) or issues of criminality (Is a visible crime worse than a secret one? Is Elizabeth Sawyer a criminal? in the same way that Frank Thorney is?). One way to drive home the limitations of looking for Hoy's authorial shares is to have one group give its presentation, to choose a specific issue the group has raised, and then to ask another group whether they can confidently identify which member of the first group contributed that point to the presentation.

Team teaching is another pedagogical strategy that can bring different styles and forms of knowledge into the classroom and can simulate for the class how these plays offer collaborative knowledge to an audience (Hirschfeld and DeNeef). To involve students in an exercise that to some extent corresponds to the conditions of early modern collaborative performance, the instructor designs an assignment that involves a group dramatization of scenes from the play (this assignment can be expanded into a much larger performance project if time and the design of the course permits). The groups end their presentations with a question period and discussion about the problems and benefits that collaboration posed for them in staging and interpreting the scene. A quicker alternative to this assignment is to give groups scenarios and have them improvise scenes to emphasize the sensitivity and responsiveness required to produce coherent collaborative meaning in performance.

Other assignments can reflect the textual component of collaborative production. For example, students can be given a photocopied scene from the play with the dialogue of one of the characters blanked out (scenes with fast-paced dialogue between two characters work best) and asked to write lines of dialogue for the blanked out character without referring to the play. This assignment can provide students with a sense of what collaborative writing entails. Collaborative essay assignments or research projects reflect the course content. Such assignments can be difficult to evaluate, but one suggestion to circumvent this difficulty is to offer a two-part assignment. Part A would involve a collaborative effort by a small group of students and would be given a mark applicable to all members of the group. Part B would be written and graded individually; it would describe the collaborative methodology employed by the group and indicate what steps were taken to integrate the group members' contributions. It would also critique the advantages and difficulties of the collaborative project and offer a self-evaluation of part A as a finished product.

The Witch of Edmonton offers opportunities to apply these methods, to defend the practice of collaborative playwrighting against its detractors, and to study its responsiveness to pressing cultural issues of the day. So that students are aware that *The Witch of Edmonton* has been criticized for its loose construction, they can be provided with quotations from scholars who have complained of the play's lack of dramatic unity. For example, Joan M. Sargeaunt's 1966 comment that the Frank Thorney plot "is quite well constructed, but very little attempt has been made to weld it and the witch plot together" (40) and Kathleen E. McLuskie's more recent complaint that "the effects of collaboration are evident in the way the action works in scenes and loose-ends of plot are left untied, but the witchcraft plot provides coherence" (*Dekker and Heywood* 145) could be placed on an overhead for the students to read and discuss. But students should also be encouraged to challenge the notion that collaborative plays are, by definition, hackwork and to examine the play for evidence of thematic richness.

The treatment of honor and promise offers just such a social and dramatic focus. The theme is a particularly apt one since at least a brief discussion of promise, especially of violated oaths, occurs in each act of the play, regardless of authorial shares. Act 1 is concerned both with Frank Thorney's perjured wedding vows (1.1.55–69) and with Warbeck's casual swearing, which Susan begs him to stop (1.2.48–53). Act 2 introduces, through Elizabeth Sawyer, the idea of oaths as curses in which one promises to do evil. Here too is the notion of broken or abused promises, an idea made explicit when Tom manipulates his word to trap Elizabeth into losing her soul (2.1.138–60). Old Carter and Warbeck reinforce the idea that oaths often lead to perjury when Old Carter, although allowing that an oath is "a kind of debt" (2.2.9), explains that Warbeck should not be upset that he cannot marry Susan, because even gentlemen break their word (2.2.11). Young Cuddy Banks enters the discussion of promise in act 3 when he reduces oath taking to a mere commercial transaction (3.1.123–28). In scene 2, Winnifride reinforces the earlier discussion of the way oaths can be used to manipulate or to mislead when she vows to Susan that she will love and care for Frank in Susan's absence (3.2.81–86). Act 3 introduces the connection between oaths and the conscience when Old Thorney suggests that the conscience must distinguish good oaths from bad (3.3.86–87); Warbeck and Somerset later concur (3.4.78–79). Swearing is further disparaged in act 4 when the First Countryman naively explains that his adulterous wife swore she was having sex with the serving man because she had been bewitched (4.1.8); oaths are now simply an excuse to avoid responsibility for one's own actions. Elizabeth Sawyer turns the discussion back to perjury when she includes in her tirade against society a vilification of those who would swear to something they could not possibly know for sure (4.1.140–46). Like Old Thorney, Warbeck, and Somerset, Cuddy Banks later connects oaths and conscience when he swears on his conscience that Elizabeth would not hurt anyone (4.1.203–04). Finally, in act 5, all the characters speak about oaths and promises, reiterating and summing up the themes of perjury, conscience, and casual swearing. In the last scene the consequences of perjury are made clear: honor and reputation are murdered (5.3.13, 77) and readers are warned to "take heed / How they believe the devil; at last he'll cheat you" (5.3.46).

The instructor may want to glance at each one of these references to promise in the play or to examine one passage in detail while pointing out the others. Either way, students should be asked to consider the treatment of oaths and perjury in the play and the way that this treatment provides thematic rather than narrative continuity. Each character swears oaths or takes vows, and all are either deceivers or deceived, regardless of how one divides up the authorship. Students might then be asked, either in small groups or individually (perhaps as a homework assignment), to draw up a short list of other possible thematic issues that cross the traditional authorial boundaries of *The Witch of Edmonton*.

Alternatively, a parallel can be drawn between the collaborative creation of the honor code and the way the witch herself is constructed by the social behavior of her contemporaries (Comensoli 121–31). Students might consider how one gets honor and who gives it. Can one be honorable if others do not acknowledge it? Students could discuss whether honorable women, like Susan, are a construction of society in the same way that vengeful women, like Mother Sawyer, are. The class might compare Susan's death scene, in which she embraces death gladly on discovering that she has been unwittingly made an adulterer and repents a sin she has been forced to commit (3.3.24–64), with Elizabeth Sawyer's final words in which she too repents her "former evil" (5.3.21–51). What do students make of the parallel between Frank's claim that he murders Susan because she is "a whore" (3.3.26) and society's claim that it may execute Elizabeth Sawyer because she is a witch? Such questions of honor provide an opportunity for wide-ranging discussion and may begin to explode the myth that collaborative plays are less rich in ideas than single-author plays.

The real challenge involved in teaching collaboration is to help students discover not so much the division of labor as the integration of labor and just how one playwright's contribution to the collective effort shaped, and was shaped by, another's. Dekker, Rowley, and Ford, like many other writers of the period, were professional men of the theater who knew one another's strengths and played to them when working collaboratively. Asking students to join with one another and with their instructor in the same spirit of co-operation can make for a lively classroom and a fuller sense of how Renaissance plays were actually written and performed.

Responding to Renaissance Drama: One Way of Guiding Students

Frances Teague

The Problem: Mistaken Assumptions

Students who enroll in a class about Renaissance drama are not, as a rule, weak. Most have experience with literary analysis, and all of them have some understanding of Shakespeare when they begin their study of his contemporaries. Often they plan to go on to graduate study in English and want to take the course as preparation for that future. In other words, a relatively esoteric course like Renaissance drama generally attracts advanced students who ought to do well. Yet precisely because they are well read and have some familiarity with literary texts, students sometimes bring assumptions to the course that can make the material difficult for them. Let me start with some comments (verbatim, save for spelling) that my students last year made about various plays:[1]

> REBECCA.   The characters in this play [Dekker's *The Shoemakers' Holiday*] are less developed, for the most part, than the characters in a Shakespearean comedy. For instance, none of the characters is given a history. The audience knows nothing about any of the characters' pasts.

Another student, Chris, commented on Wagner's arrogance in Marlowe's *Doctor Faustus*, but concluded he did not understand Wagner's "motivations" in the same way that he might try to understand a character in a novel, who is endowed with a past, as well as desires and thoughts. Wagner, however, does not fit Chris's assumptions about characterization. Instead, Wagner is impertinent or respectful because that is what a particular scene calls for, as a consequence of his social identity (as a servant), the plot's requirements (as an analogue to Faustus), and so forth. Rebecca too is having trouble interpreting character because she is assuming that the play she is reading will work like *Henry IV, Part 1* or *As You Like It*. Hammon in *The Shoemakers' Holiday* shifts his love from Rose to Jane very quickly because the play needs that movement, not because the relationship is genuine or sincere. Good students who have done a fair amount of reading may expect other Renaissance plays to work as they have been taught that a novel or a Shakespeare play does: they need to realize that they will often find it more useful to think of the personages in Renaissance drama as roles rather than characters. In fact, they may find it useful to reread Shakespeare's plays in the light of what they learn from other Renaissance dramas to recognize the similarities of technique that Shakespeare shares with his contemporaries.

WAI-WAI.   However, as who is most important in the story [of Ford's
The Broken Heart], I'm leaning more toward Orgilus at the moment, for he somewhat fits into typical "tragic" hero archetype
(though he has more than one fatal flaw . . . yes, this argument is a
bit weak).

TARA.   The thing I liked least [about The Shoemakers' Holiday] is hard
to ferret out. I think it was the two characters of Lincoln and the
(Former) Lord Mayor. They seemed to impede the progress of the
play, but I guess in every story there must be a protagonist and an
antagonist.

Both Wai-wai and Tara use a critical vocabulary ("tragic hero," "archetype,"
"protagonist" or "antagonist") and assumptions one can ultimately trace to a
model that the nineteenth-century critic Gustav Freytag first popularized (although neither they nor, in all likelihood, their high school teachers would
invoke Freytag explicitly). They have been taught that dramatic structure follows a set pattern across cultures. As a result, they assume that Renaissance
tragedy (a more important form than comedy) is like Greek tragedy and centers on a hero who has a tragic flaw and whose fate will turn on a climactic
moment. Certainly in a Greek tragedy, we might look for the tragic hero's
anagnorisis or peripeteia and contemplate its meaning. In The Broken Heart
or The Shoemakers' Holiday we gain little by looking for such elements. To
read Renaissance tragedy as if it were Greek tragedy is naive, for one will
misread even the work by dramatists who had a good classical education. As
one critic remarks, "If Jonson glanced at Aristotle's Poetics before writing
Sejanus, he put it back on the shelf" (Leggatt, English Drama 132), and that
same observation would hold true for such plays as The Jew of Malta by
Christopher Marlowe or Bussy D'Ambois by George Chapman, although Jonson, Marlowe, and Chapman were all quite capable of reading Aristotle.

Students may also try to account for their responses by drawing on what
they already know about the period. In particular, they refer to the parallels
they see to Shakespeare's plays, although on occasion they may cite other
popular accounts of the Renaissance.

LISA.   After having seen Shakespeare in Love, in which little John Webster feeds the rats to the yowling cat, act 5 of the play [The Duchess
of Malfi] makes sense, in some vague way. But act 5—how to deal
with it? How to resolve? I found it interesting that the Cardinal
kills Julia with a poisoned Bible—beyond its sheer weirdness, it's
very telling that it was a figure from the Church who used that
method of murder—if the Cardinal wasn't corrupt enough already,
right?

In studying The Shoemakers' Holiday, for example, one student writes about
the parallel to Romeo and Juliet that she finds so striking, but she seems not

to notice the powerful differences: Dekker's play has absent parents and his lovers have excellent luck at the end. Evaluating the events of a Renaissance play by comparing them with those in a play by Shakespeare is a tempting practice that one should resist, of course, but trying to understand Renaissance drama in terms of a popular fiction like *Shakespeare in Love* also creates problems. Struck by Webster's fifth act, Lisa accounts for that wonderful oddness as the contribution from the bloodthirsty (and fictional) boy in *Shakespeare in Love;* she does not move beyond that popular construction, save to condemn the Cardinal's hypocrisy.

Each of these comments points to students' intellectual discomfort with the unexpected moments in Renaissance drama, which are precisely the moments I like best. Not surprisingly, then, I find it frustrating to teach Renaissance plays to students who have been taught to believe that characters necessarily have motives, that good plots must develop organically, or that dramatic structure proceeds inexorably through some version of Freytag's pyramid (exposition, rising action, turning point, falling action, denouement). My students also find it frustrating to confront a body of plays that suggests their hard-won knowledge of literature, derived from studying Shakespeare's works, great novels, or classical drama, counts for little. My frustration matters little, but their frustration is very important. A good student who has worked hard to understand material in other courses does not want to begin a course in Renaissance drama by being accused of irrelevance, naïvete, or ignorance. Therefore I have adopted a teaching technique that allows the students to control the works they study effectively enough to understand how their preconceptions about the Renaissance, drama, or literature may fail.

The Response Papers

In my undergraduate Renaissance drama classes I ask students to prepare a series of response papers; the average on these provides ten percent of the final grade. Whenever the class begins study of a new play, each student turns in a short paper, a page or two long. Recently I moved the response papers online, asking students to post them to a bulletin board on a Web page. (That bulletin board is the source for the student comments above.) In their response papers, they answer set questions about the play; their responses vary from a sentence to several paragraphs. I alter the questions every time I teach, but in general some questions ask for straightforward information (what was the venue for the first production of this play?), while others ask for opinion (who is the central character and why do you think so?).

> Reading notes [Items 1, 3, 5, 6, and 7 are always included; items 2, 4, 8, and 9 are included depending on the makeup of the class, especially students' major subjects.]

1. Name the play and author(s).
2. What is the play's date and venue?
3. Who is the protagonist, the central character? Why do you think so?
4. What kind of play is it?
5. What is the play's turning point, the moment when the protagonist's fortunes are reversed?
6. What is the outcome?
7. What elements are notable (important speech, moment of spectacle, prominent image)?
8. If you were teaching this play, what would you emphasize?
9. If you read an essay about this play, what was the critic's central point?

Marking the papers is easy: in a few minutes, I can read through each of them, offering a comment or two and giving a mark from one to ten. (I can quickly post comments and grades to persons using the Web.) Students earn points for demonstrating that they have read and thought about the play and for completing their work on time. I do not deduct points for spelling or mechanical errors. If a student turns in a completed response paper showing firsthand knowledge on the day that we begin work on a particular play, then that individual receives ten points; if the paper arrives a day late, the maximum grade is seven points; after that, the paper can earn only five points.

Benefits

The series of response papers offers a number of benefits. From the instructor's point of view, the assignment substantially increases the amount of writing that students do without substantially increasing the time in grading. Response papers reward students for doing the reading in a timely fashion, and they provide me with a good sense of what issues need discussion, where students have become confused, and so forth. From the students' perspective, the assignment is an easy A, one area in which students have complete control over the grade they receive. Some like the idea that they can use the response papers to study for examinations or to generate essay topics. Since I have begun to use the Web page bulletin board, which allows everyone to see all the other responses, students comment that they find it helpful to know that they are not alone in finding certain points difficult. I like the fact that the bulletin board allows them to respond to and question one another. The best feature from the class members' point of view is that they can engage more fully with the reading in class discussions. All students prefer lively class discussion to those that are deadly dull. Because they come into class having done the reading and having formulated some opinions about the play, discussions are far better than they would otherwise be.

By resisting the answers that a class provides in those discussions, I can get the students to argue with me. For instance, if I have assigned *The Shoemakers' Holiday*, students will give varying answers to the question, "Who is the protagonist?" Some say Simon Eyre, while others name Rowland Lacy. If I say that I think the true protagonist is the King or Hammon, I can expect a moment of silence and half an hour of heated debate. As we go over the various arguments that students make, we find ourselves talking about what sort of play *The Shoemakers' Holiday* is: a city comedy, a romantic comedy, or a shameless effort to curry favor at court. Asking students to identify the genre of a play like Beaumont and Fletcher's *Philaster* can generate a fine discussion, as does asking them to pick out a single turning point in *Doctor Faustus*. Because all students have already taken and defended a position in the response papers, they are far more likely to enter into the debate, especially once they see that I enjoy having them correct me. (They also learn that they gain no advantage by agreeing with me: if too many of them start to argue for my position, I simply announce that the discussion has become boring and that I am therefore reversing my position so that the discussion can continue.)

Breakdown as Breakthrough

What I like best about the response papers, however, is the moment that arrives each term when the class revolts. About midway through the term, students begin to complain about the rigid questions. Why, they ask, must every play have a turning point or a protagonist or a genre? That moment exhilarates me, for they have learned on their own how conventional assumptions about drama can fail. The conversation that follows is always an exciting one. Sometimes we end up talking about why our culture seems to prefer tragedy to comedy, especially since most Renaissance plays were comedies; Jill Levenson estimates that "in the Elizabethan/Jacobean theatre [. . .] [comedy] would finally surpass tragedy by a ratio of three to one" (269). We ask what happens if the central character of a play is relatively powerless instead of being a powerful aristocratic man (allowing students to notice subversive elements in a play always works more effectively than my pointing them out to the class). We may talk about how different plays vary structurally and why the model of Freytag's pyramid has exerted so much influence. In other words, the relative rigidity of the response papers leads students to question their own received wisdom about Renaissance drama. Last term the class happened to be studying Jonson's *The Masque of Blackness* after a breakthrough discussion. One of the first responses I received was the self-conscious comment, "I hope we are not supposed to evaluate *The Masque of Blackness* using the [. . .] format established for the other [response papers], because I don't think I can pull it off!" Here are several other student responses to later plays that show, I think, how they have learned to question their initial assumptions:

> TERRI.   I thoroughly disliked Penthea. She was whining, histrionic, and extremely self-absorbed. She loved nobody except for herself and I was glad when she died. Glad, do you hear me??? Glad!! (Sorry— a little histrionics of my own.)
>
> JOSH.   Terri, I like that you're opinionated! Histrionics always make for entertaining academic work.

> JOSH.   The most curious aspect of the play [Middleton and Rowley's *The Changeling*] was its tendency toward rough transitions or even abrupt ones. I did not feel a flow to the plot until the last two pages although I was well able to follow it. The scenes struck me as jarring glimpses at the least flattering aspects of people who would have been decent in nearly any other play, but I did not feel the coherence of a morality play like Faustus.
>
> OCTAVIA.   I'm inclined to agree with Josh that the weirdest thing about this play is the way everything just seems "thrown together." I didn't really understand why the plot would shift so rapidly. Or maybe I simply didn't get it.
>
> SHAPOUR.   I think I'll go back and read this play again later. I feel like I've missed a huge part of this play after reading everyone else's response papers.

Terri resists the nobleness of Penthea in *The Broken Heart* and has enough fun doing it that Josh backs her up; this exchange makes it clear to me that we have to discuss that response. And when Josh himself makes a good point about *The Changeling*, Octavia responds to him, although she admits that she may not fully understand what is occurring. Finally, Shapour is willing to reread a play when she finds her response differs from that of her classmates. I don't want to suggest that I see these responses as terribly sophisticated, but I do see them as more skeptical about their own assumptions and more willing to consider the plays without regard to other literature.

Why does an assignment, which seems initially to be busy work, turn out so well? I would argue (along with composition and rhetoric specialists) that writing is itself a mode of learning (Emig).[2] Entering the world of Renaissance drama can be daunting for undergraduates, who must wrestle with difficult language, outré plots, and unfamiliar conventions, as well as learn about the historical and cultural milieu of the plays. Moreover, students must do all that in the shadow of Shakespeare, a presence that complicates the process by ensuring that they think they have some knowledge, however inapplicable it may be. The response paper gives them a way to manage the plays: they may have an answer upside down and backward, but if they make a good faith attempt, they will receive credit. Furthermore, by breaking down the elements of the play they need to identify, students are more able to control the key points. Since I insist they tell me why they give the answers they do, they must analyze and evaluate the work in question. The response papers also highlight problem areas: as soon as I read a set of papers on *The Broken Heart*, for example, I know how well students understand the play's assumptions about chastity and rape.

The response paper is generative. Obviously I value the discussion that the papers generate, but that is not quite what I mean. I am often told by a student that the comments I make in the margins or online are important: they establish, however laconically, a dialogue between two people. Because I have placed a check mark by an apt sentence or scrawled, "good idea," students have found essay topics that they believe they can handle well. (They seem to gain such confidence from an affirming scribble that no amount of hard work fazes them.) And if they identify an effective passage or ask a penetrating question, they can count on seeing their own insight show up as a question on the midterm or final examination. Given the discussion of Penthea and her situation in the class whose comments I have been citing, I asked them to explain why understanding Renaissance marriage customs (such as the handfast or arranged marriage) is essential if one is to make sense out of *The Broken Heart*. Their answers showed clearly who had paid attention to the discussion about the questions they had raised in their response papers. By using a Web-based system, students now receive comments and encouragement from their peers as well as from me. Moreover, the knowledge that others in the class will read what they have to say makes them more thoughtful: when they adopt another student's idea, they give credit (as do Josh and Octavia), and when they disagree, they take more care in explaining why so that their classmates will not be offended. (I do warn them at the outset to watch their tone because I will not tolerate flaming responses.) They even recognize the changes that take place in their understanding; one student wrote that she felt she had finally learned a new way of reading, while another commented that she so enjoyed one play's macabre plot turns that her pleasure in reading had counteracted the effects of cold medicine and kept her awake. The anxiety and discomfort that the class initially felt has changed to pleasure and pride in their new sophistication.

Renaissance plays demand a sensibility that appreciates allegorical action and melodramatic turns, as well as lyric speeches and clever dialogue. The response papers work well both because they allow students some control over their new reading experience and because they give students credit for being well-prepared readers. But the assignment is sufficiently rigid that it irritates students after a while. And once they express that irritation, they begin to understand that a formulaic assignment, like formulaic thinking, is simplistic and inadequate. The key, however, is that that recognition originates with the students themselves rather than with their instructor.

NOTES

[1]I am drawing on student comments from spring term 1999. My thanks to that class for their lively participation. The students I quote directly gave me their permission to reproduce their remarks, which are verbatim save for corrections to the spelling; when I summarize, I do so because the student has graduated and I have lost touch with her or him.

[2]That writing is an important part of the cognitive process is well established. In addition to Janet Emig, see Peter Elbow's influential 1983 article "Teaching Thinking by Teaching Writing" and his *Writing without Teachers* as well as work by Linda Flower and John Hayes.

Vittoria's Secret:
Teaching Webster's *The White Devil*
as a Tragedy of Inscrutability

James Hirsh

John Webster's *The White Devil* is a complex play. There is no point in teaching the play unless one confronts its complexity. Fortunately, I have found that students are willing, even eager, to make the imaginative effort required by *The White Devil* because it provokes their curiosity, their desire to analyze its implications. To explore questions raised by the play, students and I work inductively, from specific episodes to general conclusions, from explicit passages of dialogue to implicit suggestions. Once students become used to this procedure, all I usually have to do is invite them to consider particular episodes or passages, and they themselves recognize possible implications of each piece of evidence in the context of the issues we have been discussing. If I do my job well, each class session is itself a form of improvisational theater that is engaging and suspenseful.

One particularly challenging theme of *The White Devil* concerns the potential inscrutability of certain features of human experience. Characters face challenges to their powers of understanding, challenges that are sometimes frustratingly difficult or insuperable. The play presents similar difficulties for playgoers and readers, students and teachers. In approaching the play from this perspective, students and I begin by examining episodes in which characters themselves comment on the difficulties of interpreting their experience. For example, in 3.2, after Brachiano speaks cryptically of "a friend's grave" and then exits, Francisco responds, "How strange these words sound? What's the interpretation?" (3.2. 296, 301–02).[1] In this case, playgoers understand Brachiano's words when they occur, and Francisco receives an explanation only a moment later when Giovanni informs him of Isabella's death. But characters face many circumstances that are not so quickly or easily explained. Only a moment before Vittoria's and Flamineo's deaths, the following exchange occurs:

> VITTORIA. My soul, like to a ship in a black storm,
> Is driven I know not whither.
> FLAMINEO.   Then cast anchor.
> 'Prosperity doth bewitch men seeming clear,
> But seas do laugh, show white, when rocks are near.'
> [...]
> 'While we look up to heaven we confound
> Knowledge with knowledge.' O, I am in a mist.
>   (5.6.246–49, 257–58)

The lives of these characters have not provided them with adequate means for understanding their experience. The exchange offers three distinct reasons for this inadequacy. Vittoria's metaphor of a black storm suggests that human beings are not given enough light or information. But Flamineo's first aphorism suggests that clarity and whiteness may be as dangerous as insufficient light. The knowledge we derive from our limited experience is not merely incomplete; it may cast new experiences in a false light. Flamineo's next aphorism suggests, furthermore, that our knowledge can be self-contradictory. Some of our experiences lead to one conclusion, and some to another, and we are left in a mist.

These ideas are illustrated by the action of the play in a variety of ways. While Francisco is alone on stage in 4.1, the actor who has played Isabella enters. Francisco, however, rejects what would seem to be an unambiguous and welcome confirmation of life after death:

> How strong
> Imagination works! How she can frame
> Things which are not! Methinks she stands afore me
> [...]
> 'Tis my melancholy;
> How cam'st thou by thy death? How idle am I
> To question my own idleness?
>
> (4.1.101–03, 108–10)

But Francisco's assumption that the apparition is a figment of his imagination is nowhere verified in the play, and his rationale cuts two ways. If imagination "can frame / Things which are not," then perhaps Francisco's imagining that this apparition is a delusion is itself a delusion. If the apparition does have independent existence, it would present a further problem. I ask students to consider what might be suggested by the fact that the apparition arrives just when Francisco seeks to intensify his vengefulness: "To fashion my revenge more seriously, / Let me remember my dead sister's face" (97–98). Students realize that this would be a most opportune moment for a devil to take the shape of Isabella in order to encourage Francisco's vengefulness and thereby to bring about his damnation. Hamlet is troubled by a similar possibility concerning the apparition he has encountered (2.2.598–603). A further disturbing possibility raised by the episode is tied to another inscrutable element in the play, the character of Isabella. Isabella displays an apparently selfless love for Brachiano. When her husband rejects her for Vittoria, she pretends in public to be shrewishly jealous to give Brachiano a justification for abandoning her. Such selflessness is too good to be true and encourages the cynical suspicion that her pretense of bitter jealousy and anger is not really a pretense but an expression of her actual state of mind and an example of what is now called passive aggression. It is thus possible that the ghost is Isabella's spirit, damned

for wrathfulness, who now seeks to damn Francisco by intensifying his vengefulness. The episode sets off a cascading series of alternative possibilities, and
playgoers are left in a mist.

Another challenge to both characters and playgoers is set up immediately
after the departure of Isabella's ghost (whatever it may be). Francisco says to
himself, "I am in love, / In love with Corombona, and my suit / Thus halts to
her in verse" (4.1.119–21). I invite students to recall how they interpreted this
passage when they first read it or to imagine themselves in the place of a
playgoer who has not seen the rest of the play. If they are able to do this,
they realize that Francisco's declaration of love is incongruous but not incred-
ible. Like real human beings, characters in Renaissance plays sometimes fall
prey to incongruous emotions. In the midst of plotting the destruction of
Othello and Desdemona, Iago declares, "I do love her too" (2.1.291). Francisco may have become fixated on Vittoria precisely because she is beloved by
his hated enemy Brachiano. If Francisco's infatuation with Vittoria were not
credible, then Francisco's actual design in sending a love letter to Vittoria—
a design revealed later—would be pointless. As I explain to students, a fully
engaged playgoer will try to figure out what motivations would explain the
behavior of characters. But a moment after deciding on a credible explanation
for Francisco's declaration of love, such a playgoer is forced to reconsider.
Francisco instructs a servant to deliver the letter "when some followers / of
Brachiano may be by" (128–29). It now seems that Francisco sends the love
letter with an ulterior motive. His expression of love for Vittoria in a soliloquy
was presumably facetious, but playgoers were not in on Francisco's self-
directed joke at the time it occurred. I ask students to imagine what new
motive alert playgoers would most likely attribute to Francisco after his instruction to the messenger, and most students recognize that the answer is to
cause dissension between Vittoria and Brachiano—to ruin their relationship,
just as that relationship ruined Isabella's marriage and led to her death.

When the letter arrives, Francisco's design, as now understood by playgoers,
initially seems to work. Brachiano himself intercepts the letter and, merely on
seeing the salutation, immediately jumps to the same false conclusion to which
many playgoers jumped in the earlier scene—that Francisco sincerely loves
Vittoria—as well as to the further conclusion that she returns Francisco's love.
After Vittoria enters, Brachiano presents her with evidence he regards as so
"gross and palpable" (4.2.22) that it requires no interpretation: "Look upon
that letter; There are no characters nor hieroglyphics" (70–71). This episode
ironically recalls the arraignment scene in which another letter to Vittoria,
from Brachiano, was presented by Monticelso as evidence of Vittoria's adultery. In that case, although guilty, Vittoria pointed out the patent injustice of
judging her guilty on the basis of a letter addressed to her. There is perhaps
some poetic justice in the current replay of that situation with the difference
that in this case she is genuinely innocent. But Brachiano eventually comes
to believe Vittoria. To make up for mistrusting her, he arranges her escape

from the House of Convertites and decides to marry her. Francisco's apparent scheme has not only failed but backfired: the lovers are more devoted than ever. When told of the news in the next scene, Francisco reacts with appropriate disappointment: "O damnable!" (4.3.52). After his informant exits, however, he displays quite a different reaction:

> How fortunate are my wishes. Why? 'Twas this
> I only laboured. I did send the letter
> T'instruct him what to do. Thy fame, fond Duke,
> I first have poisoned; directed thee the way
> To marry a whore; what can be worse?
>
> (53–57)

I invite students to consider the thematic implications of the sequence of assumptions Webster encourages alert playgoers to make: that Francisco loves Vittoria, then that his plan is to drive a wedge between her and Brachiano, and then that he intended all along to drive them together to turn Brachiano into a social outcast. The play contains so many twists and turns, so many moments when playgoers are forced retroactively to reconsider their understanding of previously witnessed events whose meaning seemed at the time "gross and palpable," that the longer the play goes on, the less playgoers can feel certain about their understanding of anything they witness.

One episode whose meaning seems "gross and palpable" at the time it occurs is Vittoria's account of her "foolish idle dream" (1.2.230). She tells Brachiano that in the dream his wife and her husband were killed when a whirlwind blows a yew tree on top of them. Flamineo comments, "She hath taught him in a dream / To make away his Duchess and her husband" (255–56). Reminding students that Flamineo is a fallible character who generally views human behavior from a profoundly cynical perspective, I ask if there are other ways of interpreting Vittoria's behavior. First, it is not certain that Vittoria is lying about having had such a dream. If dreams are wishful fantasies, it is not improbable that a woman in an unhappy marriage would dream of her husband's death. Second, whether or not she had such a dream, her motive for describing it to Brachiano may simply be to convey that she wants to have an affair with him. To express such a wish does not constitute conspiracy to commit murder. A playgoer who convicts Vittoria of conspiring to murder Isabella and Camillo on the basis of her account of her dream has jumped to a conclusion on flimsier evidence than supports the later false conclusion that Francisco is in love with Vittoria. Such a playgoer uncomfortably resembles the Cardinal in the arraignment scene. Whether or not Vittoria intends to provoke Brachiano to murder their spouses is her secret. Perhaps Vittoria even deceived herself about her motive, telling herself that she was only idly imagining a hypothetical circumstance when she actually hoped that Brachiano would turn that hypothesis into reality. After I acknowledge that on occasion

I have been mystified by my own actions and motivations, students agree that they have had similar experiences.

The apparition of Isabella, Francisco's letter, and Vittoria's dream are merely three examples of inscrutable elements in *The White Devil*. A teacher may select or invite students to select other similarly inscrutable passages, episodes, or features of the play to examine in detail. For example, students particularly enjoy exploring the title of the play, the meaning of which first seems to be "gross and palpable" but becomes increasingly uncertain as the play progresses or as one ponders its possible implications. On every occasion when I have asked, "Who is 'the white devil' and what does the term mean?" a thoughtful student reasonably connects the title to Vittoria and suggests that a white devil is a person who looks innocent but who is in fact evil. Vittoria is called a devil by Flamineo in the second scene of the play (1.2.254), by Monticelso in the arraignment scene (3.2.216–17), and elsewhere. During their quarrel in 4.2, Brachiano calls her "the devil in crystal" (86), which seems synonymous with "the white devil." In a delirium near the end of the play, Brachiano describes what he perceives as Vittoria's whiteness: "Her hair is sprinkled with arras powder, that makes her look as if she had sinned in the pastry" (5.3.119–20). But the more one considers the question, the less certain the answer becomes.

As has often been noted, other characters in the play are called devils. Indeed, others deserve the epithet more than Vittoria does. As Brachiano's henchman, Flamineo becomes a pander and murderer. He refers to his "pale forehead" (1.2.328), and Cornelia refers to his "white hand" (5.4.80). Brachiano orders two murders, is described as being deathly pale (5.3.83), and is called "Devil Brachiano" (5.3.153) by Lodovico. His ghost (or a spirit impersonating his ghost or a figment of Flamineo's imagination) appears in 5.4. The actor presumably wore white makeup since ghosts were conventionally associated with whiteness as indicated by the following passage from *Henry VI, Part 2*: "Oft have I seen a timely-parted ghost, / Of ashy semblance, meagre, pale, and bloodless" (3.2.161–62). Francisco also qualifies as a white devil. He arranges the murder of Brachiano and invokes infernal gods (4.1.138). For playgoers, the black makeup he adopts as "Mulinassar" conspicuously conceals his whiteness. Monticelso is another candidate. As a cardinal and later as a pope, he is outwardly moral and pious, but his motives are vindictive and unscrupulous; he torments Vittoria and unjustly acts as both her prosecutor and judge. He keeps handy a book of criminals (for a purpose about which playgoers are invited to speculate) that contains "The names of many devils" (4.1.36). In the guise of a monk, Lodovico torments and brutally murders Brachiano. Zanche is called "devil" (5.1.86) by Marcello and says that her robbery of her mistress will "wash the Ethiop white" (5.3.264). Isabella may conceal genuine anger and jealousy beneath her feigned anger and jealousy; Francisco comments on her "white hands" (2.1.65), and her ghost (presumably pale) helps stir Francisco's vengefulness. Flamineo sees devils everywhere: "In this a politician imitates the devil" (3.3.16–17); "man, what a devil art thou to be tempted by that cursed mineral [gold]!" (3.3.22–23). Vittoria says, "O me! This place is hell" (5.3.181). The play dramatizes the human capacity for thinking or acting like a devil, that is, as a tempter or a tormenter. Ironically, one of the things that can make life hellish is the impulse of people to demonize other people, to regard them as embodiments of evil and therefore undeserving of pity or mercy.

The title raises other possibilities. "White devil" could be analogous to "white lie" or "white magic," terms in which the adjective carries greater weight than the noun. A "white devil" could be a person who, despite outward behavior or appearances, is not irredeemably or wholly bad and therefore who is not unpitiable. In a way, each character regards himself or herself as a "white devil" in this sense, as someone more sinned against than sinning. Most of the characters are victimized in some way or elicit sympathy. Vittoria was married to a dolt to restore her family's fortune and is treated unjustly and brutally by Monticelso; Brachiano genuinely loves Vittoria, rescues her, marries her despite public opprobrium, and suffers an agonizing and brutal death; Lodovico genuinely loves Isabella and seeks justice against Brachiano for her brutal murder; and so on. If a "white devil" is someone who is both guilty and pitiable, sometimes a victimizer and sometimes a victim, most human beings are white devils.

"White devil" has still wider implications. Commenting on his sexual arousal in the presence of Zanche, Flamineo describes his penis as a devil:

> 'Tis not so great a cunning as men think
> To raise the devil: for here's one up already;
> The greatest cunning were to lay him down.
> (5.1.88–90)

At an earlier moment Monticelso compares whores to "Cold Russian winters" (3.2.84). The image of a Russian winter is an image of endless snow, unmitigated whiteness. Sexual desire could be said to be a "white devil" in either meaning described above: seemingly good (providing pleasure and leading to selfless devotion) but actually bad (provoking violence) or a mixture of good and bad. As a metaphor for sexual desire, *The White Devil* is a fitting title for the play. The love of Brachiano and Vittoria is at the heart of the plot, and love is a powerful motive for Lodovico, Isabella, and Zanche as well. "The white devil" may be desire in general. For Flamineo, the desire for advancement is a "white devil," luring him into criminality; for Francisco his own cunning, the exercise of which gives him so much pleasure and which he uses to torment others, functions in a similar way. The entire social system provides an endless supply of devilish temptations and torments.

If I am lucky, our classroom discussions will foster students' own imaginative consideration of possibilities, and at some point a student will helpfully suggest that, in addition to connoting "outwardly good" or "genuinely good," the word "white" also might mean "colorless" or "blank" and hence "meaningless" or "inscrutable." A devil is a tormentor, and thus "the white devil" could refer to the tormenting inscrutability of experience. Passages in the play support this interpretation. Flamineo sums up experience in an aphorism quoted earlier: "Prosperity doth bewitch men seeming clear, / But seas do laugh, show white, when rocks are near." Seeming clarity and whiteness may be deceptive. The point is not that reality is always malevolent, however. That would simplify matters. When Brachiano is convinced that Vittoria has betrayed him with Francisco, he calls her "the devil in crystal," but he eventually accepts her innocence. In this case, the assumption that a character's seeming innocence (Vittoria's crystalline beauty) is actually a disguise for guilt turns out to be false. Vittoria's seeming innocence, which (from a cynical perspective) necessarily conceals devilishness, thereby ironically serves, at least for a time, to conceal her actual innocence. This situation is the converse of one described above, in which Isabella's incredibly selfless act of pretending to be bitterly jealous may be an outlet for her actual bitter jealousy. This potential inscrutability of experience is maddening. As Flamineo observes, "we confound / Knowledge with knowledge." One can be blinded by the whiteness of fog: "O, I am in a mist." I encourage students to read Melville's chapter "The Whiteness of the Whale" in *Moby-Dick* (ch. 42), which was apparently indebted to his reading of this play. Although it may refer to the potential inscrutability of experience, "the white devil" has so many possible meanings that, appropriately enough, it is itself inscrutable.

Webster's play does not answer all the intriguing questions it raises. Instead, it presents dramatic characters and hypothetical situations on which playgoers are challenged to exercise their imaginative powers. In my approach to teaching to the play, I attempt to imitate this characteristic of the play. If our class discussions generated simple and easy answers, we would falsify the complex and disturbing experience the play was evidently designed to produce. Like the play, our discussions are designed to conjure up *The White Devil*, not to exorcise it.

NOTE

[1]Quotations of *The White Devil* are from Christina Luckyj's edition.

Against the Bogeyman in English Renaissance Drama

Theodore B. Leinwand

There is a host of English Renaissance plays, both Shakespearean and non-Shakespearean, that I have come to think of as bogeyman plays, plays that feature a particularly terrifying character. In the classroom, bogeyman plays tend to work in a fairly predictable way. All attention is riveted on the predatory, villainous bogeyman. He is the hub from which all relations extend and on which all discussion centers. Whether it is because of the charisma or the banality of his evil, vice, or mere chicanery, the bogeyman casts a shadow over not only his play but also interpretation of it. The best example of what I have in mind may well be *The Merchant of Venice* with its notorious bogeyman, Shylock. It comes as something of a surprise to students when they are reminded that the merchant of Venice is Antonio, not Shylock. Did Shakespeare simply lose control? Did he start with a title and then forget it as he got more and more caught up with his Jewish moneylender? Was Marlowe's Barabas hovering over Shakespeare's shoulder? Is Antonio merely a dull foil setting off the hugely theatrical Shylock? Or might it be that the title of this play signals the expectation that we will want to come to terms with Antonio in his own right? If we read against the bogeyman—if we give equal time to other characters—will we begin to see an Antonio, and consequently a play, that we have missed as a result of our intense focus on Shylock?

I have recently outlined two distinct accounts of Antonio, neither of which has much to do with Shylock (Leinwand, chs. 1 and 4). In fact, it was only by looking away from Shylock and paying attention to Antonio qua merchant that I was able to fashion for Antonio the sort of independence and multidimensionality that is inevitably Shylock's but that Antonio achieves in performances more often than in our readings of the play. If I ask my students to think about Antonio apart from Shylock, they first notice his relationship with Bassanio. This may lead profitably to a discussion of homosocial and homoerotic bonds in Shakespearean drama and in the period. But students also begin to notice a variety of other small but telling things. For instance, some students have commented on what are to my knowledge two plural nouns thus far unremarked by critics: Tubal says that "there came divers of Antonio's creditors" and Antonio himself writes that his "creditors grow cruel" (3.1.103 and 3.2.316).[1] This multiplicity of creditors gestures toward a world inhabited by Antonio that extends well beyond the confines of Shylock's moneylending business or Bassanio's desires. Other students, now intent on Antonio, have taken up Salerio's (or Salarino's) mention of the "wealthy *Andrew* [dock'd] in sand" (1.1.27) and followed the Arden note far enough to discover the Spanish galleon *St Andrés* captured by Ralegh in 1596 at Cadiz. This clue leads us in discussion to the history of privateering, and then back to Bassanio "adventuring" (1.1.143) for Belmont's "golden fleece" (1.1.170) with the backing of the wealthy merchant of Venice. Once again, we are off the beaten Shylock path, reading against the bogeyman and for the play otherwise cast in shadow by his immense, undeniable stature.

Harry Berger, Jr., first taught us in 1980 ("Early Scenes") that if we read the opening scenes of *Macbeth* with care, a Duncan will emerge to whom we are as good as blind if we view him only as a victim of Macbeth, the tragic bogeyman (Berger, *Making Trifles* 70–97). I find that when undergraduates are asked to follow Berger's example, they not only discover a new and more disturbing Duncan but also question their abiding assumption that tragedy is always the tragedy of one tragic character. As Berger argues, "there is something rotten in Scotland [. . .] something intrinsic to the structure of Scottish society, something deeper than the melodramatic wickedness of one or two individuals" (74). Feminists and new historicists have given us ways to redirect the attention of students captivated by Iago. The allure of a bogeyman, whether he is Shylock or Macbeth or Iago, has a way of letting characters like Antonio and Othello off the hook, absolving them of some measure of their inarguable responsibility for the crises in which we find them. Resistance to the bogeyman facilitates redistribution of complicities. By leveling the character field, we begin to see a Duncan who is, after all, the king, who understands realpolitik, and who has held his own quite well in the face of waves of insurrection. We see an Othello whose anxieties are not simply induced by Iago and an Antonio who ventures widely outside Shylock's orbit.

We can also ask our students to reckon what happens when they look beyond the obvious heavies in non-Shakespearean drama. Some of the benefits that accrue may be indicated by considering two unmistakable bogeyman plays that students find quite entertaining: Thomas Middleton's *Michaelmas Term* and Philip Massinger's *A New Way to Pay Old Debts*. While once again I am interested in the horizons that open up when we turn away from what looms so large right in front of us, it is worth noting that both these plays are themselves premised on a historical dislocation that has been frequently noticed. In very broad terms, over the course of the long early modern period, contract was overriding status, achieved identity was overtaking ascribed identity, and exchange value was supplanting use value. As landed gentlemen found themselves sometimes vexingly and always complexly entangled with urban money men, considerably mediated versions of their disorienting encounters were frequently enacted on the London stage. It has been common to accept such grotesque figures as Quomodo and Overreach as representative harbingers of nascent capitalism—even though Middleton's and Massinger's monsters both have an abiding soft spot for land and landed values—but we are not accustomed to thinking about these bogeymen's antagonists as deformations of a residual economic system in their own right. This may be simply because characters like Quomodo and Overreach are so charismatic, so overwhelming, that we forget to read against the bogeyman. Or it may be that while we, the heirs of capitalism, readily equate its onset with predation, we are apt to conceive of still earlier socioeconomic formations in more benign terms. In either case, we miss the salience of figures like Middleton's Richard Easy and Massinger's Lord Lovell. These seemingly bland, undemonstrative characters have a way of turning out to be prodigies too.

Students often ask what "Quomodo" means, but few ask about "Easy." When I pose the question, straightaway someone will volunteer that Easy is "easy" because it is so easy to trick him. This is a good starting point for a discussion about gulling. Jonson, Marston, Heywood, Dekker, Middleton—all the Elizabethan and Jacobean comics knew their classical precursors, and each had a dramatist's appreciation for the theatricality of gulling. It was only necessary for them to arrive at the appropriate socioeconomic valence of the guller-gull relationships they might stage. Is the guller now a scheming merchant and the gull a prodigal heir, or is the guller a witty gallant and the gull a hapless shopkeeper? Easy certainly is gulled in *Michaelmas Term*; however, we are not yet reading against the bogeyman if we understand Easy to be interpellated chiefly as a gull. The cony is nothing but object to the cony catcher's subject. Students who grow impatient with what they perceive to be a digression in the direction of plays and jestbooks that they were not assigned for the week allotted to Middleton will refocus discussion on the text. One of them, reminding me of what I said were the virtues of close reading, will point to a line early in the play in which Easy says that he has been "*easily possessed*" (1.1.47; my emphasis). This means to be easily persuaded or, in a more modern idiom, to be easily had; but it is still to position Easy as a gullible heir. Easy possession is also, of course, a conventionally feminized orientation, what Cockstone will momentarily characterize as being "somewhat too open / Bad in man, worse in woman" (1.1.53–54). Openness may in this regard refer to unduly easy penetrability, but it speaks as well to leakiness, another putatively feminine liability (Paster 23–63). Since one relieved one's bowels on a stool of ease, the gull and the heir may be said to come together in the person of the leaky young heir shitting away his inheritance (Leinwand 57).

A student empowered by onomastic license to associate his or her way to, say, the film *Easy Rider* will be the one to move the class out of the shadow of the bogeyman. To be easy (as in "I'm easy") is to be somewhere between mindlessness (the gull) and prescience (the guller); it is to be insouciant, relaxed, what I and my friends used to mean when we said, "no sweat." Such easiness has more to do with compliance than with passivity, and even if it does shade into gullibility, it stimulates our envy, not our censure. What Easy has going for him that Quomodo simply cannot penetrate or possess is that he is "free" (1.1.47). Not free in the sense that the Lady in Milton's *Comus* is free ("Thou canst not touch the freedom of my minde" [line 663]) and not free in the sense that he escapes the economic entailments that underwrite city comedy, but anxiety-free. If Hamlet has a preternatural sense that he is a character in a revenge tragedy, Easy has the oblivious self-confidence of a comic protagonist whose balance cannot help being righted in the end.

Easy's unintended nonchalance, his country-boy *sprezzatura*, arms him against Quomodo; in fact, in the end, it comes close to maddening Quomodo. Of course, the woolen draper who rehearses his own death in order to get a glimpse of his posterity is nothing if not anxious. But anxiety must be the most predictable attribute of a swindler, a mastermind always on the lookout for the best angle, always forecasting liabilities and hectically juggling several balls at once (students may think of Doll, Subtle, and Face or might even remember Mosca taunting Volpone with the possibility that the magnifico had broken into a sweat). Never able to relax or to let down his guard, Quomodo can at best fantasize about the ease with which he imagines Easy coming up to London expecting to hold his own in the "man-devouring city" (2.2.21). An expert in the art of hazing apparent rubes ("city powd'ring" [1.1.56]), Quomodo has only vague intimations of how a less frenzied calendar might reward him. Curiously, however, these intimations do motivate him. Both his feigned death and his intended rustication on Easy's paternal estate answer to his own profound, if unacknowledged, longing for ease (Leinwand 59). The moderately ironic but, I think, quite appealing *ars vivendi*—the easiness—modeled by Easy not only trumps the bogeyman but also constitutes the *habitus* to which he aspires. Bland, inert, inattentive Easy—not sinister, conniving Quomodo— fashions the effective ethos in *Michaelmas Term*. Only Easy's obliviousness, not Quomodo's familiar commodity scam, has real power to stun. Just listen to Quomodo: "He [Easy] makes me sweat. [. . .] Was I mad? [. . .] I'm undone [. . .] confounded forever!" (5.1.104–18).

Students can arrive at such an account of Easy-ness in the play and, in so doing, redress the imbalance that derives from bogey-centered reading, but teachers have to coach them. Students should be warned that bogeymen shrewdly solicit their attention and that they should offer some resistance, or at least try to match the attention they lavish on bogies with an equal regard for seemingly obvious or undermotivated characters. Berger's conviction that complicity is distributed across the Shakespearean character field leads him to read Gaunt and Bolingbroke with an intensity that usually has been reserved for Richard II and Hal (Berger, chs. 8–11). But the procedure I have in mind is not confined to the ethical assessment that preoccupies Berger. Students invariably condemn Shylock or Quomodo and, up to a point, this is fine. I have found, however, that they lock themselves into a position from which they then impute strict moral probity or innocence to Antonio (or Portia) or Easy. To read against the bogeyman is to suggest categories that complement or round out students' often narrowly moral interpretations (this one's a good guy, that one's a bad guy). If we temporarily bracket the bogeyman (and his obvious iniquity or monstrosity) and start with a character like Easy, then we may find that a moral vocabulary does not necessarily serve us well. Easiness poses hardly any ethical challenge to Quomodo's rapacity. Rather more like what students today identify as a lifestyle, easiness uncannily insinuates itself into Quomodo's imagination, tacitly accomplishing what *The Spanish Tragedy*'s Revenge boasts of when he tells Andrea, "Yet is my mood soliciting their souls" (3.15.20). Insofar as character is concerned, we reclaim Easy from the dustbin of dramatis personae. Insofar as history is concerned, the relationship between woolen draper and Essex heir that I have described is one way of describing the development of the land market in England—the coming together of land and capital, the growth of capitalist agriculture, and the rise of the gentleman merchant. This marriage of land and market is not consummated in *Michaelmas Term*, but I think it is adumbrated. It is the shadow that Easy and Quomodo cast together.

Massinger's mighty bogeyman in *A New Way to Pay Old Debts* is, of course, Sir Giles Overreach. My students make him out to be an intimidating bully and, predictably, the main source of power in the play's Nottinghamshire. Maybe they respond this way in part because my students have urban or suburban roots and therefore recognize money more readily than land or status as the definitive criterion of influence. Or maybe it is because Overreach translates awfully well into a Hollywood-style crime boss: he has the "justice" (2.1.9) in his pocket and gloats over his having "crushed" (2.1.1) an antagonist. A seemingly familiar, sadistic thug, he aims not only to undo but also to humiliate his foes: " 'tis my glory [. . .] / To have their issue whom I have undone, / To kneel to mine as bondslaves" (2.1.81–83). When I ask students momentarily to set aside Overreach, they turn first to Frank Wellborn, the prodigal, and then to Tom Allworth, the play's love interest. About the latter, we usually find that we do not have much to say, unless it is to note that he takes his place in a long line of landed young men willing to marry hypogamously into tainted money while professing undying love and arranging an elopement. Frank Wellborn has drawn more critical attention than Tom Allworth, and students also quickly detect elements of hypocrisy and bad faith on his part. Wellborn and Allworth are for the most part Overreach's comic antagonists, by which I mean they represent the formal or structural necessity to defeat Overreach and so guarantee comic closure—they are never true counterweights to Overreach. Though clever or sneaky, they are shallow, without even a trace of the wit that we find in a precursor like Middleton's Witgood. Once again, I ask students to follow the onomastic clues of Jacobean drama: "All"-"worth" and "Well"-"born" can coast on their ascribed identity, their birthright and inherent worthiness; "Wit"-"good" must achieve an identity by energetically exercising his wit.

But Massinger's Lord Lovell stands for something different. Most students pick up on what they take to be his snobbery, and some will note that his fastidious refusal to "adulterate my blood" (4.1.223) is precisely counterposed to Overreach's masochistic abjection (his willingness to shoulder "any foul aspersion" that might tarnish Lovell's "unquestioned integrity" [4.1.91, 96]). This recognition alone alters students' sense of the power balance in *A New*

Way to Pay Old Debts and suggests the extent to which Lovell may be pro-
digious in his own right. Not only must his (though obviously not Tom Allworth's) "scarlet" (4.1.225) blood avoid the "taint" (4.1.97) of "London blue"
(4.1.226), but his "immaculate whiteness" (4.1.95) must never be "sullied"
(4.1.97). Lovell's fear of contamination leads to a self-righteous enforcement
of distinction—what Mary Douglas calls "dirt avoidance" (12), and what
Shakespeare's Bertram considers the corruption of his blood (*All's Well That
Ends Well* [2.3.116])—which explains Lord Lovell's conviction that he must
stand free of Overreach. But *must* need not mean *can*; it is Lovell's comprehensive triumph that makes him truly stand apart.

I suggest to students that to read against the bogeyman also ought to entail
skeptical interrogation of what the bogeyman has to say. There is clearly something odd about Overreach's boast to Lovell that "to maintain you in the port
/ Your noble birth [. . .] requires, / [. . .] I [will] ruin / The country to supply
your riotous waste" (4.1.105–09). It does not take long for someone to observe
that Overreach must be thinking of Wellborn, because Lovell could not possibly be guilty of "riotous waste." Or maybe Overreach cannot subscribe to
the play's fantasy of a self-sufficient landowner because the multiplicity of
indebted, overburdened landowners in *A New Way to Pay Old Debts*, let
alone in early modern England, offers so little evidence for such autonomy.
Wellborn depends on both Overreach and Lady Allworth, Tom Allworth needs
Margaret Overreach, Overreach himself needs Lovell, even Lady Allworth
stands to gain by allying herself with Lovell—only Lovell needs none of this,
not money, not advantageous marriage, not land. A careful reading against the
bogeyman does not so much diminish Overreach's admittedly stunning presence as it reveals that it is Lord Lovell who is truly extraordinary. Creditors
like Overreach were familiar; wholly unencumbered magnates like Lovell were
simply not to be found (Leinwand, ch. 3). For Lord Lovell, and for him alone,
there is not even a trace of a crisis of the aristocracy.

Quomodo and Overreach stun us, perhaps offend or even excite us, but
seemingly tepid Easy and Lovell are fantastic to a degree that only a combination of formal method (like reading against the bogeyman) and history (in
this instance, the always intertwined relations of land and capital) reveals. We
have schooled ourselves to recognize the depth or complexity of all sorts of
Shakespearean characters beyond the vital ones like Lear or Rosalind. As a
result, we expect to have something interesting to say about characters like
Edgar and Celia. In the realm of non-Shakespearean drama, however, it has
been easy to dismiss a range of characters as thin, or as foils or types. Reading
against the bogeyman may in the short term feel like an arbitrary discipline,
but its reward is the revelation of consequence in characters we and our
students may either neglect or simply not know how to address. We think we
can say something about Edgar or Celia because that old Shakespearean magic
seems to work across time and place. I am convinced that early modern the-
atergoers had something to say about Easy and Lovell because, for them, there

was more to these characters than mere instrumentality or typicality. There is a limit to what we can recover, but we have ways to make sense of English Renaissance drama beyond the bogeyman.

NOTE

[1]Quotations of *The Merchant of Venice* are from the Arden edition of John Russell Brown; quotations of *A New Way to Pay Old Debts* are from Russell Fraser and Norman Rabkin's edition; quotation of *The Spanish Tragedy* is from the New Mermaids edition of J. R. Mulryne.

"Our Sport Shall Be to Take What They Mistake": Classroom Performance and Learning

Helen Ostovich

And all shall be concluded in one scene,
For there's no pleasure ta'en in tediousness.
—*The Spanish Tragedy*

Theseus's defense of amateur acting in *A Midsummer Night's Dream*—"Our sport shall be to take what they mistake" (5.1.90)—provides the watchword for classroom performance in my early drama course. And though, like Hippolyta, "I love not to see wretchedness o'ercharged / And duty in his service perishing" (85–86), I rarely have to watch anything that bad. Since 1994, I have become a committed proponent of student stagings, for which I offer the following anecdotal rationale. My enthusiasm for classroom performance arose initially out of desperation at the dearth of filmed or professionally performed non-Shakespearean drama. In my early drama course (running twenty-six weeks over two terms), I start with a six-week unit of eight to twelve short medieval plays, which I can often illustrate from the Poculi Ludique Societas video archives;[1] thereafter, I teach one play a week, spending six weeks apiece on Elizabethan, Stuart, and Restoration and eighteenth-century drama. Each term ends with a performance class. This survey course of twenty-four to thirty plays can leave students bewildered by their discovery that other playwrights do not write like Shakespeare: the dialogue has rhythms they don't recognize, colloquial expressions they can't decipher, and ideological assumptions they cannot transfer to a modern context. As a result, students focus more on the difficulty of reading than they do on visualizing the action or grasping the issues. My goal is to achieve a classroom situation in which readers rethink their roles as audiences or viewers, uncover contextual similarities between the past and the present, and understand that drama is an elastic, not fixed, form in which the printed script provides only a part of a play's meaning. The rest comes from actors, costumes, music, set, props, and rapport with the audience. Forcing students to perform seems the best way to achieve this end.

Performance in my classroom is part of a multitiered process. To prepare for lectures and discussion, students write a five-hundred-word paper on some performance-based aspect of that week's play: staging a specific moment, or analyzing a certain speech or conversation, or recognizing the spectacular effect of parallel action or characters, as when an on-stage audience watches a play within a play. Although I require a minimum of six such papers for the course, many students choose to write more. The object is to alert the students to the play's auditory and visual cues by having them concentrate on how textual clues offer possible performance choices in a single scene: for example, they might consider the multilingual *Soliman and Perseda* in the last scene of *The Spanish Tragedy* (Hieronimo merely says, "Each one of us / Must act his part in unknown languages, / That it may breed the more variety" [4.1.166–68]); the maidservant's prevention of Frankford's violence in *A Woman Killed with Kindness* ("*Wendoll, running over the stage in a night-gown, he [Frankford] after him with his sword drawn; the maid in her smock stays his hand, and clasps hold on him. He pauses for a while*" [4.5.31.sd]); or the account book in *Everyman*, the empty pages of which become miraculously full of good deeds.[2] These short papers also form the basis of tutorials, in which smaller groups from the class meet to share and refine various performance-based interpretations of that week's play. From within the tutorial group, even smaller groups meet on their own to collaborate on a scene for performance. After the groups perform, the participants each submit a paper evaluating how well they achieved their performance goals and what they discovered about the difference between rehearsing among themselves and performing before an audience. The audience also fills out a questionnaire for each performed scene, commenting on the relation between performance choices and the text; that is, they consider how a performance has illuminated the text or changed their perception of the text. Even when a performance doesn't illuminate, the object of peer criticism is to focus on the positive elements, explain the failures, and suggest improvements that might have made the scene more effective.[3] During this process, close reading (what I prefer to think of as close imagining), writing, experiment, and discussion all work together to promote the idea of a play's elasticity—the possibility of more than one viable performance of any given scene. Within that context, the actual performance of scenes at the end of the semester contributes to a process that has consistently centered on theatrical immediacy or spectacle as the basis for comprehending a play's options.[4]

In practical terms, how does this process work? Generally, I assign about four people to a group, although the number may vary on request or by accident. I make sure each group knows how to contact its members (by distributing telephone numbers and e-mail addresses), I set a deadline by which time the group must tell me what scene they intend to perform, and I give final approval of their scene choices. I recommend that students allow plenty of time to select the scene, read it, block their movements, cut their script, discover interpretations, and consider props, costume, and set (these last, I usually suggest, should be minimal). Otherwise, beyond offering myself as a resource or mediator, I leave the specifics to the players.

I insist on approving scene choices to make sure that students have selected a scene or pastiche that will work on its own and has a beginning, middle, and end; otherwise, blind spots can derail the production. For example, in an otherwise splendidly conceived Mak and Gill sequence from *The Second Shepherd's Play*, the students stopped short of a definitive ending. In this performance, the students set Mak's cottage in a modern winter scene, with hungry gypsies Mak and Gill hiding the lamb in a large cooking pot with a ladle instead of in a cradle. The comedy of Gill's groaning labor kept the shepherds nervously outside, but when they finally entered, the suspicious shepherds quickly retrieved the lamb from the pot. As the discussion later pointed out, the shepherds might have developed more stage business by removing the lamb indignantly from the pot after a longer search, cuddling the rescued lamb while handing the empty pot back to Gill, or threatening Mak and Gill with spoons and ladles. Nevertheless, the audience enjoyed the absurdity of the tiny toy lamb (still in its woolly state) for dinner, since it altered the play's representation of hunger among the impoverished by providing very little to eat. The performance certainly brought out the comedy of the play, clarified some of the jokes, and emphasized the good will of the shepherds, especially when one shepherd tried to give birthday money to the lamb-child and was rejected by Mak. But the conclusion was problematic because, fearful of injuring someone during the blanket tossing, the students simply stopped their scene with Gill's running away, leaving Mak abandoned among the shepherds. In a room without special lighting or curtains, nothing outside of the scene itself can signify the end of the performance. In this performance, the students needed some equivalent for Mak's blanket tossing to signal closure: perhaps just covering Mak with a blanket and beating it, or beating him with the cooking implements. Although the shepherds discovered the truth, the audience didn't see them act on it by punishing Mak, and the effect was finally unsatisfying, despite the successful comedy.

At some point in the rehearsal process, I also check that students are aware of implied stage directions and that the scene itself moves toward closure. The experience of bathos in student performance happens frequently, even when a group seems to be following the script closely. In a performance of *Everyman's* confrontation with Goods, everything went well except for the finale. The set was impressive: students had defined their stage area with candles and had brought in a large trunk overflowing with purple velvets, silver candelabra, gold goblets, and mounds of impressive jewelry and coins that glittered in the flickering light. When Everyman finally realized that Goods was not going to accompany him on his journey, he turned away in despair—and Goods was oddly silent in face of Everyman's curses, not indulging in the demonic laughter that his lines demand: "I must needs laugh, I cannot be sad" (line 456). Another year, the subsequent scene with the weakened Good-Deeds also stopped short by not including the rehabilitation of Good-Deeds and thus bizarrely failed to clarify Everyman's choice of Knowledge as his new companion. Logically, the scene should end with Good-Deeds rising up, restored to health, but the vision of the still-limp character on stage implied—

against the text—that faith and knowledge don't work as a route to salvation. A performance may have a good concept, but a good concept alone, students discover, is not enough for a scene to work theatrically.

Beyond reading closely for implied stage directions and momentum, students learn through performance to value voice and actorly presence, which can release stunning theatrical energy. Seven students in one class decided to perform a severely cut version of *Cambyses*. To avoid long speeches by any one performer, the cast decided to create a Greek tragedy effect by forming a chorus out of the prologue and epilogue. The speeches were cut into small segments for each of the seven to recite while they stood still in a straight line before the audience; the effect, despite the story of Cambyses's terrifying lack of control, was to imply a greater moral control exerted over his evil. Their basic black costumes were undifferentiated until the actors took specific roles in the action. Venus, for example, pinned a pink heart on her breast; Cupid sported dark glasses and shot at Cambyses with a child's rubber-dart gun; Cambyses wore a large crown and a sword and inadvertently added to his performance by chewing gum, which the audience interpreted as brutal empty-headedness, like an ox or bull chewing cud, waiting for the next opportunity to be violent. (One of the peculiar things students learn about performance is that audiences always try to interpret what they see, even accidents.) But the biggest surprise was the prelude to the murder of the Queen: this actress managed to turn the galloping verse into almost natural sound by speaking over the ends of lines onto the next and weighting the words for sense, not metrics. Ambidexter and Cambyses, who came across as thuddingly insensitive, spoke in seesaw rhythms, a sound the audience associated finally with moral limitations. The result was powerfully moving.

Overcoming the inexperience of amateur actors makes special demands on script and audience. One group, performing the scenes involving Helen of Troy and the Old Man in *Doctor Faustus*, had an excellent concept: they delivered a modern Faustus as seedy alcoholic toyed with by a witty devil. Mephistophilis, charmingly complicit with the audience, revealed his contempt for Faustus in the double representation of Helen, first as a teasing grotesque that was really Mephistophilis in drag and then as an erotically feminine Helen, played by a student-actress, to lure Faustus away from the Old Man's preaching. The doubleness added depth to the scene, which acting alone might not have achieved: the swaying figure of Helen, eluding Faustus's grasp, also impressed the audience with Faustus's drunken delusion that he was embracing a woman whom he actually never touched. The contrast with the elegant Old Man in a well-tailored suit and hat spoke for itself: the Old Man's fragility, indicated by his reliance on a cane, emphasized not only his moral strength but also Faustus's self-induced incapacity through drink. The brown-bagged bottle, however, provided a double clue to Faustus's failed condition both as character and, unfortunately, as actor learning the part. The Faustus actor had attached his lines to the bag and kept his back to the audience in order to read them before or after swigging. This performance choice created severe reception difficulties for the audience, although the cast hoped that the audience might read the stubborn back of this faceless Faustus as a shadowy Everyman. It only worked sporadically. The actor's choice displayed an astonishing range of distrust: distrust of himself, distrust of his fellow actors, distrust of Marlowe's lines as supplying their own mnemonic cues, distrust of the audience's desire to be engaged by performance, distrust of the whole performance process. Ironically, this actor's failure made the audience all the more eager to respond supportively to the rest of the cast, who rose to a difficult situation with determination and grace.

Refusal to cooperate, or even defection, does happen within acting groups, even when grades are at stake, but students are resilient. One group, when unexpectedly diminished by the loss of cast members, resorted to a quirky, naive surrealism for performing the bower scene between Horatio and Bel-imperia in *The Spanish Tragedy* (2.4). This group capitalized imaginatively on the scene's natural buildup from romantic rendezvous to unexpected murderous attack by staging a symbolic hanging on a witness-tree. A student stand-in (who refused to learn lines but agreed to play a mute part) performed the tree as a sympathetic witness to the shy lovers' hand-holding, footsie ("thy foot to try the push of mine" [38]), "twining arms" (43), and "dart[ing]" kisses (40)—even the tree grinned when Bel-imperia's peck on the cheek rendered the Horatio actor momentarily rosy and speechless. But after the murder (committed by one actor in the conflated role of Lorenzo/Balthazar), the tree let down a rope with which Horatio was then "hanged," although he merely kneeled on the floor with his head bent over to signal his death. The audience commented on the profound sense of intrusion, violation, and betrayal evoked by the tree's unexpected support of the scripted violence. In the audience's imagination, this concept provided excellent preparation for the later scene of Isabella's cutting down the bower and for Hieronimo's acute sense of betrayal by all he had once believed in.

Another group, performing the conjuration scene in *The Puritan* (4.2), were similarly imaginative in accounting for a role for which they had no actor: Sir Godfrey appeared with a bewigged broom, identified as the "lady-stick" in the program, playing the part of Lady Plus. The audience appreciated this definition of the foolish Lady Plus: turning her into an easily manipulated but full-size puppet or dummy made an important visual statement on her role. In written responses, many spectators called for more stage business with the lady-stick, instead of the mere elimination of all of Lady Plus's lines: some of her lines could have been "repeated" or "echoed" by Sir Godfrey when he or other characters could not "hear" her. The best comedy came from the fact that no one on stage seemed to realize that Lady Plus was a broom. This fact underpinned her whole role: at one point, accompanied by thunder and flashes of lightning, the lady-stick peers around the door to catch a glimpse of the conjuration, only to tremble and disappear again at the sound of a particularly loud crashing of thunder.

Performance before a receptive audience, as students discover, makes actors respond to their roles more enthusiastically than any rehearsal might have predicted. During a performance of the Dapper and the fairies sequence from *The Alchemist* (3.5), such enthusiasm pushed both audience and actors over the edge. In this sequence, Dapper is blinded by a "smock" (line 10) and purged of his "worldly pelf" ([line 17] purse, handkerchiefs, jewelry, seals, loose coins) by fairies (played by Subtle and Face) who search him with pinching and tickling while emitting high-pitched fairy babble ("*Ti, ti, ti, ti!*"). Subtle, Face, and Dol communicated the sheer fun of squeezing more and more valuables out of Dapper and produced an appropriately rapid shift into panic when a knock at the door interrupted the robbery of their victim. At this point in the text, they silence Dapper by shoving a gag of gingerbread (a gift from his aunt, the Fairy Queen) into his mouth before he is led offstage to wait in "Fortune's privy lodgings" (line 79). Unfortunately, the actors substituted a slice of cheesecake for the gingerbread and, pumped up by the audience's laughter at the "*ti ti*" tickling sequence, pressed the cheesecake rather too exuberantly into Dapper's gaping mouth. The result blurred the margin between truth and fiction as Dapper began to choke and spew cheesecake while the audience howled at the "acting." Dapper's attempts to get off stage were hampered by an improvised bit of stage business: Subtle and Face, aroused by the audience's shrieks of laughter, completed the perverse sexuality of the tickling assault on Dapper by dropping his pants around his ankles. As it turned out, the student playing Dapper was actually choking. He barely made it to the men's "privy," where he threw up whatever was left of the cheesecake. (The other actors, sobered by what might have happened, cleaned it up afterward.) The victim himself was amazingly good-natured about having his near-death experience mistaken for great clowning, the physical gags all too literal. His willingness to be "violated," as one member of the audience expressed it, increased the level of comedy to a very close approximation of what Jonson meant by the "comedy of affliction" (*Epicoene* 2.6.33–34). Despite the successful performance of Dapper as a glutton for punishment, its very success provoked dangerous consequences that might have ended less happily.

Although students often choose to perform comedy, under the mistaken assumption that they will be laughed at anyway, a combination of comedy and tragedy affords an excellent opportunity for making theatrical points. In a performance of *The Duchess of Malfi* (3.2), the concept was simple: a loving couple in a happy household is terrorized and disabled by a brother's jealousy. The scene moved from the inconsequential banter of Antonio, Cariola, and the Duchess at her dressing table to the chilling climax of Ferdinand's threats, followed by the Duchess's question, "You saw this apparition?" (142), after her brother has exited and Antonio reenters with a pistol to protect his wife. Cariola and Antonio had been frozen in silent fear, hidden at a doorway, while the Duchess suffered Ferdinand's abuse, but their horrified reactions helped bridge the two halves of the scene. Their reentry gave a satisfying symmetry to the scene because, as one student observed later, the "scene ends with the same characters in the same place as in the beginning, but with a much changed atmosphere." The actors had spent considerable time developing their characters. Cariola performed apt stage business of sewing, hanging up clothes, assisting her mistress, and joking with the couple, to demonstrate her friendship with both husband and wife. The Duchess held the scene together with emotional changes from seductiveness to terror, echoed by Antonio's early teasing and later helpless anxiety. The ugly tension created by Ferdinand's appearance was outstanding: with a body taller and heavier than any of the other three actors and a voice dripping with malice, the actor paced in quiet rage around his victim, maintaining a blank facial expression of inhuman cruelty. The high point of horror occurred during this confrontation, when the Duchess, having fallen to the floor, cringed away from the deliberately slow-moving, slow-talking Ferdinand, who stroked her after telling her the parable of lost reputation, stage business that suggested his kinky pleasure in subjugating her. In this visually stunning moment, with her brother looming over her, the Duchess, small and alone, had no defense against his irrationality. As one student commented, "You got lost in the moment, it was that good."

Classroom performance allows students to achieve critical understanding of theatrical texts by pragmatic means. Through their own committed efforts, students learn that early modern playwrights are theatrically aware and innovative and that, although some plays seem dense or puzzling on the page, performance of the scripts opens up imaginative possibilities that inject vitality into their appreciation of drama, read or performed. They learn primarily that a play text is an elastic thing, that performers bring dimension and sensibility to characters and actions, and that readers can enrich their solitary study of plays by investing the scripts with the legacy of their group experience in theatrical rehearsal and performative choice. Secondarily, they make new friends, release one another's creativity, and gain respect for their own and others' abilities. The humanities have no better gifts than these.

NOTES

[1]Poculi Ludique Societas is a group of specialists in medieval and early modern performance at the University of Toronto. See the list of past productions and the archive gallery online at <http://www.chass.utoronto.ca/~medieval/www/pls/>.

[2]Quotations of the plays in this essay are from C. F. Tucker Brooke and Nathaniel Paradise except those from *Epicoene*, which are from Helen Ostovich's edition, *Everyman*, and *The Puritan*.

[3]In her essay "Teaching Shakespeare through Performance," Miriam Gilbert comments, "We can learn from what doesn't work as well as from what does" (607).

Gilbert's essay appears in an issue of *Shakespeare Quarterly* with several other useful articles on classroom performance.

[4]G. B. Shand describes play texts as "sites of constant and normal negotiation between textualized obligation and multiple legitimate performative options" ("Reading Power" 245) and the students who learn to appreciate the enriched meanings derived from such negotiation as "perceptively empowered readers" (244). See also Shand's earlier rationale for classroom performance in "Classroom as Theatre: A Technique for Shakespeare Teachers."

Teaching Cary's
The Tragedy of Mariam
through Performance

Laurie Maguire

I teach Elizabeth Cary's *Tragedy of Mariam* at the end of a fourth-year honors seminar, Women and Society in Renaissance Drama. We read plays by Middleton, Webster, Ford, and Shakespeare, paying a lot of attention to dramaturgy as well as social issues. *Mariam* is the first and only play we read written by a woman; it is the first and only closet drama we read; and it is the first and only play we read in an unmodernized edition (we use the Malone Society Reprint). The play is therefore triply unfamiliar to the students, and they don't quite know how to deal with it.

I usually do an introductory class dealing with Elizabeth Cary's life (I don't do biographies of other dramatists, but I find the students get excited about Cary's conflicts and consciousness) and the historical background of the play. I deal with this latter material in the most hands-on way I can: I draw an extensive family tree on the chalkboard but leave the name boxes blank, giving the students large adhesive flash cards with character and historical names and inviting them to use the argument at the beginning of the play to place the cards in their correct position on the board. This process usually involves a lot of frustrated discussion as we discover the errors in the argument, collate the information with that in scene 1 of *Mariam* and with our biblical knowledge, and get confused by onomastic duplication (the Aristoboluses, for instance). It is a fun exercise, the students see me figuring the story out too (even after years of teaching the play I regularly lose my placing of its historical characters), and it equips us for Mariam's reaction in scene 1 to the information given directly before it in the argument.

I then devote an entire class to scene 1, which I conduct as a drama workshop. Usually I have at least one drama student in the class willing to be directed by me in the role of Mariam, but if I don't the workshop approach works equally well as a discussion. It may seem strange to talk about teaching *Mariam*—a closet drama—as performance, but critics frequently comment on the dramaturgical sophistication of this play. Thus Josephine Roberts: "*Mariam* reveals a knowledge of stagecraft that suggests Cary's familiarity with popular as well as closet drama" (69). And here are Margaret Ferguson and Barry Weller in their introduction to the California edition of Cary's play: "whether or not *Mariam* was intended for performance, it seems to have been written with an ear for dramatic inflection, variety, and emphasis" (153). Certainly, when one thinks of films such as *Sex, Lies, and Videotape* or Alan Bennett's monologues *Talking Heads* or the Nicole Kidman video head-shot sequences in *To Die For*, it is clear that *Mariam*'s moment—a play of speech rather than action—has come.

The first two acts of *Mariam* concern characters' reactions to the rumors of Herod's death. In scene 1 Mariam has just received this emotionally turbulent news. What are our definitions of "just"? Five minutes? One hour? Five hours? Probably the bombshell has occurred immediately before the scene begins; she wants to process it. The students' difficulty in following Mariam's speech comes from the monologue's vacillation, its ambivalence, its changes of opinion. We observe the number of times "but" and "yet" and other such conjunctions occur, to help us see how the structure of Mariam's language reveals her conflicted mind; and we talk about the line "one object yields both grief and joy" (11) as a key to the scene (and the play).[1]

As we work through the scene line by line, we use practical theatrical exercises to help us. We discuss what actors call "objectives." Objectives have to be actable (something you do rather than feel) and they have to be self-oriented (you can make yourself do something but cannot necessarily make someone else do something). For example, to deal with duality or to reconcile private and public life is not a valid objective because it is not actable, but to escape from Herod's tyranny can be an objective because it is both actable and self-oriented. We consider an actress's possible scene objectives in 1.1: to cry, to be alone. This leads us to discuss location. Mariam needs privacy. Where would she go? Where can a queen go to be alone? A palace courtyard? A dressing room? Obviously Mariam is somewhere where she can be accessed because Alexandra interrupts her thoughts. We imagine the scene taking place on an unlocalized Jacobean stage but with props that suggest a domestic interior such as a bedroom or a dressing room. In one class I used modern props—photographs, a handmirror, handkerchiefs—to help the students see how Mariam's wildly changing emotions could be cued by props in her vicinity. For example, plastic photo frames with *TV Guide* pictures of movie stars functioned as personal photographs of Herod, Aristobolus, Hyrcanus, and a wedding photograph of Mariam and Herod: Mariam's changes in attitude were triggered by her catching sight of one or another of these loved family photos, which provoked her memory. This worked well given the stress on the opposition of the two relationships between Herod and Aristobolus and Herod and Mariam in the speech and Mariam's vacillating emotions toward Herod. When we imagined her in the garden, we used class members as statues of Julius Caesar ("Rome's last hero" [2]) and Herod. In another class a student made a taped compilation of snatches of romantic pop classics based on duality, paradox, tears, and joy ("Only the good die young" [Joel], "I can see clearly now the rain has gone" [Nash]). She played the tape to prepare the students, in the way performance music would, for the paradoxes of Mariam's dual emotions.

Having thought about location and timing, we then score the script for beats (changes of objective). We identify what the speaker, Mariam, wants and when what she wants changes; we identify what stands in her way at a particular moment (love, society, conscience); we articulate why it matters to her (serenity, integrity, freedom, women's rights). The monologue's rhetorical structure—chiasmus, anaphora, rhythmic changes (e.g., the four strong monosyllables in line 25: "And blame me not"), contrasts, conjunctions—provides the actor with clues in this exercise. We consider emotional choreography: At what point(s) does Mariam cry? Why? There are no right answers, and we don't take the time to score all eighty lines, but the students usually emerge with an understanding of Mariam's jagged mental and emotional gear changes.

Before we work on the text of the scene and its emotional beats, we often do a theatrical exercise in intuitive analogues. What would Mariam be if she were an animal? a color? food? wine? a car? an event? a musical instrument? a season? etc.? The students respond with gut reactions, which they must then defend textually. Suggestions and rationales have included the following: Mariam is a mouse at the start of the play, a lioness at the end; she is a conflict of red and white color; she is *sole veronique*—a fish caught but presented beautifully; she is an entrée in phyllo pastry, where the outside conceals what is inside; she is made of pure, organic ingredients—full of integrity, nothing artificial or synthetic; she is a red wine—an intellectual and sensual experience, something smooth but stronger than it appears, a drink requiring discipline but with the opportunity for intoxication. (Interestingly, all the students suggested alcoholic rather than soft drinks for Mariam, and this in itself became a topic of discussion: an anodyne soft drink was not suitable, they insisted, but neither was a fancy cocktail.) She is a Plymouth Horizon (simple); a Cadillac, but without keys; a Morgan (custom-built and elegant but not showy). As an event she is a play (with inner conflict and dialogue), a tennis match (a ball going back and forth between evenly matched opposites), a symphony orchestra. As a season she is autumn or spring (in transition). As a musical instrument she is a lute or violin. All students can join in such a discussion without fear of failure, and their responses are usually based on some subliminal textual understanding. We conclude with suggestions for actresses to play Mariam (Natasha Kinski, Sarah Jessica Parker, and Juliet Stevenson have all been proposed) and by this stage the students usually want to cast themselves in her role.

The point of all this is fivefold. The intuitive exercise gets the students talking—even those who have found the play difficult—and makes them realize that they have often understood more than they realized. The theatrical work on scene 1 makes the students aware that *Mariam* is actually not that different in terms of theatrical viability and accessibility from the other plays we have read, although it looks different. The focus on the competing emotions in scene 1 gives the students a strong thematic foundation for understanding the rest of the play's psychomachia and dialectic of obedient and disobedient wives, private and public voice, grief and joy, innocence and blame: they know Mariam and her milieu. Focusing on scene 1 also creates a nonthreatening, cooperative classroom atmosphere. And above all, it reminds us that plays that were not performed are not, ipso facto, unperformable. Elizabeth Cary's theatrical influences and stagecraft are topics worth investigating further.

The students appreciate the focus on text and character after the heady new historicist and gender politics that have occupied us for so much of the term, and, having been introduced to the play in this user-friendly fashion, they now find it easy to tackle the complex interpretive work on race and gender that is the subject of the next class.

NOTE

[1]Quotations of *The Tragedy of Mariam* are from A. C. Dunstan and W. W. Greg's edition.

Teaching History, Teaching Difference, Teaching by Directing Heywood's *A Woman Killed with Kindness*

Ric Knowles

What are we teaching when we teach early modern drama through performance? When the dramatist in question has been Shakespeare, the answer has most often seemed self-evident: we're teaching "Shakespeare." And this pedagogical goal has been considered, more or less by definition, to be a Good Thing. But it has also rested for the most part on the assumption, pointed to by Ann Thompson, that both "Shakespeare and the student [. . .] stand somehow outside history, society, and politics" (142). To direct student productions of early modern plays that reject this assumption is a fraught and problematic exercise, and it remains unclear exactly what students involved in such productions learn about early modern plays, about the cultural or theatrical contexts through which they produced their meanings, or about the cultural roles they played then and play now in the academy and the world.

Teaching through performance, at least as most of its proponents have articulated it, involves the conflation of neo-Stanislavskian acting methods (which fetishize the authority of author, text, and director together with the unmediated presence of the actor) with appropriative modernist modes of what Richard Halpern calls "historical allegory"(1–14), disseminated through the Royal Shakespeare Company but ultimately derived from F. R. Leavis's Cambridge and T. S. Eliot's formalist criticism (McCullough). The effect of Method acting, Stanislavskian or American, which appropriates the past and encourages "making the character your own," which focuses on similarity rather than difference, is to efface the differences among early modern, modern, and postmodern understandings and constructions of character, role, class, race, gender, and sexuality in the interests of contemporary relevance— what Alan Sinfield calls "Shakespeare-plus-relevance" (176). Fundamentally modernist staging techniques and theories based on historically and culturally transcendent human values dominate the contemporary classroom and rehearsal hall, notably through the influence of the Royal Shakespeare Company, its outreach programs such as ACTER, publications of interviews with actors (which W. B. Worthen discusses as the last outpost of character criticism [125–50]), and, with overwhelming impact on pedagogy, John Barton's book and widely circulating video series *Playing Shakespeare* (Worthen 166–68). These techniques and theories work to swallow historical difference in a seductive ecstasy of identification and empathy, in which familiarity to the students' own psyches and circumstances serves as the measure of Truth. The philosophical and ideological underpinnings of the approach rest in the belief that, as Eliot argues about understanding Ben Jonson, "we must see [the early modern playwright] as unbiased by time, as a contemporary," which "does not so much require the power of putting ourselves into seventeenth-century London as it requires the power of setting Jonson in our London" (69).

What can a teacher and director do who is committed to teaching historical and cultural difference and to showing students how their intellectual labor in the theater is grounded in a specific historical moment and shaped by the material practices of a particular theatrical and cultural site? An obvious first step, perhaps, is to avoid Shakespeare for the time being and to work with scripts by Jonson, Middleton, Marston, or Heywood, where the problem of the Bard as cultural fetish (Garber) and authority (Worthen 1–43) is somewhat diminished, the cultural stakes are different, and the manifest strangeness of the work can be productive: students can feel free to acknowledge a lack of familiarity with or appreciation of both text and context that is not automatically attributable to inadequacies in their education or deficiencies in their sensibilities. A second, more conceptual step is to choose a period setting and shape a research exercise as a process in translation among cultures rather than as an exegesis of canonical texts with universalist meanings, asking not only what the text means or even what it means to the student but also what it meant in its original and subsequent contexts and how it can be made to mean in this particular place and time of performance. A third step is to historicize the rehearsal process itself and the theatrical techniques and conventions it employs while at the same time interrogating the different theatrical and pedagogical roles (director and actor, teacher and student) and social positionings of the participants. Each of these steps, moreover, has to be taken in full and divided consciousness of the relation between the learning processes of student participants and the experience of student audiences, who experience the production only once, as product. It is too easy, otherwise, unconsciously to separate out the processes of research and those of rehearsal, to confine historical awareness to the intellects of the students working on the show without allowing it to shape their or their audiences' ways of thinking and producing meaning.

Through the remainder of this essay I want to draw on the successes and failures of each of the steps I have outlined in two student productions of Thomas Heywood's *A Woman Killed with Kindness* that I have directed at Canadian universities. The first, at Mount Allison University in New Brunswick in 1989, was an extracurricular production involving English and drama students; the second, at the University of Guelph in Ontario in 1992, was a single-semester course in a drama program that combines acting, directing, design, technical theater, dramatic literature, theater history, criticism, and theory. Although sets and props were 1980s and 1990s brass, glass, and crystal, the period and place setting for the productions, signaled by costuming, was the immediate wake of World War I in the nearby United Empire Loyalist cities of Fredericton, New Brunswick (in 1989), and London, Ontario (in 1992), to which an unwelcome modernity arrived suddenly with the return of disaffected soldiers from the Great War. Both productions opened with the interpolated arrival of Wendoll carrying a suitcase and wearing the uniform of a private in the Canadian army.

Heywood's play seems to serve the first step well. Firmly rooted in place and time, with neither the apparent familiarity or cultural authority of Shakespeare nor the difficult liabilities that Eliot found in Jonson's determined historical specificity and with neither the rhetorical flourish nor the antique grandiosity of a concern with kings and princes, but with the linguistic simplicity and immediate populist appeal of a "prose Shakespeare," a play such as *Woman Killed with Kindness* seems appropriate grist for the pedagogical mill of student production.

Yes and no. While the scenes among the servants and the subplot's scenes of falconry, prison, and early modern usury are sufficiently unfamiliar to prompt both dramaturgical research among students and the awareness of historical difference, they are also extraordinarily difficult to stage and extremely tempting to cut heavily. Meanwhile, the main plot's scenes of seduction, accusation, and repentance read and play very clearly and seem, to most student actors, dangerously transparent. Not surprisingly, of course, these are the scenes on which classroom exercises are most likely to focus and to which student actors are most immediately (and unmediatedly) attracted. These are also the scenes that serve as the uncut core of most contemporary productions, including student ones. But it is important that students pay attention to what they might be tempted to regard, in an unfortunate contemporary television analogy with *Upstairs Downstairs*, as the play's below-stairs scenes of early modern domesticity, both because of the foreignness of these scenes and because of the context that they provide for understanding the main plot and the public character of the early modern household. It is similarly important that students learn to complicate the apparent transparency of the main plot by reading it through the lenses of early modern (rather than contemporary) domesticity and kinship networks.

Most students are comfortable understanding the play's concerns with the exercise of control through kindness, understood as the conferring of obligation. The method is familiar from the operations of charity in maintaining industrial and postindustrial capitalism, as it is familiar as one of the engines of late-twentieth-century parent-child relations. Most student actors are also comfortable reading the main plot through the lens of contemporary soap-opera melodrama as a story of heterosexual temptation, betrayal, and repentance. In rehearsal, these two levels of comfort manifest themselves as willingness, even eagerness, to explore such things as gendered and classed power relationships as they play themselves out in private scenes between individual characters (which of course the early moderns would have considered to be either persons or roles), as student actors often take the initiative in presenting resistant rereadings that they find available in the writing and its frequent silences. At the University of Guelph, just such a rereading was given by the actor playing Ann, at the end of the temptation and seduction in scene 6; she resisted her character's apparent passivity and took the initiative in leading Wendoll offstage to begin their sexual relationship. The choice, in contemporary acting terms, was logical: not only did the actor see no written barrier to it, she found justification in the arc of her consistent Stanislavskian character. The later Ann, she reasoned, would need something substantial about which to feel so repentant. Is this the ingenious uncovering of contemporary, interventionist, and feminist relevance, as I thought at the time, or a thoroughly contemporary misreading of early modern gendered power relations? Or both? What was learned at this moment by student actors and audiences? What were the responsibilities of the (contemporary male) teacher and director in this situation?

Moments like this require the teacher and director to encourage careful historicization of both the past and present as they concern domestic power relations, sexual politics, and what is now anachronistically called character. In the example given above, the play's interest in Wendoll's violation of homosocial bonds, kinship networks, and codes of friendship between men demands this attention to history. If the production of early modern plays is to be meaningful and culturally productive, particularly in teaching situations, it will achieve this goal not by erasing historical difference but by learning from it. And the teacher can do this by denaturalizing students' universalist readings of what many of them assume, in the case of *Woman Killed with Kindness*, are heterosexual, middle-class, and private relationships between characters who are fundamentally normal, as they presume themselves to be (and by implication they presume themselves to be unlike anyone in the room—or ultimately the audience—who feels silenced by such normative assumptions). The combined effect of a rehearsal-hall search for contemporary relevance and the suturing of character with actor identification in the main plot of *Woman Killed with Kindness*, together with the tendency to cut, revise, or mug in the play's scenes of early modern domesticity, is to downplay the play's focus on the public nature of the late sixteenth-century household and of Ann and Wendoll's offense—an offense against the homosocial order, the traffic in women among the early modern gentry, and the early modern sex/gender system. As Rebecca Ann Bach argues, *Woman Killed with Kindness*, far from anticipating a middle-class heterosexuality familiar from postwar television shows such as *Leave It to Beaver*, "reveals the *absence* of that structure of thinking in early modern English domestic tragedy" (518; my emphasis).

I am not arguing here for either side of the traditional binary in debates about the period setting of early modern productions: modern-dress updatings can efface historical and cultural difference, but museum-style attempts to replicate Elizabethan staging without the benefit of early modern audiences are equally misguided. One potential way of maintaining the theater's unique role as a place- and time-specific site for the negotiation of cultural values while keeping historical (and other) difference alive for students in the research processes of design and rehearsal, in rehearsals themselves, and in the consciousness of audiences is what I am calling step two, the three-period solution. I found it useful to set *Woman Killed with Kindness* in a resonant third period (in this case Canada in 1919) while maintaining and acknowledging frame elements of the contemporary world of the actors and audiences (in this case 1990s props, furnishings, and elements of the present reality of the backstage and auditorium), even as the text remained early modern. While audiences often experience cognitive dissonance early in modern dress productions of early modern texts, they tend to settle in over the course of the show. The three-period solution tries to avoid this acclimatization by keeping three historical settings alive and in tension in the actors' and spectators' minds as the different settings interhistoricize and defamiliarize one another. This solution, then, can help to avoid the problems with Brechtian quoting, which disrupts character-actor identification by placing fictional actions and characters in history but which can nevertheless essentialize and dehistoricize the actors, who seem to quote from a fixed point outside the action (and outside history).

By mapping historical change over three periods, this solution also has the advantage of placing both the fictional past and the actors' and audiences' shared *present* within history. In the research and rehearsal process, students are faced with an intermediary disruption in the they're-just-like-us-after-all instinct instilled by acting classes. They find themselves unable to rely on their appropriative instincts as they explore inevitably inexact analogies and disruptive differences among the circumstances of 1603, 1919, and 1990s versions of their characters, while at the same time falconry rubs shoulders with batsmen and usury with high finance.

But it isn't enough to historicize the present through content alone, when the whole theatrical enterprise operates in history and the meanings produced on the stage and in the audience are as much a function of historically specific techniques and practices as of conscious interpretation: the very role of the director was a modernist invention; the acting techniques learned by students as neutral and value-free were designed for productions of Anton Chekhov in the late nineteenth century and adapted in the United States for use in the plays of Tennessee Williams and Arthur Miller; the processes of design and technical theater are dictated by contemporary industrial guidelines, safety regulations, and technological developments; and rehearsal processes are shaped by organizational and stage management practices determined by twentieth-century labor relations and notions of efficiency. My third step, then, is to draw attention to the construction of the rehearsal hall itself and the historically specific roles, relations, and hierarchies that it stages and contains (including those, always inflected with differentials of power, between teachers and students; among races, classes, genders, and sexualities; and among directors, designers, actors, stage managers, and technicians). This step also involves interrogating the ways in which these historically specific techniques, practices, and relations shape students' understandings of human subjectivity (and therefore their roles), social relations (and therefore the relationships among the characters), and interpretative practices (and therefore actors' and audiences' production of meaning) in ways that would have been opaque to Heywood, his actors, and his audiences.

The most difficult role to cast and perform in a student production of *Woman Killed with Kindness* is that of Susan, simply because it is both central and extraordinarily discontinuous and unnatural for a contemporary actor. In each of the productions I directed, I cast the most accomplished actor available to me in this role, which also unfortunately meant the actor most skilled at applying, or imposing, contemporary, post-Stanislavskian techniques and conceptions of character. A skilled student actor in this role who is trained to find Stanislavskian through-lines, to play Stanislavskian objectives across linked beats and units, and to come to a unified understanding and performance of Susan through close attention to what the character says, how she speaks, what she does, and what others say about her can construct a psychologically unified contemporary characterization of Susan from her lines. This can be done despite Susan's leaps first from the doggerel and apparent naïveté of her first scene (sc. 3), then to her intelligence and dignity in the petitioning scene (sc. 9), and finally to the abrupt reversal from humiliation and hatred to apparently unconflicted love in her capitulation to Sir Francis (sc. 14). But without understanding that the character so constructed is not found in the lines but made of them, and made out of techniques that the actor has learned and understood to be neutral and ahistorical, she surrenders the opportunity to perform active and conscious negotiations among diverse conceptions of character, role, gender, sexuality, and social relations. For example, because she does not perform the various (women's) roles presented to her by the script, she loses the opportunity to provide valuable commentary on the action, including that of the main plot. This difficulty is exacerbated by efficient contemporary rehearsal practices that encourage the rehearsing of different plot strands separately, by not calling full-cast rehearsals until late in the process and, therefore, by focusing on linear actions and isolating plots from one another that might otherwise be considered intellectually or emblematically related. It is also exacerbated by a rehearsal context in which the role of teacher and director is gendered male, the cast dominated by men, and the actor playing Susan further isolated as the only woman involved in her particular plot strand and therefore the only woman negotiating gender in what contemporary theatrical culture constructs as an exploratory rehearsal process.

Student reviews of the Guelph and Mount Allison productions point to their mixed success at foregrounding historical and other difference. While Michael Barclay complained in Guelph that "there was no real indication that London, Ontario, had anything to do with the script," Derrick Sleep, in a lengthy review of the Mount Allison version, articulated in some detail the production's "displacement[s] in time," noting that "the viewer is immediately assaulted with four centuries of historical images, each with its own distinctive flavor. Your mind is forced open with the collision of what you are seeing and what you are expecting to see" (13). But the difficulties, frustrations, and partial successes involved in attempting to teach and enact resistant difference through the mounting of a single production, within the context of the contemporary Canadian educational and theatrical industries are also signaled in the reviews. Although one found confusing "the efforts of director Ric Knowles to bring some sort of modern-day feminist angle to [the production]" (Barclay) and the other found the play "relevant, regardless of its historical context" (Sleep 24), both reviewers felt most comfortable praising the acting of their fellow students in quite conventional terms. It seems clear, however, that the pedagogical successes and failures of both productions related directly to the degree to which they were able to resist the lure of too easy familiarity or too facile relevance and—in Thompson's terms, with which I started—to keep "history, society, and politics" alive and active in both the process and the product for actors and for audiences.

NOTE

I would like to thank my research assistant, Sheena Albanese, for her help with this paper, and Christine Bold, for her helpful commentary on an earlier draft. And of course I would like to thank all the students and staff at Mount Allison and Guelph who contributed to both productions.

Webbing Webster

C. E. McGee

"It's all right, Dad. I'll just check it out on the Web when I get to school."
So my ten-year-old daughter assured me a few years ago when, not knowing
the answer to her question, I offered to drop into the college library to get
the information she needed. For me this exchange provided a glimpse of a
future generation of students who, I imagined, would turn first to the Internet
to do their research just as automatically as I head first for the bookshelves
of the university's libraries. That quick exchange also occasioned a more con-
certed effort on my part to encourage undergraduate students to examine the
resources of the Internet—to test its usefulness for research, to analyze its
rhetoric, to assess the quality of the material there, and, most important for
this essay, to produce material for that medium. Webbing Webster was one
form this pedagogical endeavor took.

Several other factors shaped the project. One was the work of the Education
Committee of the Stratford [Ontario] Festival Board, then just starting to
develop the educational pages of its Web site to enrich the experience of
school groups that regularly attend festival productions, especially of Shakespeare. Closer to home, the English program of the University of Waterloo
underwent a major transformation, adding to its program in literary studies a
specialization in rhetoric and professional writing. This curricular revision
aimed in part to help students bridge studies of literature to those of language:
producing a Web site on Webster seemed a way of encouraging them to do
just that, to develop their knowledge of dramatic literature while practicing
one kind of professional writing currently in demand. Finally, there was the
wider public discussion of the value of a liberal arts education, in which many
argued that the secondary gains of such an education are the development of
marketable skills in critical thinking, problem solving, research methods, and
the use of the English language. The primary purpose of the humanities remains both the intellectual engagement with issues and the acquisition of
knowledge of, say, philosophy or history, *Beowulf* or Beckett. Preparing a Web
site, however, realigns the order of these aims. It makes explicit the importance and the parameters of the writing project itself, so that the development
of students' facility with a new technology and its discursive practices can share
the stage with the development of knowledge of, in this instance, *The Duchess
of Malfi*.

Out of the combination of these forces came the following essay topic included among those suggested for an introductory-level course dealing with
literary representations of rebellion and for an upper-level course on the history of English drama to 1642:

> Prepare 8–10 pages of educational material on John Webster's *The
> Duchess of Malfi* as if for inclusion on the Stratford Festival Web site.

Assume that the main audience of the site will be secondary school students who are studying the play in class and will be attending a performance of it at the Festival Theatre. Your aim should be to provide helpful information both about the play and about its performance possibilities. Depending on the number of people interested in this option, workshops will be arranged with the university library and the Arts Computing Office to help students search electronic databases and solve technical problems presented by HTML (hypertext mark-up language).

Implicit in the guidelines is the desire to ground the project in an existing theatrical context. Students were expected to have some knowledge of the conditions specified: the aims (to teach the play in a way that would prepare for a performance and to learn by teaching); the audience (high school students planning to see the show); the medium (the Internet—a medium of notes, visuals, sounds, and links); the Web site (that of the Stratford Festival, which has its own institutional objectives and cultural status); and the theater (the conventions and physical features of which govern staging and theatergoing). To ask undergraduates to write for reasonably bright high school students is to ask them to address themselves to an audience from which they are removed, but not far removed. The undergraduates should have some knowledge of the language and concerns of the high school audience; in fact, many of my students would have had the experience of a school trip to see a Stratford Festival production as one part of their study of a play. The university students would, I hope, give us the benefit of their own high school experience in developing a Web site that responds to the interests and the needs of our target high school audience. But any theater or audience will do: one might ask for materials to help a group of seniors, all with years of experience of seeing Shakespeare's plays on stage and screen, take in a production of *Duchess* at one's university playhouse or in a local "gymnatorium." What is crucial is that the conditions of the writing be specific and recognizable.

This project assumes that students will complete many other courses in their major field of study to fulfill the requirements for a degree and that for most of their courses traditional academic essays will be written. Such essays usually involve sustained analysis and subtle thinking about complex issues. A successful Web site, however, especially one pitched primarily at secondary school students, has other criteria to meet. Whereas traditional essay writing prizes coherence and unity, Web sites comprise fragments of information. The information is normally introductory and the units of thought brief; ideally the style should be clear, informal, and, given the imagined professional context in which it is to appear, free of basic errors in grammar and usage; the text is usually enriched by the integration of visual material; the site is normally elaborated by means of links to related, often more specialized and detailed, sites. Of course, representing basic ideas clearly and succinctly presents its own challenges, and meeting them helps the undergraduate program in English as a whole achieve one of its general aims—to develop versatile writers.

Working on a play by Webster or any early modern playwright except Shakespeare facilitates this endeavor because there is so little that is useful on Webster or his works on the Internet, and what little there is is frequently rudimentary, course-specific, narrowly focused, out of date, or inaccessible. Any number of Web browsers can help one conduct a survey of potentially relevant sites, and helpful criteria for evaluating them can be found in print and online (Hawkes 4–5). Doing a search for Webster quickly reveals some of the limitations of the Internet as a tool for research: typing in "John Webster" will produce over a thousand matches, almost none dealing with the dramatist, and the few that do are hard to ferret out. However, searching for "*The Duchess of Malfi*" produces hundreds of matches, including enough pertinent ones to get a sense of the range of material available: production photos, reviews, analytical notes, actors' profiles, advertisements and order forms for texts and videos, student projects, course outlines, essay topics, and full texts of the play (promised but not yet delivered). Consequently, while students are writing for the Web, to do well with this project they have to be reading the scholarly literature on the play. Indeed, the only way for students to avoid published research entirely is to immerse themselves in the play itself (a most desirable option) so that they come up with their own insights and with the textual evidence to communicate those insights to others.

The topic as set down above provides little direction about what aspects of *The Duchess of Malfi* should be covered. This silence about the content deliberately encourages students to determine what is significant about the play and to organize those findings successfully. To do so, they have to read not only the play but also their audience. Of the three questions that often inform teaching and research—what do we know? how do we know what we know? and so what?—the last question matters most to high school students. They are, in general, quick to pose the question of relevance, and they do so not only of a Web site but of every screen presented on that Web site. Their insistent "so what?" should help those designing a site decide what to include and exclude. It is difficult to exaggerate how important it is to hold that focus on the question of relevance if one is to resist the allure of links. Links to other Web sites have a powerful appeal because they seem to add great blocks of information at the click of a mouse, but they create more problems than they are worth if high school students cannot apply the information available at these other sites to the play in question. Links to sites providing historical background, reviews of past productions, biographical notes on cast members, or texts of plays by Webster's contemporaries have often proved to be one of the main potential pitfalls for students who undertake this project.

While shedding light on the play as dramatic literature, the projected Web site aims also to help high school students appreciate it as dramatic performance. This goal is more easily met if a production of *The Duchess of Malfi*

is actually being mounted, since students can then obtain interviews with actors, directors, designers, musicians, technicians, and other theater personnel
involved in making the many decisions shaping a production. *The Duchess of
Malfi*, however, is not often performed and discussion of the play as a performance must address playable possibilities. Some of the signifying features
of a production of *Duchess* are obvious in the script: what features of actors'
bodies are given prominence? what stage properties are used? how? when?
and why? Other aspects of a performance may be connected to conventions
of Jacobean staging. The large, relatively bare thrust stage of the Festival
Theatre in Stratford, like the stages of Elizabethan and Jacobean public playhouses, relies on language, costumes, music, and the comportment of the
actors to establish the atmosphere of the play. Reviews of productions, productions far removed in time and place from students' experience, can be
made relevant here as long as they illustrate the effective use of such devices.
Urjo Kareda's account of the Stratford Festival *Duchess* of 1971 does; after
praising the decision to leave the stage bare, he writes that the director
"clothes his actors in rich silvers and golds, dark, heavy velvets, sensuous furs,
but all subtly burnished and fringed, a rich golden world already in decay."
Costumes, not sets, were crucial to the design of this production, but, being
a modern venue, the Festival Theatre also draws on current technological
resources, especially for lighting and the amplification of sound. It is important
that students about to attend a performance see the material conditions and
customary practices that theater uses to make its meanings.

Act 1, scene 2 of *The Duchess of Malfi* provides a particularly useful concentration of many of these performative elements, the discovery of which is
important for the design of a Web site, for brevity is the soul of the Internet.
The Duchess rebels against the authority of her brothers and proceeds, despite "frights and threatenings" (55).[1] Wooing Antonio, she closes the physical
space between her and him even to the point that she notices that one of his
eyes is bloodshot. Bringing out her ring, she makes use of a stage property
that has both customary and specific symbolic value. " 'Twas my wedding ring,"
she says, "And I did vow never to part with it / But to my second husband"
(113–15). Slipping the ring on Antonio's finger, she engages in a ritualistic
form of action (one recognizable to most students), just as she does when
Antonio kneels and she, his lady, raises him up to her level (a ritual not
immediately recognizable to students). Besides revealing how actors deal with
their individual objectives in a particular scene, the manipulation of stage
space, the interpretation and uses of props, and the modulations of naturalistic
and ritualistic action, this scene may help students see even larger patterns of
scenic design (if the staging points these up in performance), since "Julia's
proposition to Bosola parodies the Duchess's proposal to Antonio both in
language and in action" (Belsey, "Emblem" 105). Sharply focused on one
event, the commentary should bring together various aspects of Webster's art
that students may or may not see realized on stage.

When students seek advice about what aspects of the play they should develop on their Web site, I direct them to contexts in which teachers, editors, and critics situate Webster's works: the author's life; the social history of his day; the sources he used; the genre he inherited and the structure he designed; his distinctive style of language; the play's cast of characters, setting, dramatic conflict, and major issues. These are not topics that must be touched on but departure points for investigation. Webster's biography, for example, is too sketchy to provide a sustained analysis of *The Duchess of Malfi*. Similarly, uncertainties about the date of composition and about the content of the play as first performed make it difficult to demonstrate precise connections between the play and its times. One student, however, succinctly invoked both these contexts by adding to her Web site a copy of the "Vertuous Widdow" in Webster's *New Characters*. Doing so clarified the contemporary teaching against the remarriage of widows, the peculiar motives for Ferdinand's antagonism to his sister's, and her rebellious defiance of her brothers' wishes (1.2.49–56). Since, as John Russell Brown observes in his introduction to the play, "letters, documents, treatises, and pamphlets of James' reign could illustrate abundantly the court setting of the play" (xl), students might easily develop a *Duchess of Malfi* Web site by accumulating evidence of the traces of Jacobean England in Webster's Italy, but by doing so, they run the risk of producing a site too heavy with text to hold the attention of their audience.

Other students used the visual resources and linking mechanisms of the Internet more effectively. Rather than work toward a hypertext version of *Duchess* by linking it to a myriad of early modern illustrative materials (see McGann, esp. 34–40), they produced their own graphics to structure their analysis. One student developed a map of Italy with the names and relevant images of places in the play on it. While this map began as a way of establishing the plot insofar as it is tied to the comings and goings of characters, specific places clarified other aspects of the action. The shrine to Our Lady of Loretto, for instance, symbolized the Duchess's questionable use of religion to escape the violence of her brother. Ancona epitomized the Cardinal's exercise of his power, which he used to compound the tragic oppression of Antonio and the Duchess. Another student attempting to design an entrée into the world of the play created a little gallery of framed portraits of Ferdinand, the Cardinal, the Duchess, and Bosola. Doing so mimicked Webster's own strategy of having Antonio do character sketches of this group to deliver on his promise to make Delio "the partaker of the natures / Of some of your great courtiers" (1.1.85–86). While the portrait gallery served as a composite of Calabrian court life (analogous to the overview of the French court in Antonio's first speech), each portrait led to a more detailed account of each character. Attending to Webster's strategy—his telling rather than showing of character—also prepared students for the complexity of this scene in performance, a scene in which Webster reveals the characters of Delio and Antonio in action, while they tell us about other characters, who are shown simultaneously in the ceremonious leave-taking of Lord Silvio. In both these cases, the students created effective visual ways of organizing introductory information about the central characters and their world.

For students in the course The Rebel in Literature, the scene of the Duchess's final torment and death is thematically crucial because it contains the Duchess's famous affirmation of her identity, "I am Duchess of Malfi still" (4.2.142). That she defends herself aligns her with classic rebel figures. More important for a Web site aimed at high school students, she introduces a recognizable concern—identity—and she does so in terms significantly different from those used by most of these students. Whereas the Duchess identifies herself by gender and class ("Duchess") and by surname ("of Malfi"), most students identify themselves by given, or first, names and by family names. Moments of concentration provided by statements such as "I am Duchess of Malfi still" dramatize the immediate struggle of the tragic hero, raise questions about the social implications of naming for all the characters, and introduce a topic that students may be able to respond to in the light of their own experience of language and the construction of identity. One of the most interesting uses of this moment on a Web site was by a student trying to come to terms with the difficulty of Webster's language, which many students claim is much harder to comprehend than Shakespeare's. To overcome this difficulty, she developed a list of the Duchess's "simple" lines and "clear" statements. The list included the following: "I'll never marry" (1.2.12); "We now are man and wife" (1.2.192); "I have youth / And a little beauty" (3.2.137–38); "Sir, your direction / Shall take me by the hand" (3.3.311–12); "I am not mad yet" (4.2.22); "I am Duchess of Malfi still" (4.2.142); "Pull, and pull strongly" (4.2.228). As a whole this list helped track a through-line in the Duchess's role, that is, a series of choices culminating logically in her encouragement of the executioners to take her life. Like the gallery of portraits discussed earlier, this understanding of the coherent development of the Duchess over the course of the play provided a framework for additional observations. Each quotation, since none was as simple as it appeared, had a fuller explanation and interpretation that could be read by clicking on a key word in it. Many of these specific notes were also performance oriented. They alerted students to questions that a prospective production would answer: How old is the Duchess of Malfi? Or, in terms of the actor's body as Bosola describes it, how gray is her hair? How are hands used throughout the play? And, in the absence of specific stage directions in the text, how is the Duchess finally strangled? What began as a commentary on simple statements in a piece of dramatic literature fans out into theatrical questions about the actor's body, stage violence, and significant patterns of stage business.

Although this project began as an option on a list of essay topics, it has been most effective when taken up not by individuals but by a tutorial group. Of the twenty or so students who tried their hand at preparing a Web site, only two produced excellent results. Often the results were imbalanced because students who gathered helpful information about the play failed to come to terms with its performance possibilities and vice versa. Often the sites developed by the students most adept with the technology were most disappointing because their energies went into designing icons, captions in pop-up boxes, complex color combinations, sound effects, and a plethora of links. All the razzle-dazzle threw into relief how little insight these students had into the texts of the play and productions of it. Webbing Webster was most effective when undertaken by a group of students, each one of whom was responsible for dealing with a specific aspect of performance. The group as a whole came to terms with the play through its discussions, shared the responsibility for searching for Internet and library resources, collaborated (as many professional writers must sometimes do) in the writing, and kept one another alert to the audience for whom they were writing and its insistent "So what?"

NOTE

[1]Quotations of *The Duchess of Malfi* are from Fred B. Millet's edition.

Arden and the Archives

Arthur F. Kinney

Thomas Arden was murdered by his wife, Alice, and her fellow conspirators in the parlor of their home in Faversham, a small market town in northern Kent about twenty or thirty miles from London, on 15 February 1551; at the time of his death, Arden was forty-three years old, his wife was sixteen. Such a crime was thought especially horrifying because it was unnatural, upsetting the family order, which was analogous to political and social order, and because it reversed the customary sense of hierarchy and authority. Legally, the crime of a wife murdering her husband was therefore considered petty treason. With a certain briskness, a commission of oyer and terminer—"to hear and determine"—was appointed on 5 March, and perhaps without precedent on the very same day Edward VI's Privy Council sent letters arranging that two of the murderers should be punished in London, two more in Canterbury, Kent, and still two more in Faversham. They argued that Arden was a royal official as the customs collector of Faversham and moreover the son-in-law of a nobleman and Privy Councillor while Alice and two of her servants were guilty of a crime whose punishment was clearly spelled out by statute. Such a crime was strikingly rare, regardless of who the participants might be—the surviving assize records for all of Elizabeth's long reign (1558–1603) note only about twenty women convicted of such a crime. But, sensational in its own day, the murder became a cause célèbre throughout Elizabethan and Jacobean England because of the popularity of the play based on it, *Arden of Faversham*, written and staged probably by 1591 and printed by 1592.

When we first read the play, we discuss in class how complex the characters are, judged both by the lines that convey their thoughts and by their actions: all of them seem caught up in human passions that are divided between their own self-interests and their desire to foster relationships with others. Arden is buffeted by his desire for a wife, we note, his disgust at her adulterous behavior (which nevertheless he seems to condone by permitting it), and his ambition to amass a greater fortune (as if in part to demonstrate more pointedly his superiority over the lower-born Mosby). Alice in turn is torn between her desire to free herself of her husband, whom she has come to dislike, and her passionate attraction to Mosby, and both these feelings are countered by the danger and loss of status that could result from Arden's death and a remarriage or liaison with Mosby. Mosby himself finds his attraction to Alice both forceful and fatal. Usually a student asks, early on, if the nine attempts to kill Arden don't make the play a farce and thus deemphasize, perhaps even discredit, taking the play seriously as domestic tragedy. But then I (or someone in the class) suggest that the play lingers on the possibility of murder to measure the effects of crime before it is committed: What is sufficient cause for murder? Do the failed attempts only increase the desire for crime? Do they give us a better, richer view of the psychology of criminality? Finally, what is the play chiefly about? Is it a study of infidelity and cuckoldry as much as selfish rebellion or murder, a study of marriage in a society that does not recognize divorce, or a portrait of a greedy landlord whose love of money is greater than his love of his wife? Although Arden commodifies everything in his life, thus encouraging or justifying his murder, his actions (particularly those permitting his wife to be alone with Mosby) may be viewed as a kind of self-flagellation, a kind of willed suicide. Arden himself seems confused about his own behavior and its motives:

> As for the lands, Mosby, they are mine
> By letters patent from his Majesty.
> But I must have a mandate for my wife;
> They say you seek to rob me of her love.
> (1.300–03)

Yet even this confusion may be partly or wholly mitigated I suggest because Mosby himself seems to be a social climber, and as we examine textual references in the play concerning this possibility, we will find he is analogous to Arden, which suggests his self-indulgence.

These are difficult, controversial, and troubling matters, but it is nevertheless clear to all my students that this celebrated crime has deep, intricate connections to the culture that witnessed it. I then propose that we go to the archival materials, which still exist in abundance, to better understand, interpret, and judge the play's characters and events. The earliest representation of the murder is in the anonymous *Breviat Chronicle* for 1551:

This year on S. Valentine's daye at Feversham in Kent was commyted a shamefull mourther, for one Arden a gentilman was by the consente of hys wyfe mourthered, wherfor she was brent at Canterbury, and there was one hanged in chaynes for that mourther and at Feversham was (two) hanged in chaynes, and a woman brente, and in Smithfielde was hanged one Mosby and his syster for the same murder also

(Hyde 92)

Somewhat later Henry Machyn saw the event much the same way, entering in his diary:

The fourteenth day of Marche was hangyd in Smyth-feld, on John Mosbe and ys syster, for the death of a gentyll man of Feyversham, one Master Arden the custemer, and ys owne wyffe was decaul[ed] and she was burnyd at Canterbury and her servand hangyd ther, and two at Feyversham and on at Hosprynge, and nodur in the he way to Canturbery, for the death of Master Arden of Feyversham. [. . .] and at Flusshyng was bernyed Blake Tome for the sam deth of M. Arden.

(Hyde 92)

I photocopy these reports and circulate them in class to discuss what these observations reveal about the time and culture, and I pass out copies of Raphael Holinshed's fuller account (in the 1587 edition with marginal notes the playwright seems to have known and used) for them to study before the next class.

In the next class, with Holinshed in one hand, the play in the other, we go over the recorded perception of the event popularly distributed before the play was written and compare the two. There are a number of differences, giving a changed view of the characters, that sooner or later students themselves discover and advance. Arden for instance is hardened. He fosters adultery, Holinshed reports, for his own gain: "bicause he would not offend hir, and so loose the benefit which he hoped to gaine at some of hir freends in bearing with hir lewdnesse [. . .] he was contented to winke at hir filthie disorder [. . .]" (*Arden* 149). Moreover, he bought all the lands of the dissolved Faversham Abbey and then moved the annual town fair there "so reaping all the gaines to himselfe, and bereauing the towne of that portion which was woont to come to the inhabitants" (*Arden* 157). But Alice's portrait is also coarsened. After Arden's death, she callously "caused hir daughter to plaie on the virginals, and they dansed, and she with them" before suggesting the "game at the tables," backgammon (*Arden* 156). Here Mosby is not someone interested in upward social mobility, nor is he a coward in contemplating Arden's death. There are other differences between the potential source of the play and the play itself: the playwright creates Franklin (who has no historic precedent), fuses Alice's maid and Mosby's sister into Susan, and substitutes for Alice's dinner guests in Holinshed the grocers Prune and Cole, the characters Bradshaw and Adam Fowle. Tellingly, perhaps, he allows the roles of Bradshaw and Lord Cheiny and Clark and Reede to be doubled, inviting new speculations.

But as Patricia Hyde has discovered after years of accumulating all the archival records extant, the chroniclers (including Holinshed) and the playwright (perhaps innocent of the truth) have both diminished and simplified Arden, and when the class learns about what the records now show—either by reading assignments in Hyde's book or by hearing my elaboration of those facts in class—they can yet again reread the play and see new meaning lurking in what is left unsaid or distorted for dramatic effectiveness. Thomas Arden was born in Norwich in 1508, the son of a mother who spent her days begging about the city. Since she was never arrested or detained, she must have had strong social or personal connections with the Norwich magistracy, so that Arden himself must have had some privileges as well as, we can suppose, some considerable embarrassment. His first appearance in the documents, however, is not in Norwich but at court. A warrant of Richard Rich and John Onley was issued to the treasurer of the Augmentations on 12 July 1537, to pay "£6-13-4 to Thomas Arderne, one of the clerks of Edward North Esq., Clerk of Parliament, in recompense of such pains as he and his fellows have taken in and about the writing and making of certain books of Acts of Parliament for the King's Highness concerning as well the suppressed lands as the King's Highness purchased lands" (Hyde 28). North must have liked Arden, for he not only initiated his career at court but also arranged for Arden to marry his stepdaughter Alice. According to the arrangements they made, Arden was to stand bound to North for 1000 marks sterling (£666) either to make her a jointure of £40 a year for life or else to appoint it to her by his last will and testament. Although we might conjecture that North's motive was to gain a bright, loyal son-in-law who could serve his turn in various court appointments, we can perhaps more securely ascertain Arden's: he came from no background at all (and so his taunts about Mosby's class status in the play are self-reflexive) and stood only to gain in money and position. As Stow adds to Holinshed, Alice "was the Lord Northes wyves dowghtar. And hir husband and she havynge therefore often recowrse to my lord Northes [. . .]" (Stow, "History" 719). Stow is also more specific about Arden's ambitions:

> Arden, perceyvinge ryght well theyr familiaritie to be muche greatar then theyr honestie, was yet so greatly gyven to seke his advauntage, and caryd so lytle how he came by it, that in hope of atteynynge some benefite of the Lord Northe by meanes of this Mosby who could do so muche with hym, he winked at that shamefull dysorder and bothe parmyttyd and also invited hym very often to be in his howse.
>
> (Stow, "History" 719)

The elision here may not be apparent immediately to the class, but soon they will discover the motive is as political as monetary and that Mosby is the key link Arden has to North, suggesting that his marriage was (at least from Arden's perspective) insufficient to guarantee him the success he anticipated. The suggestion is that Arden finds Mosby's attachment to Alice not desirable but vital.

Within two years, Arden also acquired another patron—Sir Thomas Cheyne, lord warden of the Cinque Ports, whose power was based in Kent. He too must have been crucial in Arden's rise because by 1540 or shortly afterward Arden was appointed Henry VIII's customer (that is, collector of customs) for Faversham, gathering customs levied on merchandise that was both imported to and exported from the town's port. These political associations served Arden well; by September 1541, he was also appointed the king's comptroller of the wealthier port of Sandwich, appointments renewed by Edward VI. He got a further bonus in 1546 when he was given half the value of forfeited cheese, which amounted to £69 13s. 4d.

Arden converted his income into investment in land, concentrating on property in Kent. Although at first he and his partner, William Walter of Putney, bought lands in Warwickshire—the manor Lambertisland in Hernhill for £268 14s. 4d.—he went on to accumulate the manor of Otterpool in Lympne on 3 July 1545; the parish of Saltwood and property in the suburbs of Canterbury; the five-acre site of the Carmelite friary of White Friars in Sandwich, including "the whole church, belfry, and cemetery" as well as the messuages, houses, buildings, barns, stables, dovecotes, ponds, fish ponds, fishery, fruit gardens, orchards, and other gardens; the manor of Ellenden-in-Hernhill; Flood Mill and Surrenden Croft in Faversham, once property of the dissolved abbey; and, from Cheyne, the site of the demolished abbey itself. But, contrary to Holinshed and to the play, the abbey had owned land all over the town of Faversham and Arden did not own all of it; in fact, proportionately, he owned very little of it. He owned some 30 acres out of a total of 2,847.

Nor was Arden entirely despised by Faversham. The wardmote book records that in the second year of Edward VI's reign, on 26 March 1548, Thomas Arden became the town's mayor. In the dawn of the Reformation, his first problem was to adjudicate disputes over objects taken from the church. He issued a statute for the making of laws ordering that only the mayor, jurats, and twenty-four of the common council should be called to the wardmote to make laws and statutes unless the mayor decided to call others; twelve of the twenty-four were chosen by the mayor, twelve by the town's freemen. He arranged for the appointment of the common carrier to deal with the removal of contagious filth such as dung. He reexamined the wages paid the parish clerk. He oversaw an act for the paving of West Street, Preston Street, and Key Lane; introduced an act to handle hogs and swine wandering loose on town streets; and passed an act dealing with the goods of orphans. Then, perhaps suddenly, in December 1550, he was disfranchised. Arden was said to have "gone aboute and labored by dyvers wayes and meanes to the utermost of his power to infrynge and undo the said frauncheses, liberties and freedoms. That therefore the said Thomas Arden shalbe deposed from the benche and no more to be juratte of the said towne. Butt from hensforth to be utteryle disfraunchesed for ever" (Hyde 74). He had become unpopular; Hyde believes it may be because he had made deals with his political allies in London and elsewhere on their behalf (74–76). He must have been popular to be elected mayor; he must have been disliked to be so ignominiously dismissed. Alice Arden is recorded as encouraging Thomas Morsby to kill him, saying, "he was so evil belovd that no one would enquire after his deathe"(Hyde 84). Just as suddenly, on 20 December 1550, Thomas Arden made out his last will and testament, although there is no indication he was ill. He left money for an annual sermon, requiring the preacher from the Protestant Christ Church, Canterbury, from whom he had leased Faversham parsonage, or some other learned man to name him as the "causer" (Hyde 80) of the sermon. He left the remainder of his property, worth only £22 7s. 8d., held in free socage and the 5-shilling fee from Saint Valentine's fair, to his daughter Margaret (who is not mentioned in the play). His wife was named executrix; Sir Edward North was named overseer, for which he was willed Arden's best horse. Hyde thinks that Alice had hoped for a settlement to her marriage and was continually frustrated in not obtaining it (80). There are implications that Arden's political allies in London found him no longer useful (76). Thomas Arden, then, was a man who climbed socially by climbing politically, not just economically; the theme of commodification (of goods and of wife) is the playwright's interpretation. What does he gain by this? I ask the class. The question always leads to fruitful discussions of rank and gender as well as the restrictions of the marital bond. It is quite possible, we often conclude, that the purpose to which the story of Thomas Arden is put in 1592—when the first of the bad harvests made survival a harsh and inescapable issue for some—are purposes his life and death could not sustain in 1551. The intentions of a playwright, that is, need not be entertainment or profit, but propaganda.

Another way of judging attitudes toward the historic Thomas Arden is to see what the punishments meted out to his executioners tell us. Thomas Morsby and his sister Cicely Ponder, found guilty of murder, were imprisoned in London and then transported by public procession in a cart to Smithfield where they were hanged. Elizabeth Stafford, as a servant of Arden's, was also declared guilty of petty treason and was burned at the stake in Faversham (although Hyde suspects she was first strangled as an act of mercy [94]). Michael Sanderson, another servant guilty of petty treason, was tied to a hurdle, drawn behind a horse from prison to a place of execution in Faversham, and then hanged, drawn (he was cut down while still alive, stripped naked, had his genitals cut off and stuffed in his mouth, and his entrails pulled from him and burned), and quartered (with the parts of his body and his head parboiled and dispersed). John Grene was hanged in Faversham as well, but his body was cut down, immersed in boiling tar or pitch, and suspended on a gibbet, fitted out in chains. Black Will was never returned to England but burned to death in Flushing. The painter, William Blackbourne, and Shakebag escaped. As for Alice Arden, Machyn notes that she was "decauled"—an obscure word that Hyde thinks may mean "her entrails were ripped out and burned for her adultery, because people believed that these had given rise to her wicked thoughts" or, "alternatively, she was pregnant by Morsby and the foetus was being torn from her and burned" (98). She herself was burned at the stake in Canterbury and her property forfeited to the town of Faversham. Such a series of gruesome deaths suggests it took nine prosecutions and seven executions to compensate for Arden's murder. Was this out of social necessity, unavoidable statute, personal vendetta, or respect for Arden? The play, with its sense of miraculous discovery and stigmata of his death, puts him on the side of providence.

Discrepancies and contradictions within and among archival documents suggest that no extant record can tell us everything we would like to know, nor can it explain everything. These inconsistencies alert my class to the problems of documents in the archives, which are at best partial, at worst narrowly and even misleadingly propagandistic. They are never value-free. By such lights, we cannot expect the play *Arden of Faversham* to be free of its own designed meaning and its intention to persuade through dramatic narration. We conclude our time with the play by returning to the text to uncover, as best we can, the attitudes and values of the anonymous playwright. Then, if there is still time, we turn from Arden, the person about whom we perhaps know too much, to the person about whom we know virtually nothing. We attempt to describe Anonymous, the playwright.

"This Strumpet Serves Her Own Ends": Teaching Class and Service in Early Modern Drama

Jan Stirm

My students have a difficult time understanding the term *class* even when applied to our own period; trying to apply it to a preindustrial society adds to their confusion. David Scott Kastan clarifies the issue by pointing out that *class* is a nineteenth-century term that correlates with none of the early modern definitions of social stratification (101). While class today specifically refers to separation based on income and occupation, early modern definitions relied on rank and status (related to occupation, of course). But Kastan's most interesting point relates to the fact that early modern actors cross-dressed class as well as gender, since all the actors were (technically) servants, though they played parts representing an array of social positions. He demonstrates that early modern arguments against professional players reveal anxieties about class cross-dressing reminiscent of the state's attempts to control apparel of citizens through sumptuary laws. Happily, some of the documents revealing these anxieties, such as Phillip Stubbes's *Anatomy of Abuses* (London, 1583) and Stephen Gosson's *Playes Confuted in Five Actions* (London, 1582), may already be familiar through feminist work on gender cross-dressing, so that if students are also trying to understand gender cross-dressing, tying the two ideas together is likely to be helpful. How, then, do we teach students to understand the representations they read (and sometimes see or act) as representations and not reflections of society? I start by asking my students to conceive of class, like gender, as a type of performance.

Early modern literature and drama assumes a ready knowledge of the social organizations and the linguistic and clothing signs that reveal characters' relative positions. I assume that my students know these signs for their own culture, though they may not have thought about them in this way, so I begin by asking them to identify clothing that they associate with specific social positions—maids, judges, politicians, businesswomen, and so forth. We then practice staging the opening scene of Thomas Middleton and William Rowley's *The Changeling* so that students can work on reading physical positioning as a sign of social status.

Modern students, perhaps familiar with domestic service through movies or modern practices, tend to think of household servants in early modern drama as having their own households away from their service. I try to change students' assumptions about early modern service by explaining that between 1574 and 1821 some sixty percent of the population aged fifteen to twenty-four were in service (Kussmaul 3). Most surviving evidence about relationships between mistresses and female servants comes from the writings of men, especially in letters and diaries, which represent women mediated through a male viewpoint. And in a way, this mediation seems especially appropriate for students learning about early modern drama, a genre written by men (with few exceptions) and practiced on the stage by male actors. One such text, a letter to Susan Coke (also spelled Cook or Cooke) from her uncle, John Holles, introduces many of the issues important to representations of women in the drama. The letter (which I have on reserve for my students) exposes and counters students' expectations. Here, Holles answers a letter (which does not seem to have survived) from Susan Coke to his wife, Ann:

> To his neece Mrs Susan Cook with my Lady of Harford [Frances Howard, countess of Hertford]
>
> 29 June 1615
>
> Susan Cooke you writt to my wyfe to buy yow 19 yards of damask for a gown, for which yow had sent 8li and because yow suppose that sum to fall short, yow requyre her or my self to disburse the rest: I will spek plainly to yow, both in your fathers behalf, and my owne, and putt yow in mynd that service is no heritage, and if yow be to pressing uppon us who must provyd for yow futurely, yow only will loose by it: yow ar allowed 25li a year, and sum small helps yow have had besyd: your father hath a great charge, and hath the provision of your portion uppon his aime. I have allso many to care for; I know yow ar placed with an honourable and a bountifull Lady, who looks uppon yow with a liberall ey, both in the respect shee caries to me, and your owne merit: if yow can benefitt your self sum little (as they say) at the years end, it is well, other wise if yow be nothing indetted, and have your fethers to boot, the matter is not great, save the loss of so muche time, and youth: when my Lady, and I spoke together concerning your cumming to her, I little imagined yow should be her second woman, which nevertheless I passed over, how be it, seeing it is so, yow must proportion your self accordingly without equaling your superior, who peradventure allso may have her portion, and marriage in her owne hand: be therfor moderate in your ways, advised, and howsoever yow pleas others, pleas God, and a good conscience, in a word, as wise as a serpent, and as innocent as a dove, God grant yow understanding, and his grace 29 June 1615. Your very loving unkle, Jhon Holles.   (1: 71–72)

I like starting with Holles's letter because it challenges the immediate identification my students usually make with mistresses (rather than servants) in the plays they're reading. Further, the letter introduces my students to the importance of a good place and the difficulty of attaining it. Holles's stress on Coke's good fortune in being with an "honourable and a bountifull Lady" gives a sense of the mistress's role in the relationship. Young women in service expected to learn from their mistresses important adult skills, including domestic management and social practices, and they also expected a place in society where they might make social connections, including connections with potential marriage partners. Further, my students can quickly see that Holles's letter centers on finances (this from a man who spent some fifteen thousand pounds to become the first earl of Clare!), and not only on the money Coke spent on nineteen yards of damask. He notes that Coke is allowed twenty-five pounds a year, and while hopeful that she "can benefit [her] self sum little," concedes that it would be sufficient if she "be nothing indetted" at the end of the year. But Holles, while slightly concerned about Coke's personal finances, shows a strong awareness of the predicament of Lady Hertford's first woman, "who peradventure allso may have her portion, and mariage in her owne hand." In other words, the other serving woman may be in service to earn money, and Susan Coke shouldn't press her into an "arms race" of clothing. For both, Holles assumes, service is a temporary state, leading to a marriage that will probably put the serving woman into a position as mistress of her own household. Thus my students can see that service not only enabled women to learn adult skills but also gave them opportunities to save for a dowry. (Students can find information about marriage and dowry practices in Alan Macfarlane's *Marriage and Love in England: Modes of Reproduction 1300–1840.*)

The point that service leads the servant out of service and toward marriage makes conflicts between masters or mistresses and servants understandable. For both men and women, marriage marked a drastic change from social subordination as children to (relative) independence as adults. For members of the laboring class, this change meant moving from the relative security of a yearly contract to less secure seasonal labor. For husbandmen and women, it meant moving to an independent (and probably smaller) holding and working for themselves. For members of the gentry or merchant class, it meant supporting themselves with whatever portions their families had assigned. Women might be culturally circumscribed, but they were likely to have more freedom as a partner in the household than as a servant. Thus the tensions between servants and mistresses could grow as servants reached adulthood, found potential partners, and moved toward marriage and independence. The goal of female servants, in a sense, was to successfully identify with their mistresses by marrying and becoming mistresses of their own households.

In plays, domestic serving women work in the home, managing a wide variety of tasks. Some of the most obvious of these—meal preparation, laundry, cleaning, and caring for children—are rarely represented on stage. Sewing, especially in the form of needlework, is more often represented (Orlin, "Three Ways" 192). But the most usual work of serving women on stage is to manage access to their mistresses and to ensure their mistresses' privacy and chastity. Thus a serving woman enabled a mistress to travel, meet male acquaintances in her bedchamber, or even attend plays without provoking censure. The dramatic serving woman thus has tremendous power in her relationship. She is at the same time subject to her mistress's socially sanctioned power (Frances E. Dolan teases out the complexity of household violence as one aspect of this power; see esp. 210–15).

Rather than see exploitation of one character by another as exemplifying the exercise of power in subversion or containment, I ask my students to read the mistress-servant relationships in plays such as *The Changeling*, *The Second Maiden's Tragedy*, and John Webster's *The White Devil* as exemplifying the breakdown of interdependent relationships, the misrecognition of characters' interdependence with their female "partners." This misrecognition causes individual female characters to attempt (usually without success) to inscribe themselves into very different gender and class positions. Traditionally, the servants in these plays—Diaphanta and De Flores in *The Changeling*, Leonella in *The Second Maiden's Tragedy*, and Zanche in *The White Devil*—have been seen as parallels to their mistresses or masters. In contrast, reading with a focus on class and service reveals that these characters play central parts in tragedies of class position in which their interests as servants conflict with the interests of their mistresses and masters.

In short, one plot of *The Changeling* features Beatrice-Joanna, betrothed to Alonzo de Piraquo, but in love with Alsemero. She hires De Flores, her father's waiting-gentleman, to kill Alonzo, paying for this favor by having sex with him. Jasperino, Alsemero's servant, claims to have heard Beatrice-Joanna and De Flores together while he himself was in a private part of the house awaiting "private conference" with Diaphanta, serving woman to Beatrice-Joanna (4.91–92).[1] So, before marrying her, Alsemero gives Beatrice-Joanna a virginity test, which she passes only by discovering it, trying it out on Diaphanta, and copying her reaction. She then convinces Diaphanta to spend the wedding night with Alsemero for a thousand ducats (money Diaphanta identifies as a portion that will enable her to marry "a justice" [4.2.125–27]). But when Diaphanta remains in the bedroom too long, De Flores starts a fire, rousing the house and providing an opportunity for him to kill her. In the final act, Alsemero challenges Beatrice-Joanna as an adulterer, claiming that Diaphanta revealed as much. Alsemero shuts her in a closet with De Flores, who stabs her. When Alsemero releases them, Beatrice-Joanna confesses her sin before dying; De Flores then kills himself. The parallel plot, in contrast, features a chaste, married woman, Isabella, who manages to deter the advances of a man, who is aided by her husband's male servant.

After our initial work staging the first scene of the play, which encourages students to see how Jasperino sees Diaphanta as a kind of double of her mistress (helping to determine that stereotypical reading), students and I focus on act 4, scene 1. We consider the typical representation of the servant as more sexually knowing, more ribald, especially in response to Beatrice-Joanna's expression of concern about her wedding night, when Diaphanta acknowledges that:

> 'Tis ever the bride's fashion towards bedtime
> To set light by her joys as if she ow'd 'em not.
> (4.1.65–66)

My students see that Diaphanta correctly interprets Beatrice-Joanna's behavior here as acting, indeed, as a kind of acting common to those in Beatrice-Joanna's position—soon-to-be married upper-class women.

Beatrice-Joanna overcomes Diaphanta's belief that her mistress is acting a part only by offering to pay a thousand ducats to another woman to spend the wedding night with Alsemero. That the effective issue is financial reasserts the class relation between the two women: one labors and the other pays for that labor. Diaphanta reveals her financial dependence as she wants the money for a dowry that will enable her to change her social position; she will have

> [. . .] the bride's place [Beatrice-Joanna's place in bed]
> And with a thousand ducats! I'm for a justice now,
> I bring a portion with me, I scorn small fools.
> (4.1.125–27)

Bringing Holles's letter to the table, my students see that Diaphanta reveals a desire to become, in a way, Beatrice-Joanna—a bride, a woman with higher social standing, a mistress rather than a servant. They note that Beatrice-Joanna and De Flores see this conflict at the beginning of act 5, scene 1 when Beatrice-Joanna complains that she had to trust someone (5.1.15).

Like *The Changeling*, *The Second Maiden's Tragedy* has a tragic plot concerning a serving woman and mistress. And like *The Changeling*, it includes a parallel plot. In both *The Second Maiden's Tragedy* plots, a man (the Tyrant, Votarius) attempts to seduce an attached woman (the Lady, the Wife) in spite of her fiancé or husband (Govianus, Anselmus) and is aided by a pander (Sophonirus, Leonella) (Levin, *Multiple Plot* 27–34). Significantly, in the second parallel plot, the pander (Leonella) is the Wife's waiting woman, whose control of private space factors in the Wife's seduction. Leonella interests my students especially because she brings her own lover into her mistress's home, allowing him to penetrate the space in a kind of metaphoric rape. As with *The Changeling*, where Isabella remains chaste despite the efforts of a male servant, in *The Second Maiden's Tragedy*, the Lady remains chaste (though she dies in the process) despite the efforts of a noble in the court acting as a pander. Most tellingly, the noble argues that the Lady's "want of a woman's counsel" meant that she wasn't encouraged to allow the Tyrant to seduce her (4.3.100). In both plays, the woman with a waiting woman (who should provide security and safety) falls in part because she thinks she can trust her waiting woman, while her waiting woman clearly indicates her desire to advance, even at her mistress's expense. My students see this when the Wife says:

> There's many a good knight's daughter is in service
> And cannot get such favour [a man's company] of her mistress
> But what she has by stealth; she and the chambermaid
> Are glad of one between them.   (4.1.74–77)

Reading these lines in conjunction with the Holles letter and *The Changeling* and learning to pay attention to the waiting gentlewomen help my students understand the complexity of early modern representations of class. They also become more aware and suspicious of their identifications with characters, especially with characters from the uppermost classes.

I like to have my students read *The White Devil* with *The Changeling* and *The Second Maiden's Tragedy* to help them become aware of the racial identifications that parallel the usual class identifications. Questioning these identifications by studying class relationships in the plays exposes constructions of class and race in the broader culture, which helps students consider how these constructions come to seem natural to their cultures. (Like *class*, *race* is a term fraught with complexity. Most broadly it describes a group "connected by common descent or origin" [*OED*]. Depending on usage, however, it might be seen as roughly synonymous with the modern scientific term *species*, as in the concept of the human race.) In *The White Devil*, my students recognize the pattern of a serving woman used by men to enable one of them to seduce her mistress. In this play, however, Zanche, the serving woman, is a Moor, and thus all the more vulnerable within the racist culture of the play.

Coming to *The White Devil* after working with *The Changeling*, my students see Zanche's familiar position as a pander to her mistress, Vittoria, in act 1, scene 2. There Flamineo (Vittoria's brother, who is trying to help Bracciano seduce Vittoria) tells Bracciano that he has arranged a meeting with Vittorio for him: "I have dealt already with her chamber-maid / Zanche the Moor, and she is wondrous proud. / To be the agent for so high a spirit" (13–15). Further, in act 5, they recognize the familiar power Flamineo gains over Zanche because she expects to marry him; after he rejects her, her attraction to Francisco (disguised as Mulinassar, a Moor) as a potentially viable alternative makes sense to them as well. For Zanche, marriage and sexuality are matters not of passion or romance but of economics. She assumes that Mulinassar's expressed intention not to marry would not prevent his willingness to take her as a lover, but she implies dissatisfaction with a sexual arrangement that would not include marriage and a consequent change in social status. Later she reiterates her concerns about marriage, commenting that the money and jewels she has stolen form "a dowry, / Methinks, should make that sunburnt proverb false, / And wash the Ethiop white" (5.3.260–62), and plans to use this wealth, along with her knowledge of Isabella's death, to try to convince Mulinassar to marry her.

Like Diaphanta and Leonella, Zanche dies as does her mistress. Here, then, is one aspect of their relationship in which the servant parallels her mistress's position, much as she wishes to parallel her position as mistress by taking a partner. By the end of act 5, my students are able to use what they've learned about servants to make sense of the class valence of Zanche's representation. Their understanding of the conflicts between mistress and servant in this and other plays helps them understand the construction of racism in *The White Devil*.

Working with John Holles's letter introduces my students to some of the complexities of the relationships between serving women and mistresses and helps them resist identifying too quickly or easily with the mistresses' positions in early modern drama. It also allows us to historicize and recognize that being a servant was a changeable position because a servant might readily expect to marry and start a household with a mate. Working from this knowledge, my students can read the parallels between serving women and their mistresses in *The Changeling*, *The Second Maiden's Tragedy*, and *The White Devil* more effectively, recognizing that the serving woman's death is a tragedy of position, enabled by the conflicts that develop between the female characters in the plays. I find that my students can use the experience they gain from working with these plays to read class position in other early modern texts as well.

Selected Other Early Modern Plays Featuring Interesting Servants

Francis Beaumont and John Fletcher, *The Maid's Tragedy* (1619); George Chapman, *The Widow's Tears* (1612); John Ford, *The Chronicle History of Perkin Warbeck* (1634) and *The Lover's Melancholy* (1629); Thomas Heywood, *A Woman Killed with Kindness* (1607); Ben Jonson, *The Staple of News* (1631); John Marston, *The Dutch Courtesan* (1605); and John Webster, *The Devil's Law-Case* (1623).

Other Early Modern Resources Available in Modern Print Editions

The Church of England's "The Sermon against Idleness" (1574); Lady Margaret Hoby's *Diary* (1599–1605, esp. 7, 80, 199); and Ralph Josselin's *Diary* (especially entries for June through December 1645).

NOTE

[1]Quotations of *The Changeling* are from George Walton Williams's edition; those of *The White Devil* are from John Russell Brown's edition.

Teaching the Details of Race and Religious Difference in Renaissance Drama

Rebecca Ann Bach

Many professors who set themselves the task of teaching race and religious difference in early modern drama use texts such as *Othello*, *The Tragedy of Mariam*, *The Merchant of Venice*, and *The Jew of Malta*, plays that focus on or at least foreground such differences. However, early modern drama that does not foreground these issues can also be effective for teaching race and religious difference. Most of early modern drama's references to nonwhite or non-Protestant groups are peripheral to the main action and are often overlooked, but they are important precisely because they are peripheral; they speak to the common sense, in the Italian Marxist theorist Antonio Gramsci's terms, of early modern England. Early modern drama's peripheral references to whiteness and normative Christianity also speak to the period's dominant ideologies. Such references are ubiquitous in non-Shakespearean drama (as well as in Shakespeare). Attending to these offhand references to race and religious difference in the classroom can open up discussion of how white Anglican identity was formed in the early modern theater. These details also point to the ways that racial and religious categories are inflected by and help produce gender and rank categories. In addition, attention to these details bears pedagogical fruit when it shows students how groups regarded as other were stereotyped in relation to one another.

I write from my experience teaching Renaissance drama at two levels: as part of the sophomore survey of early English and Irish literature, a course in which I have taught *The Duchess of Malfi* and *The Roaring Girl*, and as the primary material in a course on Renaissance drama for seniors and master's students, in which the texts include *Epicoene*, *The Duchess of Malfi*, and *A New Way to Pay Old Debts*. However, the pedagogical method I describe is not limited to the plays and examples I cite; instead the approach works as a way to teach the issues of race and religious difference in any text.

Teaching race and religious difference seems vital in both teaching contexts, although for slightly different reasons. In the sophomore survey, students can see a developing ideology of racial difference as we move from the Anglo-Saxon and Celtic worlds to an England involved in the slave trade. Religious difference is obviously central to early English and Irish literary and cultural history, since the time periods include the Reformation and involve perennial English hatred and fear of Jews and Muslims. Because I teach a Renaissance play in the survey course as a part of those histories, I want to attend to racial and religious differences in the drama. My Renaissance drama course has always focused on social and cultural issues, and, since these differences were integral to early modern English culture, I discuss them in the classroom.

Although I can't always bring scholarly work directly into the classroom, many critics have informed my teaching of race and religious difference. Kim Hall's work, especially her book *Things of Darkness*, has educated me in attending to racial difference and the construction of blackness and whiteness in Renaissance texts generally. The other book that has informed me on the issue of white identity is Richard Dyer's *White*, a book that takes seriously both how texts talk about whiteness and don't talk about whiteness and that explains how the omissions as well as explicit references help construct white identity. *The Stripping of the Altars*, by Eamon Duffy, made me understand the English Reformation from a social perspective that enhances the political perspective anthologies like the Longman or the Norton provide. Finally, James Shapiro's masterful *Shakespeare and the Jews* has been vital in helping me understand Jewish history and the perspectives toward Jews that were available to the dramatists I teach. I often refer to works like these in class, and at the upper level I have had students read these books themselves. The bibliographies of these books point to a mass of other important work that a teacher coming to these issues for the first time might want to consult.

At both the sophomore senior, and master's level, I teach the details of race and religious differences by pointing to patterns of reference in texts. In upper-level classes, I ask students to read for these patterns. Generally at the end of class I give three or four questions or topics that students should think about when they are reading a new play for the next class. I usually ask students to collect either a word or references to a particular subject. For example, I might ask them to collect references to Jews when reading *The Duchess of Malfi* or to collect uses of the words *white, fair*, and *negro* when reading *The Roaring Girl* or *A New Way to Pay Old Debts*. This practice serves three heuristic purposes. First, it makes students pay close attention to the words they are reading. They can't collect words if they haven't read carefully enough to find them. Since I teach at a commuter campus with a slightly older student body and most of my students work and are taking care of their families, they are generally tired. But enough of them are challenged by the idea that they can find and understand something specific in a difficult text that they look carefully and bring their discoveries in. Often just asking them to collect something makes them curious about its importance. Second, asking students to collect references or words lets them bring their knowledge to class. Students gain a sense of mastery when they bring the information they have gathered into the classroom. Finally, the assignment makes them attend to the particular details they have collected; often that means that students have thought about what those details might mean and have arguments prepared for class discussion.

For example, I may ask an upper-level class to collect references to whiteness and blackness when they are reading Dekker and Middleton's city comedy *The Roaring Girl*, a play that ostensibly has little to do with skin color. I let the class know that the word "fair" can signify as white-skinned in the period—here Hall's work is vital. I already have collected references, so that I can fill in with any the class has missed; but usually the class collectively gathers everything I have found, and often students find things I have missed or might not have associated with a topic. A particularly astute student reader may show the class that *The Roaring Girl* actually opens with a reference to Mary's whiteness. Sir Alexander Wengrave's servant, Neatfoot, in a dialogue full of sexual references (on his part), calls Mary "fairest tree of generation" and assures her that he will deliver his master's son Sebastian to her "most white hand" (1359).[1] This reference can start a discussion of how the play purifies Mary in relation to Moll, since Mary never participates in sexual banter. The reference also shows how the play links white skin with purity. Mary's chastity, which Neatfoot mentions in the same scene, and especially her attention to her own marriage bonds are clearly associated in this scene with her whiteness. A student may note that in the next act Sebastian complains that his covetous father, Sir Alexander, "called [Mary] not fair, / And asked what is she but a beggar's heir?" (1361). At this point, the class can discuss how the category of fairness is linked to status. This reference also brings up the question of Sir Alexander's pathetic faith in appearances, which is questioned throughout the play. As with the previous detail, Sebastian's usage of "fair" demonstrates how racialization is imbricated in other categories of difference, and at the same time it can open up discussion of the play's central themes.

A student may also bring up Sebastian's assessment of Moll when he says, overheard by his father, "Well: why suppose / The two-leaved tongues of slander or of truth / Pronounce Moll loathsome; if before my love / She appear fair, what injury have I?" (1377). The references to whiteness and fairness in *The Roaring Girl* introduce the more sophisticated questions the play provokes. For although Sebastian posits Moll's fairness for his eavesdropping father, he never really considers Moll as a marriage partner, and the play makes sure that its audience clearly understands that she is out of Sebastian's orbit, not "fair" enough for serious consideration. Thus the fairness reference in this case points to the play's bedrock ideology, which is not as progressive as it might seem to a late-twentieth-century audience of students. These students can see a triumphant "roaring girl," unmarried, in control, and tricking men, and assume that the play champions fundamental challenges to the patriarchal hierarchy.

The detail of Moll's apparent fairness became evidence recently in my survey class. At this level, I have students complete study questions on each text. The handwritten answers, which I grade only for content, ensure that students complete the reading and also become the basis of class discussion. For *The Roaring Girl*, one of the study questions reads, "How is Moll described? Be specific and collect page references." The students are able to complete this relatively easy task, and I can use their responses to show them the patterns of reference to fairness and ask them to interpret those patterns in class. Thus, at the lower level, I show them the initial reference to Mary's white hand and ask if Moll is as fair as Mary in Sebastian's eyes. Then we can discuss both what this means about how the play portrays Moll and what it means about race and status in the Renaissance.

Details in *The Roaring Girl* and other Renaissance plays can introduce a discussion of the fundamental status categories in the Renaissance—the categories of nobility, gentility, and citizenry that determine who will marry whom in the plays. Details can also show how racial categories and nomenclature, recognizable from modern terminology, were already coming into play in early modern England. In *The Roaring Girl* Sir Alexander laments his failed efforts to reform his son, saying, "I wash a negro, / Losing both pains and cost" (1367). When a student brings up this detail in class, discussion shows students what, unfortunately, may be familiar to them from more modern racial discourse: that skin color was already being used to categorize people and that brown skin was both associated with dirtiness and seen as a permanent mark of difference. The same points can be made with a detail from Massinger's *A New Way to Pay Old Debts*, a play that I love to teach in my upper-level class. In this play, the young gentleman Alworth praises his beloved Margaret to Lord Lovell; Alworth tells his master that Margaret's father's riches make her a marital prize:

> O my good lord, these powerful aids, which would
> Make a misshapen negro beautiful
> (Yet are but ornaments to give her lustre,
> That in her self is all perfection), must
> Prevail for her.   (3.1.87–91)

At this moment in the play, students hear blackness spoken of as the ultimate ugliness, akin to deformity. Since Alworth and Lovell are good characters in the play, my students learn what was acceptable discourse on the stage. Read with the reference to race in *The Roaring Girl*, students are able to understand that characters like the worthy Alworth as well as disreputable characters like Sir Alexander mouth the same racial language.

Students have also pointed out, however, that Alworth leaves open the possibility that with enough money and land a "misshapen negro" is conceivable as a marriage partner. Although Lovell is wedded to an ideology that can't accept marriage across status lines and so rejects Margaret as a bride, the play does not see the racial line as a boundary that would not be crossed by anyone. Alworth's reference to a "misshapen negro" can help us discuss the play's deep interest in who is marriageable and why. In addition, potentially the detail can initiate a discussion about how racial ideologies change over time.

I think this is an important point to be made in the early-twenty-first-century classroom. As a professor of Renaissance drama who attends to racial and religious difference in the texts, I ultimately aim to help students understand both historical difference and the related idea that racial ideologies are constructed and only achieve material effects by being continually reinforced. When my classes talk about details such as the Alworth reference to Margaret's attractions, we can discuss how attitudes toward mixed-race marriage have changed over time. I make sure that students understand how unspeakable such an idea became by the nineteenth century. And I either make or draw from the students the links with England's involvement with the African slave trade (Hall). Thus students have to contend with a more complicated understanding of history than seeing history as a continual record of progress to the enlightened present. And they also understand that literary reference is linked to the material conditions of people's lives. In a related manner, I work toward giving my students the ability to denaturalize the connections between darkness and evil and whiteness and good that have undergirded racial ideology since its earliest developments. It is often more difficult to get students to see the construction of whiteness. Recently I had a class in which students brought up almost every possible defense against this view, desperately wanting not to see fairness and whiteness as a racial category. I find Dyer's analyses very helpful on this point, and with his understandings in mind I was able to facilitate the students' discussion until they finally realized that their arguments—that whiteness was only a status category and that tans became fashionable in the twentieth century—all led back to the same point: that whiteness is a constructed marker of racial difference.

My class discussions of race in the plays greatly benefit from the presence of persons of color in my classroom. Most African Americans don't need to be prodded to see white skin as a racial category. At the University of Alabama, Birmingham, I don't have all-white classrooms, but I did when I taught as a graduate student at the University of Pennsylvania. At Penn I had to work harder to bring the category of race forward; as Dyer discusses, white skin privilege is much harder to see than blackness. At the University of Alabama, Birmingham, I can rely more on students at least supporting me in my arguments about race in the plays. As professors we should be conscious of the racial dynamic in the classroom, and we also might want to talk about our own racial privilege or lack of privilege. As a white Jewish woman I can't talk for or as a black character or a black reader, but I can talk about my relationship to black people. To some extent, I can use my Jewish identity to talk about dynamics of racism, like internalized oppression. But I think everyone can talk about themselves as existing in a system of white-skin privilege and about the place of Renaissance drama in the construction of that system.

My Judaism comes to the fore when I approach the subject of religious difference in Renaissance drama. As in the discussion of race, different student populations affect how I approach the topic. At Penn, a school with a large Jewish student population, students picked up Jewish slurs without my even asking them to collect references. When we read *The Duchess of Malfi*, they would ask about Bosola's inclusion of "Jews' spittle, and their young children's ordure" in his list of noxious substances to be found in the closets of women who paint their faces (2.1.39–40). Their attention to this detail enabled us to discuss the history of anti-Semitism and where these plays fit in that history. Now that I teach in the heart of the Bible Belt, my students are less able to see the commentary on Jews embedded in such details. But when I ask them to attend to references to Jews and Christianity in *Duchess*, they notice this detail among others, and because I am Jewish I can open the discussion with them in a way that usually precludes hateful commentary in the classroom; generally students are not eager to offend the teacher and many students genuinely like me. Quite a few of my students in Alabama think they have never seen a Jew before, and my presence in the classroom is an educational experience in itself. This can be painful for me, but it is also often empowering for those of my students who feel somehow different from the norm. Because almost every Renaissance text deals with religious difference, especially Catholic and Protestant differences, my Judaism becomes a way to talk about stereotypes of religions from an outsider perspective. Just the fact that someone can see Christianity from the outside teaches my students to become aware of religious difference.

Of course, not everyone will come into the classroom from an outsider religious position, and, as my experience teaching at Penn indicates, an outsider in one academic setting is an insider in another and vice versa. But I encourage professors to bring their religion or atheism into the classroom so that students understand that religious difference in the plays is connected to personal religious conviction four hundred years ago and also today. In our (sometimes) tolerant society, our students can forget the force of religious struggle in the Renaissance. I remind my students that people were being burnt for religious difference and that murder by state or local authorities is sanctioned by a common sense that one group or another is noxious.

In my upper-level classes, Ben Jonson's *Epicoene* has been a great text for teaching religious difference. Again, while *Epicoene* is not a text about religion per se, its details reveal the "common sense" of early modern English culture, the acceptability of religious stereotyping, and the perception of non-Christian people as other. Jonson is a particularly interesting playwright to teach with these terms in mind, since he converted to Catholicism in his lifetime and later rejoined the established church. Teaching *Epicoene*, I ask students to collect references to religious and national difference (often these categories are intertwined). Students bring in a detail such as Truewit's comparison of Mistress Otter to a radical Protestant: "No Anabaptist ever railed with the like licence" (126). Truewit's characterization depends on his audience understanding that radical Protestants are socially offensive. But Truewit also uses the larger category of Christian when he asks Sir John Daw to be "merciful" to Sir Amorous La Foole for, "he is a Christian, as good as" Daw (152).

Although the play is unmercifully parodying both Daw and La Foole in this scene, the detail shows that the category "Christian" functions in the play as a human being incapable of murder. This detail sets into relief Morose's admiration of the Turk for keeping mute servants (109). Morose—a character students love to hate—laments that "the princes of Christendom should suffer a barbarian to transcend them" in silence (110). Discussion of this detail helps my students see how the play treats Morose as other through his love of Turkish customs. When we put these and other details from the play together in class, students can see that *Epicoene*'s discourses rest on a given hierarchy of human religions in which Christianity as a whole is purified in relation to a barbarous Muslim world. And they also see the debates within English Christianity fought out within the stereotypes Jonson expected his audience members to understand.

Teaching the details of race and religious difference lets students confront issues that still shape our lives. And it shows students how popular entertainment has always contributed to shaping peoples' lives. It is not always a comfortable task, but it is always exciting, and for me it is crucial.

NOTE

[1]Quotations of *The Roaring Girl* are from *The Longman Anthology of British Literature*; quotations of *A New Way to Pay Old Debts* are from T. W. Craik's edition; quotations of *The Duchess of Malfi* are from Elizabeth M. Brennan's edition; quotations of *Epicoene* are from Robert M. Adams's edition.

Historicizing Gender:
Mapping Cultural Space in Webster's *The Duchess of Malfi* and Cary's *The Tragedy of Mariam*

Christina Luckyj

I hand my students a questionnaire when I want to begin talking about gender in early modern drama. The first question, If you could be magically transported back to England in 1600, what do you think you would notice about women's lives?, gets a remarkably unanimous response. Women were "unequal," "slaves," "kept in the kitchen," "not respected as real people," "not involved in politics," "did everything around the house and were therefore inferior to men," and lacked "an independent voice." The next question, What do you hope to discover about early modern women?, also gets a fairly consistent response: while some students claim simply to desire knowledge, others have an agenda, seeking to discover "strong and independent thinkers," "hidden heroines," women who were "on the inside screaming to be heard," and "not as passive as I think." Based on their sources—which they identify as Shakespeare, movies, and "intuition"—my students are attempting to historicize, though I suspect their early modern woman is grafted onto the 1950s homemaker and the 1960s radical feminist. A few basic assumptions surface immediately: woman's private, domestic space is assumed to be rigidly distinct from the public world, inequality is automatically conflated with slavery, and "an independent voice" is an unassailable good. I ask my students to acknowledge their preconceptions and fantasies about early modern gender so that we can establish a reference point, a site to which we will return in order to map how far we have come. What is clear is that my students begin by believing that material conditions for women in early modern England were entirely negative and oppressive yet that women themselves might transcend them. Despite almost two decades of new historicism in the academy, the popular mind still imagines the early modern woman as something like Virginia Woolf's "very queer, composite being [. . . who] dominates the lives of kings and conquerors in fiction; [though] in fact she was the slave of any boy whose parents forced a ring upon her finger" (49). While I doubt that I can convince my hopeful young students of the determinism of culture, I can encourage them to remedy the "scarcity of facts" (50) of which Woolf complains by exposing them to a wide range of early modern cultural texts that place women in multiple, sometimes paradoxical, positions. If early modern dramatic characters such as John Webster's Duchess of Malfi or Elizabeth Cary's Mariam frequently appear to be transcendent, ahistorical heroines, I can help my students relocate them in their culture, thereby (with luck) modifying their over-simple view both of early modern culture and of these apparently protofeminist figures.

I give my students a sheaf of documents that have been photocopied from the microfilmed *Short-Title Catalogue* (where possible). I work from the *STC* partly because I can't find in a single anthology the selections I consider most useful (though Kate Aughterson's *Renaissance Woman: A Sourcebook* is a marvelous resource) and partly because I want my students to have that experience of difference, strangeness, and surprise that comes with reading old texts. I include excerpts both from Puritan conduct books (William Gouge's *Of Domesticall Duties*, Robert Cleaver's *A Godly Form of Household Government*, William Whately's *A Care-Cloth*) and from women's texts (diaries of Lady Anne Clifford and Lady Grace Mildmay; the life of Katharine Stubbes as written by her husband, Phillip Stubbes [*Crystal Glass*]). By examining male-authored constructions of women alongside female-authored works, students can see both men and women manipulating and negotiating common cultural codes—good preparation for our study of plays produced by a man, John Webster, and a woman, Elizabeth Cary. They also gain an understanding of how cultural directives are absorbed into women's representations of their lives.

Once my students have looked over these cultural materials, I divide them into groups of five or six. I ask the groups to find evidence to support opposing points of view: for example, the first group (A) may be asked to argue that early modern women were entirely silent, subordinate, and submissive, while the second group (B) must maintain that early modern women were not entirely silent, subordinate, and submissive. Subtle this approach is not, and it is not designed for graduate students—yet such positions, however oversimplified, encourage students to focus their discussions and select their evidence judiciously, in preparation for an engaging final debate. The tyranny of my authority in disallowing them to make their own choice simulates the overarching determinism of culture. Equally important, however, are the radically disjunctive positions possible within culture; for this reason, I ask my students to switch places part way through the debate and, like Tudor schoolboys, argue on both sides of the question. The evidence deployed for either side of the debate will look something like this when it comes from the conduct literature:

A: "Nature hath placed an eminencie in the male over the female: so as where they are linked together in one yoake, it is given by nature that he should governe, she obey" (Gouge 270).
B: "of all degrees wherein there is any difference betwixt person and person, there is the least disparitie betwixt man and wife" (Gouge 271).
A: "God hath committed his power, of giving a daughter to a son, or taking a daughter for a sonne, unto the Parents. [. . .] If crosses come, whither

must the afflicted person run for comfort, but to Parents and friends?"
(Whately 70).

B: "why did *Rebeccaes* Parents deny her to *Isaack* [. . .] before such time as
they had asked her consent [; . . .] do they not plainely shewe, that both
the law of Nature, and the law of God taught them, that this consent was
of great moment and absolute necessitie?" (Cleaver 116); "there shal be
in wedlocke a certaine sweet and pleasant conversation, without the which
it is no marriage, but a prison, a hatred, and a perpetuall torment of the
mind" (Cleaver 171).

A: "silence is the best ornament of a woman and therefore the law was given
to the man, rather the[n] to the woman, to shew that hee should bee the
teacher, and she the hearer" (Cleaver 100).

B: "silence, as it is opposed to speech, would imply stoutnesse of stomacke,
and stubbornnesse of heart" (Gouge 282).

A: "As the *Eccho* answereth but one word for many, which are spoken to her;
so a maides answere should bee in a word" (Cleaver 101).

B: "*Salomon* describing a right wife, saith: *She openeth her mouth with wise-
dome: and the law of grace is in her tongue*" (Cleaver 102).

A: "Because God hath placed them under their superiors, they will in all
duty manifest that subiection which their place requireth" (Gouge 27).

B: "*If an husband require his wife to doe that which God hath forbidden, she
ought not do it*" (Gouge 328).

What becomes clear quickly from the debate format is that the same text can
provide ample evidence for diametrically opposed positions and thus that early
modern patriarchy was in no way univocal or monolithic. Mary Beth Rose
points out, "Absolute spiritual and social equality between the sexes, coexisting
with the equally absolute subjection of women that is decreed and then
subverted—the logical inconsistencies that now appear so glaring, particularly
given their consequences, seem never to have occurred to the Puritans" (*Expense* 129). Of course, these inconsistencies were probably not registered as
such because most women managed to manifest both obedience and self-
possession. Close examination of women's texts similarly illuminates potentially conflicting codes held in careful balance:

A: Katharine Stubbes "obeyed the commandment of the apostle who biddeth
women be silent, and to learn of their husbands at home,"

B: yet "if she chanced at any time to be in any place where either Papists or
atheists were and heard them talk of religion [. . .] she would not yield a
jot, nor give place to them at all, but would most mightily justify the truth
of God against their blasphemous untruths" (Stubbes, *Crystal Glass* 238).

A: Grace Mildmay praises her mother-in-law as "a virtuous woman and dutiful
to her husband, in all chastity, obedience, love and fear towards him"
(Mildmay 219),

B: yet Mildmay describes her governess thus: "all good virtues that might be in a woman were constantly settled in her; for from her youth she made good use of all things that ever she did read, see or hear, and observed all companies that ever she came in, good or bad, so that she could give a right censure and true judgement of most things, and give wise counsel upon any occasion. And she could apprehend, and contrive any matter whatever propounded unto her most judiciously, and set her mind down in writing, either by letters indited or otherwise, as well as most men could have done" (Mildmay 214–15).

In Anne Clifford's diary group A might well note her submissive relation to her husband: "Sometimes I had fair words from him and sometimes foul, but I took all patiently, and did strive to give him as much content and assurance of my love as I could possibly," but group B could point to Clifford's subsequent feisty remark: "yet I told him that I would never part with Westmorland upon any condition whatever" (Clifford 265). Indeed, Anne Clifford is a particularly useful choice, because, as Katherine Osler Acheson points out, she herself is "a paradoxical and conflictual figure," who both anticipates and utterly refutes "nascent feminism" (31, 40). After students debate these points, further discussion invariably follows—usually about the kinds of agency that were available to early modern women. These women were not feminists, and this may well disappoint some, but most students emerge from this exercise with a more nuanced and inflected view of the culturally approved maneuvering room for women: the significance of consent in marriage, of moral integrity and duty to God, of wisdom and good judgment balanced against the predictable calls for submission and subjection. Indeed, Gouge's insistence on what he calls women's "*voluntary* subjection" as distinct from their "*necessary* subjection" illuminates his assumption of a female subjectivity or will, however he construes it as "willingnesse to yeeld" (27). In the classroom, additional contradictions can be noted and shelved for further use: Cleaver, for example, when giving advice on the choice of a good wife, maintains that "an honest woman dwelleth at the signe of an honest face" but marginally notes that "*[u]nder faire faces, are sometimes hidden filthie mindes*" (100). This ambivalence about female beauty is matched by a similar ambivalence about ideal female conduct. If female obedience is clearly desirable in most conduct books, so are female honesty and integrity—and drama often explores what happens when such potentially variant codes come into conflict (Rose, *Expense* 131).

Set side by side, John Webster's *Duchess of Malfi* and Elizabeth Cary's *Tragedy of Mariam* seem initially like mirror images of each other: the former features a woman who defies her male relatives to marry the man of her choice, while the latter shows us a woman who defies her husband by defending her male relatives. Both plays maximize the authority of their female protagonists by according them the most powerful position available to women

in early modern society: that of widowhood, "a time of maximum female autonomy" (Mendelson and Crawford 180). Even though the Duchess remarries
in act 1 and Mariam's husband is later revealed to be alive, both women begin
their respective plays with an enlarged cultural mandate as women not subject
to male authority—a mandate extended by their status as aristocrats and rul-
ers. The death of her first husband allows the sexually experienced Duchess
to woo her steward, "like a widow [. . . with] but half a blush" (1.2.373–74);
there is no doubt that she is the "lusty widow" (1.2.259) Ferdinand accuses
her of being.[1] The supposed death of Herod allows Mariam to discover her
complex feelings about her husband (1.1) and to share them spontaneously
with Sohemus (3.3.127–80), an act that is declared tantamount to adultery by
the Chorus (3.3.227–44). For many students tackling the plays for the first
time, such sexy, assertive women appear to be either valiant, protofeminist
rebels ahistorically transcending their patriarchal culture or (as some critics
have argued) cautionary figures indubitably censured for their transgressions
(Jardine; Peterson). After this exercise in historicizing gender, however, students should be able to steer clear of both the Scylla of culturally determined,
total subjection and the Charybdis of ahistorical transcendence. I ask them to
develop a more inflected awareness, to use what they have learned from nonliterary sources to imagine how early modern culture could both produce and
accommodate these acts of apparent female insubordination. What existing
cultural spaces did these women occupy?

Initially, the culturally informed student will note that in both play worlds,
the same acts of self-assertion that are derided by some are defended by
others and thus are comprehensible in early modern terms. Here a student
may recall Anne Clifford, who, during her long fight for her right to inherit
her father's estates, records that "many did condemn me for standing out so
in this business, so on the other side many did commend me in regard that
I have done that which is both just and honourable" (266–67). It is quite
likely, however, that Clifford's determination not to be "dispossessed of the
inheritance of [her] forefathers" (254) was understood by her contemporaries
not as protofeminist verve but as feudal loyalty to kin. Public opinion in both
Webster's and Cary's plays is similarly divided but for different reasons: the
Duchess is allegedly hailed as "a strumpet" (3.1.25) by the people even as she
is staunchly defended by two anonymous pilgrims (3.4.25, 33), while Mariam
is called both "guiltless" and guilty of "disgrace" (3.3.181–83) by her servant
Sohemus and by the Chorus (3.3.215–50; 5.1.272). Catherine Belsey notes the
latter "contradictions" as "symptomatic of the play's consistent unease about
its heroine's right to speak" (*Subject* 173), but these make more sense when
placed in the broader cultural context explored in the classroom. That context
suggests that, even as women violate one cultural code (that of submission to
male authority, whether brother or husband) and are hence judged guilty,
they occupy another sanctioned cultural space: in the Duchess's case, that of
consensual companionate marriage and (subsequently) virtuous widowhood;

in Mariam's (like Clifford's) case, that of virtuous transparency and family loyalty. Moreover, both women are increasingly authorized by religious language that suggests, as Gouge claims, that they are "truly informed by God's word" (328) in their particular acts of resistance.

Even though the Duchess herself constructs the space of her willful marriage as an uncharted "wilderness" (1.2.278), her audience would no doubt have accommodated it to current models of female consent to Gouge's "voluntary subjection." For in many ways this marriage is quite conventional and comfortably within the "circumference" (1.2.384) of culture; indeed, the Duchess herself points out that she has "not gone about, in this, to create / Any new world, or custom" (3.2.111–12). Far from rejecting "all vain ceremony" (1.2.372), the Duchess actually insists on ceremony, on "a contract in a chamber, / *Per verba de presenti*" (391–92), and, as Ann Cook tells us, "*de praesenti* vows bound a couple immediately and irrevocably as partners" (154). This marriage clearly bears out Cleaver's edict that "there shall be in wedlocke, a certaine sweet and pleasant conversation" (as we see in 3.2.1–65). But its harmony is at least partly based on the Duchess's willingness to subject herself to her husband, to make him her "lord" (1.2.347), and to be led by his hand (408). She thus carries out Cleaver's advice: "And she ought to consider, that no distinction or difference of birth and nobilite, can be so great, but that the league, which both Gods ordinance and nature, hath ordained betwixt men and women, farre exceedeth it: for by nature woman was made mans subiect" (146). This subjection is extended later in the play, as the Duchess follows Bosola's suggestion of feigning a pilgrimage (3.2.311–12) and submits to "Heaven's scourge-stick" (3.5.77), declaring herself "Bent to all sways of the oppressor's will" (3.5.142). Her outburst of cursing (4.1.95–107) comes just after she believes Antonio to be dead, when she identifies herself immediately with the self-immolating Portia, "the rare and almost dead example / Of a loving wife" (4.1.73–74). Now a virtuous widow, the Duchess translates her social subjection into spiritual terms. Seizing on Bosola's proffered religious metaphor of prison as bodily confinement (4.2.127–31), the Duchess increasingly represents herself as submissive to the will of Heaven, as her wilful cry "I am Duchess of Malfi still" (4.2.139) yields to "I have so much obedience in my blood, / I wish it in their veins, to do them good" (165–66) and "I would fain put off my last woman's fault" (222). Webster thus exploits orthodox notions of female virtue to authorize his protagonist.

Once students can align the Duchess with feminine submission, however, they can easily also locate her in the roomier paradoxical cultural spaces mapped earlier. She may retreat into the "silence" (4.1.9) of approved female virtue, but it is a silence that Ferdinand quickly recognizes as "disdain" (12)— Gouge's "stubbornnesse of heart" (282)—rather than submission. She may increasingly adopt religious language, but she uses it as a means of refusing to recognize or submit to the corrupt authority of her brothers. Her final gesture, as she kneels submissively to enter "heaven gates" (4.2.228), also asserts physical agency and makes the executioners' task more difficult. Perhaps the best example of this paradox comes in the echo scene (5.3), in which the Duchess's voice literally reproduces that of her husband, thus fulfilling Cleaver's prescription for feminine virtue: "As the *Eccho* answereth but one word for many, which are spoken to her; so a maides answere should bee in a word" (101). However, in the very act of echoing her husband, the Duchess asserts her own agency, as when Antonio's fatalistic remark "you'll find it impossible / To fly your fate" becomes the Duchess's command: "O fly your fate" (5.3.34–35). This agency is also well within the parameters of a good wife's wise counsel: "So much is the wives wil subiect to her husband: yet it is not meant, that the wife shuld not employ her knowledge and discretion which God hath given her, in the helpe, and for the good of her husband" (Cleaver 220–21). Indeed, that a wife must subject her will means that she has one: as the Chorus in *The Tragedy of Mariam* puts it, " 'Tis not so glorious for her to be free, / As by her proper self restrain'd to be" (3.3.219–20).

Elizabeth Cary frames Mariam as culturally legitimate in several ways. Like Webster, Cary also relies on the model of companionate marriage—or, rather, on its violation. When Mariam utters an agonized cry on hearing of Herod's return, "And must I to my prison turn again?" (3.3.151), she echoes Cleaver's description of loveless marriage as "a prison, a hatred, and a perpetuall torment of the mind" (171). Mariam's subsequent open defiance of the ideology of wifely submission finds its legitimacy partially in the widespread fear of female hypocrisy, of that "beauteous body [which] hides a loathesome soul" (4.4.178). Assuaging cultural fears like Cleaver's, that under *"faire faces, are sometimes hidden filthie minds"* (100), Mariam insists, "I scorn my look should ever man beguile, / Or other speech than meaning to afford" (3.3.165–66). Then, when she actually faces Herod, Mariam represents her defiance not as an assertion of personal autonomy but rather as an act of loyalty to her male relatives, killed by Herod (67; argument). This is surprising, since on hearing that Herod is alive, she cries to Sohemus, *"Foretell the ruin of my family, / Tell me that I shall see our city burn'd: / Tell me I shall a death disgraceful die, / But tell me not that Herod is return'd"* (3.3.127–30; emphasis mine). Yet Mariam's privileging of her family of origin at this crucial moment (significantly reiterating her mother's view expressed in 1.2) both implicitly devalues the marital authority of Herod as "parti-Jew, and parti-Edomite" (1.3.235) and aligns her with the patriarchal family, those "Parents and friends" who arrange marriages and "comfort" those they fail (Whately 70). Furthermore, by persisting in wearing "dusky habits" (4.3.90) after Herod's return, Mariam, like the Duchess, embodies and manipulates a cultural paradox: she inscribes herself simultaneously as loyal mourner (of her brother and grandfather), as widow (anticipating her refusal to acknowledge her husband's authority), and as modest, virtuous woman (adopting the "honest and sober raiment" recommended by Puritan preachers [Cleaver 103]). Finally, Mariam's position, like the Duchess's, is ratified by the spiritual authority accorded to women as bound ultimately only to God; indeed, Mariam becomes an explicit type of Christ, as "the sun-admiring phoenix' nest" (5.1.24) who imagines her own resurrection (5.1.77–78). As in *The Duchess of Malfi*, Cary carves out a space for her protagonist that fully exploits the cultural paradoxes suggested in the historical material. And, just as the Duchess both echoes her husband and finds her own voice, conflating obedience with agency, so Mariam is reported to have "smil'd, a dutiful, though scornful, smile" (5.1.52) on her way to execution. However, the kind of integrity Mariam asserts is neither proto-feminist nor transcendent; it is firmly rooted in the codes of early modern England. In the classroom, I aim to expose my students to a range of cultural material that illuminates just how multiple and unstable those codes could be.

NOTE

[1]Quotations of *The Duchess of Malfi* are from Elizabeth M. Brennan's edition; quotations of *The Tragedy of Mariam* are from Barry Weller and Margaret W. Ferguson's edition.

Tragedy and the Female Body:
A Materialist Approach to
Heywood's *A Woman Killed with Kindness*
and Webster's *The Duchess of Malfi*

Lori Schroeder Haslem

Students who have seen much popular film in recent years are perhaps accustomed to bodies (whether whole or in parts) being at the center of action, but they often have not considered the ways in which physical bodies are spectacularly and conceptually central to much early drama. Given that cultural material concerning the human body is a growing field of critical study (e.g., Paster; Sawday; P. Parker), a teacher of Renaissance drama could defensibly and profitably structure an entire senior or graduate seminar around the topic while also finding—as I have with teaching undergraduates at small liberal arts colleges—that a materialist approach appeals broadly to students, who tend to be intrigued by the bodily matter of these plays. Students are interested in how one regards the characters' bodies given that they are simultaneously actors' bodies, curious about how or if the original audience regarded bodily processes and body parts differently from how students themselves tend to, and eager to draw connections between early modern cultural outlooks on the body and larger interpretive issues in the plays. Indeed, even when a teacher does not specifically address the centrality of bodies in the plays, students come to class and ask about Shakespeare's "obsession" with lopped-off body parts in *Titus Andronicus*, about the pregnant Duchess of Malfi's devouring of manure-tainted apricots, or about Vindice's rather necrophiliac attachment to his murdered lady's skull in *The Revenger's Tragedy*.

For those not wishing to offer a course thoroughly focused on bodily matters in Renaissance drama there are also benefits to teaching, as I often have, at least a pair or cluster of plays from a mainly cultural materialist approach. Such an approach instructs students how to apply one of many legitimate theoretical approaches to the drama of the period. (I often select other pairs or clusters and help students tackle them mainly from Marxist, psychoanalytic, or structuralist and deconstructionist approaches.) With this essay I concentrate on but one way a teacher may successfully follow the latter plan, by pairing two plays—Thomas Heywood's *A Woman Killed with Kindness* and John Webster's *The Duchess of Malfi*. In important ways, these plays focus tragic action particularly in, on, and around the female body, thus calling attention to concerns of both gender and body. A teacher who introduces students to relevant cultural material about bodies and gender is providing them not with a simplistic, titillating, or pedantic way of arriving at a common conclusion about the plays' larger meanings but with an engaging and increasingly creditable technique for cracking frequently debated critical issues in these plays. And indeed the cultural material complicates as well as illuminates these issues.

Without fail, my undergraduate students are surprised to learn that there was much ado about female sexuality in the early modern period. Their assumptions tend to be that people back then just didn't think or talk much about sexuality, and I regularly even hear them suggest that female sexuality didn't become a topic of cultural interest until, say, the 1960s—that up until then everybody was trained in the Victorian mode of repressing sexuality. Thus before students begin studying much Renaissance drama (and especially before studying these two plays), they are well served by reading overviews of early modern conceptions of women and their bodies, especially those concerning a woman's sexual body—a key signifier in both *Woman Killed with Kindness* and *Duchess*. I often start this unit (which stretches over five or six class periods) by assigning *Woman Killed with Kindness* together with "The Social Contexts" chapter of Katherine Usher Henderson and Barbara F. McManus's widely available *Half Humankind* (which I put on reserve). This chapter—which surveys orthodox and popular notions about female sexuality, marriage, and societal expectations for women in early modern England and provides ample supporting excerpts from the Tudor and Stuart pamphlet wars—piques students' interest in the Frankfords' marital relationship and thus primes the pump for the first day of class discussion.

To prime this pump just a bit more, I usually start this first class with a minilecture on Peter Stallybrass's "Patriarchal Territories: The Body Enclosed," which summarizes several early modern cultural discourses in which the female body typically becomes a "site of conflict" (123). Drawing on Mikhail Bakhtin's notion of the female body as grotesque, Stallybrass explains it is "unfinished, outgrows itself, transgresses its own limits," and identifies three major areas of early modern "surveillance" of women—the mouth, chastity, and the threshold of the house—that were "frequently collapsed into each other" (126). Women were viewed as naturally—because bodily—transgressive, and thus they had especially to be policed at these three areas. I then ask students to watch for surveillance of these three areas—as well as for the lack of it—in the plays and to consider just how and why the female bodies do become sites of conflict. I also urge them to consider the female characters' own responses to perceived conflicts in, on, and around their bodies. Do they themselves accept this need for female body surveillance, or do they contest it, and to what ends?

With these general questions in mind, we begin discussing *Woman Killed with Kindness*. There is always at least one astute student who notes that, contrary to Stallybrass's view, Frankford is not much interested in monitoring Anne's chaste body, that he is seemingly neither paranoid nor jealous even when he evidently should be. We talk about why this might be so and what Heywood might be indicating about Frankford here. Some argue that Frankford's lack of jealousy means that he is a model husband who trusts Anne implicitly—a trust that arguably builds our sympathy for him when he is cuckolded. Others, noting either Stallybrass or the assigned "Social Contexts" chapter, contend that Frankford must be regarded at least in part as foolish, given the typical early modern view that a man who doesn't have enough sense to distrust his wife with another man in his own house is just asking to be cuckolded. Still others are suggestible to the idea (one that I sometimes have to introduce myself, citing some of the criticism) that Frankford's lack of jealousy and suspicion is owing to his lack of any sexual interest in Anne in the first place (D. Cook; Canuteson) or to his implied preference for Wendoll over Anne as a companion (Bryan).

On this first day too students tend to target the very problems that have been central to the play's criticism over the years: What are Anne's motivations, first for so readily cuckolding her husband with his best friend and then for starving herself to death when found out? How do the main plot and subplot interrelate? Is Frankford a heroic protagonist, or is his kindness ironic? As these points are developed in discussion, one hears students again and again frustrated by their uncertainty whether they are analyzing the play's action and characters from their own or an early modern cultural stance. After encouraging them to follow this theoretical question for a while—is it somehow wrong to analyze the play from one or the other outlook? why or why not?—I ask them to participate in an exercise for the next class period. I divide them into groups, asking each group to read from and report back on a different set of primary cultural texts. To make this exercise as trouble-free as possible (given the limited holdings of my institution's library) I put on reserve a number of widely available texts and also instruct students how to access certain primary texts on the Internet (e.g., the quite relevant "Elizabethan Homilies" at the *Renaissance Electronic Texts* site). For each of the categories listed below, the assigned group locates and reads between two and four cultural texts with an eye toward describing the outlooks on the female body given (or implied) there. I tell students that these reports will pertain to *Woman Killed with Kindness* but perhaps also, later, to *Duchess*.

> *The wife's body.* Conduct books and popular treatises on the topic of marriage, for example those by Juan Luis Vives, Desiderius Erasmus, and William Perkins (all excerpted in Klein); or Heywood's *Gunaikeion* (which, if it cannot be located, is partially surveyed in articles by Bromley; Panek; and Lewis); *The Homily of the State of Matrimony* (Klein; see also "Elizabethan Homilies"); The *Book of Common Prayer* wedding ceremony; and a useful chapter on Puritan marriage by Margo Todd.
>
> *The adulterous wife's body.* Conduct books, treatises, homilies, and laws on responses to adultery, for example, Perkins's *Christian Economy* (Klein) or *Homily against Whoredom and Adultery* ("Elizabethan

Homilies"). A good overview of the conduct books' stance on adultery can be found in an article by Jennifer Panek. And a look at Lawrence Stone, Martin Ingram, or Alan Macfarlane, on ecclesiastical laws against and surprisingly light sentences for adultery is also worthwhile, these sources being easier to access than the laws and case records themselves.

The fasting body and chastity. Robert Burton's *Anatomy of Melancholy* and other material on fasting, especially that which links fasting with chasteness and purgation of sin (again, see "Elizabethan Homilies").

The fasting body and the supernatural. Material on the connections between fasting and exorcism, on the one hand (Gutierrez), and miracles, on the other, for example historical accounts of many early modern "fasting girls" who elicited both awe and suspicions of demonism by living apparently without food (Vandereycken and Van Deth, *From Fasting Saints* and "Miraculous Maids?").

On the second day of class, after students have reported on the contents of these various texts, I return to some of the key interpretive issues of the play that students themselves raised earlier. At this point students begin to see how the cultural material can provide them with illuminating ways of thinking about these issues. By our second or third class meeting, I can try to direct discussion around the following sets of questions:

1. Given what the cultural material presents and what characters in the play describe (e.g., in the opening wedding scene), do the Frankfords have a model middle-class marriage until Anne shatters it with adultery? Many of the treatises stress the importance of friendship and companionship within marriage as well as the need to channel lust into a procreative drive: Do the Frankfords display this view of their marriage? Is Frankford's regard for Anne and her sexual body in sync with what the marriage texts recommend for husbands? Is Anne's outlook on her own sexual body in sync with what is recommended for wives? Does the subplot construe marriage and a woman's chastity in the same or different way than the main plot does? What does the status of Susan's chastity in the subplot make one think about the status of Anne's chastity in the main plot?

2. The texts on adultery are contradictory: ecclesiastical rhetoric ("The Homily against Whoredom and Adultery" ["Elizabethan Homilies"]) suggesting that adultery deserves death runs against other popular treatises and manuals (as well as actual practice) advocating public humiliation and repentance followed by mercy. How does this material inform one's understanding of how or why Frankford doesn't punish Anne physically? Or does he implicitly punish her physically? How does the material help one understand Anne's initial desire for physical punishment and later her suicide by starvation?

3. The material on fasting raises important questions about Anne's demise since she takes a purportedly righteous act to the extreme of suicide. Is Anne's act of self-starvation to be regarded as a desperate suicide of the sort described in Burton's *Anatomy of Melancholy* (942–49) or as an admirable purgation or penance through fasting? If not an act of despair, does her suicide suggest exorcism? canonization? With this act is Anne demonstrating a complete loss of control over her body, surrendering her body to the redemption of her soul? Or is she taking final control over her body in a way she has hitherto been incapable of? Does the willfulness of her act heroically defy male surveillance and ownership of her sexual body, or does it merely capitulate to and reinforce the need for such surveillance? How is one to regard Anne's emaciated dead body on stage?

By the close of our discussion on these topics, students are entirely aware of the point I made at the outset of this essay, namely, that involving relevant cultural material in our discussion of the play does not limit possible critical interpretations of it but rather helps both to inform and to complicate those interpretations. I myself do not take a hard stance in answering any of the questions I pose. My goal is to get students to use the cultural material in partial support of the interpretations they find most compelling, and I usually receive a host of very well researched and well argued papers as a result. As we prepare to move on, I tell them that we will surely revisit some of the points we have covered and debated in connection with *Woman Killed with Kindness* in our discussions of *Duchess*, a play in which a woman's sexual body is under surveillance for related and yet quite different reasons. I remind them to look for the three interconnected areas of potential female transgression: the threshold of the house, the mouth, and chastity. We realize in looking back at *Woman Killed with Kindness* that all three points of entry were precariously guarded in Anne's case—indeed, that transgression in the first two areas evidently led to the ultimate transgression of chastity—adultery: Wendoll was first admitted across the threshold, then invited both to sup and to converse regularly with Anne, and finally accepted into her bed.

With almost the opening scene of *The Duchess of Malfi* (which we start discussing around the fourth day of the unit), the need for monitoring the Duchess's sexual body—partly for dynastic reasons and partly for much more personal reasons—is conveyed with great intensity by her brothers, Ferdinand and the Cardinal. I start by emphasizing how different Ferdinand is from Frankford. Where Frankford is arguably too lax in safeguarding his wife's chastity, Ferdinand is obsessed with policing the sites of his sister's potential sexual transgression. Should he be? I have found over the years that this question can open a very provocative discussion, in part because it often yields rather surprising answers from students unless they have already read pretty far into the play. Students encountering the Duchess and her brothers for the first time often think that with the Duchess Webster gives us the incarnation of the stereotypical lusty woman, or widow, so often described in both literary and nonliterary works of the period. They often remark on how willful and sneaky the Duchess is in the opening scenes: she tells an outright lie to her brothers about her lack of sexual desire for a second husband and then, almost as soon as they leave, swiftly offers herself body and soul to a lowly steward.

If students are encouraged to discuss this simplistic assessment of the Duchess's behavior, they usually begin to see that Webster is not encouraging his audience merely to adopt either the Machiavellian Cardinal's or the psychopathic Ferdinand's views. But what does the play say about the Duchess's sexuality, about the body of this lusty widow? And what does her own insistence that she be regarded at least in part as a sexual body have to do with her heroic or tragic status? In the end, does Webster run entirely counter to the brothers' view, unequivocally exonerating the Duchess's lustiness? Or does the play present a more complicated tension, sometimes reinforcing typical early modern anxieties about the female sexual body that call for surveillance of it while at other times offering a more revolutionary and ultimately heroic view of female sexuality?

I submit to the class that, as with our study of *Woman Killed with Kindness*, we cannot take on some of the most compelling and most frequently debated critical issues in *Duchess*—for example, What is the nature of the Duchess's suffering? Is Bosola changed by his interactions with the Duchess and, if so, how and why? What can explain Ferdinand's character and his final madness? —unless we first consider what cultural attitudes toward the female sexual body the play is either propounding or challenging. Our opening discussion of *Duchess*—as with *Woman Killed with Kindness*—has already highlighted several points that make students feel unsure whether they are analyzing from their own or from an early modern cultural stance. I suggest that we once again turn to selected primary cultural texts that can help inform and energize our discussion of the central interpretive issue—the Duchess's sexual body.

At this point, I sometimes return to assigning reports on the material and other times survey some especially relevant cultural contexts myself, since students now understand the hows and whys of involving the cultural material. I offer three categories of early modern material this time around.

1. *The appetitive female body.* In part, students can here review material from the earlier report on early modern connections between gastronomic and sexual overindulgence (e.g., the homilies or Burton's *Anatomy of Melancholy* on fasting). In addition, it is useful to point them to the medical and obstetrical texts (e.g., summarized in Eccles or Maclean) that describe the increased likelihood of hysteria (defined as a wandering womb) in widowed women given their uteruses' newly unmet appetite for semen. Widows were usually advised to take another husband to sate this uterine sexual appetite. I also refer students to the humanist treatises on marriage that emphasize the prominent place of procreation in a good marriage. So, we observe, the brothers clearly have self-interested, political reasons for dissuading the Duchess

from taking a husband and are not giving her sound medical or social advice. We then discuss the various passages in the play that might support the notion of sex as a healthy and natural experience for a young married woman (e.g., the Duchess's many lines describing her life with Antonio and her children as something as natural as the life of birds or other animals in the wild), and we analyze whether this view is seriously countered by the Ferdinandian view that the Duchess's sexual appetites and indulgences are base precisely because they are like those of animals. With this discussion in mind, we turn to the famous apricots scene, where the Duchess's gastronomic and sexual appetites and functions are arguably collapsed.

2. *The reproductive female body.* To help us discuss the apricots scene, I once again direct students to overviews of medical treatises on pregnancy (e.g., Aughterson; Eccles; Maclean), especially those that liken pregnancy to disease or that elucidate the believed dangers associated either with meeting or failing to meet a pregnant woman's cravings. (For instance, pregnant women should be refused the harmful substances they often crave; however, if they don't get what they crave, their imaginations run rampant in ways that can endanger or affect the unborn child.) In the play, of course, Bosola uses the apricots trick to detect whether or not the Duchess is pregnant. Her devouring of the fruits (their skins tainted with manure) is taken as a clear sign of her pregnancy but also ostensibly throws her directly into labor, which she passes off as gastric upset and which Antonio suggests is a poisoning. The medical material helps students realize the probable uneasiness of Webster's audience at this scene, a scene that after all helps cultivate a more Ferdinandian reaction to the Duchess's appetites. They see that the scene may well reinforce anxieties about the female sexual function that the play elsewhere discredits. Indeed, in just this way—and as the Stallybrass piece has helped them understand—the Duchess's body emerges as the play's central site of conflict.

3. *The diseased body.* As various social and gynecological texts of the day make clear, pregnancy is often regarded either as disease or as impending death by early modern women and physicians alike (Aughterson; Eccles; Maclean; Paster). But Webster's play highlights a number of other aspects of diseased and tortured bodies too, for example, medical purges, madness and treatment of it, death by strangulation or by poison, torture practices, and lycanthropia (the bizarre form of melancholy that afflicts Ferdinand). Time allowing, one can ask students to research cultural texts on any of these aspects, all of which—I stress—inevitably focus attention on the Duchess's assertion of her sexual body and the central interpretive question about the diseased or healthy nature of that body.

After considering some selections from and overviews of such texts (e.g., Burton on purges; Enterline on Elizabethan descriptions of lycanthropia; Hunt on curative therapies), we turn to a series of culminating questions. How is the play's central tension over positive and negative outlooks on the Duchess's body complicated when Ferdinand, employing various demented techniques for purging her body of its sexuality, runs himself mad in the process? or when the Duchess threatens to starve herself (shades of Anne Frankford) to avoid her brothers' tortures and implies that their murdering her amounts to a kind of incestuous feeding upon her body: "Go tell my brothers, when I am laid out, / They then may feed in quiet" (4.2.236–37).[1] Does Bosola's changed attitude toward the Duchess somehow resolve this tension? And, finally, has the Duchess's own regard for her body changed throughout the play? Does her behavior in the face of shame parallel that of Anne Frankford? Why or why not? Does the Duchess exercise ultimate control over her body? And how does one regard her dead body on stage? Ideally, these final questions leave students grappling with the implied larger concerns of this unit, namely, why the female sexual body should be such a compelling site of conflict in early modern culture to begin with and why staging this conflict made for such popular tragedy.

NOTE

[1]Quotation of *The Duchess of Malfi* is from Elizabeth M. Brennan's edition.

Sex Matters

Mario DiGangi

To teach about sexuality in Renaissance drama, one must first grapple with the problem that sexuality, in its narrowest historical meaning, did not exist in Renaissance England. The problem cannot be solved simply by ignoring all evidence of same-sex sexuality in the drama and focusing only on male-female relations, on the grounds that it was only homosexuality that did not exist in the premodern era. For if homosexuality did not exist in this period, then neither did heterosexuality, a thesis that has been argued in various studies of early modern and modern sexuality (DiGangi; Goldberg, *Sodometries*; Katz; B. Smith).

If it is anachronistic to speak of heterosexuality or homosexuality in the early modern period, then in what terms might we discuss those matters of gender definition and erotic desire that were as densely woven into the fabric of social and political life in Renaissance England as they are today? How can we analyze dramatic representations of marriage without the distorting lens of modern assumptions about the heterosexual couple or the normality of heterosexual desire? And what sense can we make of same-sex affection in a culture that had sodomy laws but no conception of sexual orientation or identity? Such questions have direct bearing on the interpretation of individual plays. To understand the conflict between king and nobility in Marlowe's *Edward II*, for instance, we need to appreciate not only the intensity of Edward's love for Gaveston but also the culturally specific discourses of male friendship and royal favoritism from which that love derives its social and political meaning. We have to understand, in other words, that it is an expression of love for Edward to arrange a marriage between Gaveston and his own niece (2.3.256).[1]

I presented these interpretive conundrums to my students in an upper-level undergraduate course, Sexuality and Gender in Renaissance Drama. My primary goals in this course were to expose students to the wide variety of plays written by Shakespeare's contemporaries (Cary, Dekker, Jonson, Lyly, Marlowe, Middleton, Webster); to introduce them to recent theories of sex, gender, and eroticism; and to demonstrate to them the value of historicist paradigms for the study of literature, culture, and sexuality. To provide historical perspective, I paired the plays with secondary critical readings or with excerpts from primary documents (sermons, conduct books, pamphlets, other literary texts). Whereas in the course I avoided the anachronistic segregation of same-sex from different-sex issues, in this essay I focus, for strategic purposes, on my approach to three plays in which various kinds of homoerotic representation are central: Lyly's *Gallathea*, Middleton and Dekker's *The Roaring Girl*, and Marlowe's *Edward II*. What I hope to convey is why sex matters for teaching these plays both as compelling theatrical works and as sites of social and ideological conflict.

A basic premise of the course was that the insights of theorists and historians of sexuality can help engage student interest in Renaissance drama, especially non-Shakespearean drama, which they are more apt to regard with skepticism or indifference. I therefore began the course with a unit on gender, sexuality, and history, which emphasized that sexuality in fact has a history and that notions of biological sex, gender, and sexual desire are socially constructed, not universal or natural.

This unit began with David Halperin's "Is There a History of Sexuality?" In this highly readable essay, Halperin describes the organization of sexual relations in ancient Greece to demonstrate that sexuality is a not a universal fact of nature but a "cultural production" of the nineteenth century (416). Halperin's essay is especially useful for locating Renaissance notions of sexuality between ancient notions of sexuality (as a manifestation of social power and as a personal taste) and modern notions of sexuality (as a "separate sphere of existence" and as a "principle of individuation in human natures" [419]). I introduced these abstract concepts through a collective mapping exercise that involved placing three rubrics on the board—sex, gender, sexuality—and asking students to name the components of or associations they have with each. Building on Halperin's narrative of the historical transformation of sexuality, I then put another set of rubrics on the board—ancient, early modern, modern. Traditional period designations are instructive here: *early modern* emphasizes the period's link to the *modern*, whereas *Renaissance* suggests its classical legacy. If early modern cultures, like ancient cultures, had no sexuality, then how did they define and organize sexual experience? And how were early modern ways of defining and organizing sexual experience different from ancient Greek ways? At this point I stressed that our reading of Renaissance drama would require a dialectical process: mapping the various sexual systems of the culture (its rules, conventions, ideologies, institutions), while determining what kind of agency was possible within those systems. How did different persons operate within, manipulate, or subvert them? How did they benefit or suffer from them? And, most pertinent, how did dramatic texts represent this struggle?

After Halperin, we read excerpts from Eve Sedgwick's *Epistemology of the Closet* (22–35) and Bruce Smith's *Homosexual Desire in Shakespeare's England* (2–15), which put further pressure on any belief that sexuality has a singular meaning or mode of expression. Sedgwick presents two axioms—"People are different from each other" (22) and "The study of sexuality is not coextensive with the study of gender"(27)—that reveal the inadequacy of our conceptual tools for analyzing erotic desire. Compiling a wryly provocative catalog of the vagaries and indeterminacies of erotic desire, she suggests that sexuality runs along much messier paths than those traced by the neat binaries of homosexual and heterosexual. She observes, for instance, that "even identical genital acts mean very different things to different people" and that "some people like spontaneous sexual scenes, others like highly scripted ones, others like spontaneous-sounding ones that are nonetheless totally predictable" (25). Sedgwick's uncompromising insistence on *difference* not only alerts students to the nuanced variants of erotic desire represented in dramatic texts but also licenses skepticism about the viability of concepts like natural or universal in regard to sexuality. Whereas Sedgwick demonstrates the variance within modern sexual identities and practices, Bruce Smith examines the variety of sexual discourses in the Renaissance. He shows how legal, moral, medical, and literary discourses each produce a different understanding of sexual desire, as revealed, for instance, in the discrepancy between the literary idealization of male-male friendship and the legal condemnation of male-male intercourse as sodomy.

Having emphasized the importance (and the difficulty) of using historically accurate and theoretically precise terminology to analyze matters of sexuality, I devoted two weeks to our first play, *Twelfth Night*. Although the course focused primarily on non-Shakespearean drama, I began with *Twelfth Night* to ease students into the less familiar material and to establish a point of contrast: not all Renaissance playwrights treated cross-dressing, erotic desire, or comic plotting in the same way. Aside from *Twelfth Night*, this unit on the economics and erotics of cross-dressing included *Gallathea* and *The Roaring Girl* as well as several important essays intended to establish a critical foundation for the rest of the course. I used the first chapter of Stephen Orgel's *Impersonations* (1–30) to introduce Renaissance concepts of gender difference, particularly as it was represented in plays performed by all-male acting companies. Materialist feminist work by Jean Howard ("Women") and Kathleen McLuskie (*Renaissance*) drew attention to the social and political import of women's attendance at theaters. Acknowledging that playgoing offered women pleasure and power, Howard and McLuskie also problematize any ahistorical attribution of feminist sensibility to Renaissance playwrights. Finally, I taught Stephen Greenblatt's "Fiction and Friction" chapter from *Shakespearean Negotiations* in conjunction with Valerie Traub's "The (In)Significance of 'Lesbian' Desire in Early Modern England," because each gives a different account of Renaissance anatomical lore—that is, the one-sex model according to which male and female genitalia were structurally homologous—and of the relation of such lore to attitudes about female sexuality.

Traub's essay, through its detailed elaboration of the "radical discontinuity" that obtained between different understandings of female homoeroticism in the Renaissance (79), provides an indispensable critical vocabulary for interpreting plays like *Gallathea* and *The Roaring Girl*. Traub contrasts the dominant image of the female sodomite, or tribade—a highly visible, threateningly phallic woman who usurps male gender roles—with the discourse of "femme-femme" love (69), an affection that unites conventionally feminine women and thus avoids the appearance of social or sexual transgression. Whereas the tribade appears in medical and legal tracts, feminine homoeroticism usually appears in plays, typically in the form of a close girlhood bond that dissolves upon marriage. The homoerotic desire in such relationships is invisible, Traub argues, because erotic relations between women did not signify unless the women took on recognizably male sexual roles or neglected to fulfill their proper female roles as submissive wives and fertile mothers (77–78).

I asked my students to apply Traub's paradigm to Lyly's *Gallathea*, a pastoral comedy in which two girls, Gallathea and Phyllida, each disguised as a boy and each confused about the other's actual gender identity, fall deeply in love. Cupid exacerbates the girls' predicament by causing Diana's virgin nymphs to dote on them as well. When the girls finally discover the truth, however, they insist on the validity of their love; to clear the way for the expected comic marriage, Venus need only announce that she will transform one of the girls into a male. Is each of the girls therefore an equally feminine participant in the kind of socially innocuous homoerotic relationship described by Traub? Or does female homoeroticism instead enter into visibility in the play as a transgressive desire that must be contained?

While confronting students with the implications of Traub's analysis, I also had them read a more traditional historicist approach to the play, Ellen Caldwell's essay on *Gallathea*, "A New Rhetoric of Love for the Virgin Queen." Caldwell regards the play as a psychological allegory of the conflict between the desire for independence (chastity) and the desire for union (love) in the mind of a woman, perhaps Queen Elizabeth herself: "That desire to be free of either a life-threatening female identity or of a confining male disguise seems to motivate the women far more than the satisfaction of mere sexual passion, something which only the nymphs are forced, comically, to endure in the play" (70). Hence Caldwell concludes that the "transformation which Lyly celebrates is not the sexual one, which allows the marriage, but the psychological one, which reconciles oppositions as much within the individual as between the physically incompatible couple" (73). As an in-class writing assignment, I asked students whether they agreed with the thesis that Lyly explores a psychological rather than a sexual conflict and to what degree the political issue of Queen Elizabeth's virginity might have influenced Lyly's depiction of erotic desire. Is Caldwell right to argue that Gallathea and Phyllida do not feel the kind of sexual passion for each other that Diana's nymphs feel (albeit only comically) for them? Is it necessary to minimize the sexual argument in order to make the political or psychological argument, as she does here?

By placing Caldwell's assumptions against Traub's, I hoped to convey that the cross-dressing in *Gallathea* might be understood both to produce and to restrict homoerotic desire. Gallathea and Phyllida interrogate and woo each other with titillatingly ambiguous dialogue that blurs distinctions between male and female, homoerotic and heteroerotic:

> PHYLLIDA.   I say it is a pity you are not a woman.
> GALLATHEA.   I would not wish to be a woman, unless it were because thou art a man.

PHYLLIDA.   Nay, I do not wish thee to be a woman, for then I should not love thee, for I have sworn never to love a woman. (3.2.7–13)

Even though two girls can clearly love each other, it is impossible for them to marry and produce a child: Phyllida thus despairs that "if she [Gallathea] be a maiden, there is no hope of my love" (4.4.46–47). The problem that must be resolved for Gallathea and Phyllida is not overcoming a stigmatized lesbian desire but, as in the subplot of the three masterless brothers seeking employment, finding a proper social place. Phyllida wants to express her love for Gallathea in the conventional language of heteroerotic courtship because only such a language would be publicly intelligible as love: "Seeing we are both boys, and both lovers, that our affection may have some show, and seem as it were love, let me call thee mistress" (4.4.17–19). To be socially authorized, such a courtship must, of course, conclude in marriage and reproduction, which (unlike an erotic relationship) requires one male body and one female body. Caldwell argues that this marriage between two formerly female characters symbolizes a union of equals, a gesture through which Lyly seems to diminish the husband's power over his wife. Alternatively, the transformation of one girl into the other one's husband might be considered a reassertion of the patriarchal authority that had been disrupted by the transgressive courtship of two temporarily masterless cross-dressed girls. Whatever their final gender identities, both Gallathea and Phyllida are subjected to the imperative of reproductive sexuality, the precondition for the orderly transmission of property and family name. The play concludes, moreover, with Gallathea's injunction that the ladies in the audience themselves "yield to love" (line 5; epilogue). Yet whether or not this love must be expressed through marriage still remains open to question, for the play has also potentially validated the chaste love between two women as well as the virgin community of Diana, the mythological type for the Virgin Queen herself.

In *The Roaring Girl*, center stage is occupied not by girls disguised as boys but by an independent woman who openly dons male attire, to general shock and fascination. Unlike *Gallathea*, an elegant pastoral comedy presented before Queen Elizabeth by one of the boys' companies, *The Roaring Girl* is a popular comedy of London life. Middleton and Dekker put on stage a broad class spectrum—from gentry, citizens, and criminals to the notorious Moll herself—and represent various facets of social, sexual, and economic life in Jacobean London. This topical content can be colorfully addressed through readings from the 1620 polemics "Hic Mulier" and "Haec Vir." Attacking city women for imitating the fashions of men as well as of noblewomen, these pamphlets excoriate not only gender transgressions but also the economic transgressions associated with conspicuous expenditure in a rapidly growing urban center. To further illuminate how contemporary anxiety over cross-dressing might have reflected larger transformations in gender and social relations, I assigned a selection from Jonathan Dollimore's *Sexual Dissidence* (284–99) and Jean Howard's essay "Power and Eros," which examines the controversy over cross-dressing in the "Hic Mulier" and "Haec Vir" pamphlets and in plays like *Twelfth Night* and *The Roaring Girl*.

In his analysis of *The Roaring Girl*, Dollimore argues that subversion and containment are not simple binary forces but "always in play, each an intrinsic dimension of social process and in a dynamic interrelationship" (299). Consequently, efforts to contain, repress, or discipline social deviance are never completely successful. I asked students to test Dollimore's thesis against a particular scene from *The Roaring Girl* in which Sebastian kisses his fiancée, Mary, currently in male disguise, as a cross-dressed Moll comments on how "strange this shows, one man to kiss another!" (4.1.46). Having attempted to thwart his son's marriage, Sir Alexander instead creates an opportunity for further trespass against his authority as Sebastian enlists the aid of the disreputable Roaring Girl. Should this homoerotically charged scene between a future husband and wife thus be considered sexually transgressive? If so, does Sebastian's marriage to Mary contain the transgression? Does Moll's refusal to get married disrupt any sense of conservative closure the play might achieve? The political implications of Moll's independence are especially difficult to judge. Despite the lurid fascination of characters who speculate on her outlandish sexual tastes, assume that she is a whore, and condemn her as a hermaphroditic "monster" (1.2.137), Moll's masculine identity gives her a social mobility and an erotic autonomy—"I love to lie o' both sides o' th' bed myself" (2.2.39)—that serve to bring about the comic marriage and familial reconciliation.

In *Edward II*, a play I taught in the unit on sexuality and social disorder, cross-dressing is not at issue. Instead, the intimate relationship between king and favorite becomes the site of contention, in part because the physical signs of male friendship in the Renaissance were so hard to distinguish from the signs of disorderly sodomy (Bray). The difficulty of distinguishing socially orderly same-sex relationships from socially disorderly sodomy arises in the opening speech of the play, Gaveston's monologue, which I presented for class discussion. Whereas Edward's address to Gaveston as his "dearest friend" implies an equivalence of status and desire (1.1.2), Gaveston's self-identification as "the favourite of a king" (1.1.5) suggests dependency and political expediency. Describing the supreme "bliss" of being a favorite (4), Gaveston regards as "amorous lines" (6) Edward's invitation to "share the kingdom" with him (2). Gaveston's desires might seem merely self-serving; however, he also evinces a personal desire for and dedication to the king whom he "hold[s] so dear" (1.1.13). From the start, the desire for intimacy and the desire for power are inextricably linked.

Because the relationship between the king and his favorite is itself an authorized and conventional one, as Mortimer Senior's catalog of the "mightiest kings" and their "minions" acknowledges (1.4.390), it is necessary to explain why Edward's devotion to Gaveston should seem so transgressive. Would the peers and Isabella resist Edward so bitterly if he had a female instead of a male lover? The argument can go either way. Edward's intimacy with Gaveston appears socially transgressive (or sodomitical) because Edward places his personal desires before his public duties: as an object of erotic passion, a mistress might effeminate the king just as much as a male lover. But a mistress would not acquire the political power of a male favorite. Fierce rivalry for political power—obtained through access to the monarch's body—explains the peers' hatred of Gaveston, whom they disparage in status terms as a "base peasant" and "base groom" (1.4.7, 2.5.73). Even so, any attribution of unnatural sexuality to Edward and Gaveston is complicated by the absence of a consistent moral standard in the play: Kent, for instance, describes Edward as "unnatural" for cherishing favorites, yet later describes himself as "unnatural" for rebelling against Edward (4.1.8, 4.5.18).

In two provocative adaptations of Marlowe's play, the film *Edward II* and the accompanying text *Queer Edward II*, Derek Jarman openly challenges what can be considered natural in the realm of sexuality. Jarman's modernizations (or "improvements") of Marlowe exaggerate the sexual politics of the play in productive ways. First, the flagrancy of the alterations required to turn *Edward II* into a tale of homophobia, homosexual identity, and queer activism reveals the anachronistic distortion involved in reading a Renaissance play in terms of modern sexual categories. Whatever the dramatic or political value of such an interpretation, a sixteenth-century audience would not understand *Edward II* as a play about the conflict between a dominant and a minority sexuality. At the same time, by so audaciously appropriating Marlowe's play for his own political purposes, Jarman simply makes obvious and glamorous the less visible, more mundane currents of self-interest that lie beneath all acts of interpretation, no matter how historical.

I encouraged students to explore such questions of history, politics, and interpretation more fully in their final paper for the course. For instance, an assignment based on our discussion of Jarman's *Edward II* invited them to describe and justify their own cinematic interpretation of another play we had read. Another assignment asked students to compare, in Renaissance and contemporary American culture, the presumed relationship between cross-dressing and homosexuality, the degree of popular interest in male as opposed to female cross-dressing, and the class and gender politics of transvestite (drag) performance. Specific questions incorporated the theoretical vocabulary from the critical readings: for example, Does cross-dressing always "subvert" a culture's gender and sexual norms, or are there situations in which it might actually reinforce those norms? Aside from revealing what students had learned about Renaissance drama over the course of the semester, these topics were designed to give students what I hoped would be a valuable opportunity to articulate for themselves how issues of sexuality had come to matter to them.

NOTE

[1]Quotations of *The Roaring Girl* and *Gallathea* are from Russell Fraser and Norman Rabkin's *Drama of the English Renaissance*; quotations of *Edward II* are from W. Moelwyn Merchant's edition.

Teaching Drama as Festivity:
Dekker's *The Shoemakers' Holiday* and Beaumont's *The Knight of the Burning Pestle*

Phebe Jensen

Phillip Stubbes's attack on ungodly practices in the 1583 *Anatomy of Abuses* unwittingly provides a model for teaching the very drama Stubbes so decries, since Stubbes categorizes "stage-playes and Enterludes" together with "other kinde[s] of play[s]" that constitute traditional holiday entertainments: Lord of Misrule festivities, May games, church ales, and wakes (146). Taking Stubbes's indiscriminance as a guide and relying on both François Laroque's *Shakespeare's Festive World* and Michael Bristol's *Carnival and Theater*, I have designed courses that ask students to think of formally scripted plays as one aspect of the larger festive culture of early modern London—a culture that, as Laroque demonstrates, both looks back nostalgically on increasingly prohibited medieval festive traditions (4) and creates new forms of festivity to express the emerging social formations of Elizabethan and Jacobean London (32–73). The primary pedagogical benefit of this approach is that it allows students to discover for themselves how dramatic activities in general—and specific plays in particular—both shape and reflect the social, economic, and dramatic culture in which they are performed.

I've used this approach for a course on medieval and Renaissance drama that begins with medieval mystery and folk plays, then continues with Elizabethan and Jacobean plays (including *Midsummer Night's Dream, Twelfth Night, The Shoemakers' Holiday, Knight of the Burning Pestle, The Duchess of Malfi,* and *Bartholomew Fair*) read alongside ancillary texts such as *The Queen's Entertainment at Killingworth, Kemps Nine Daies Wonder,* lord mayor's pageants, and court masques. This model can easily be adapted to teach one or two plays in a differently oriented syllabus. Dekker's *The Shoemakers' Holiday* and Beaumont's *Knight of the Burning Pestle* lend themselves particularly well to this approach because festivity is an important theme in both, and the festive culture particularly relevant to them can be quickly and easily introduced.

Stubbes can be especially useful in the classroom as a way to acquaint students with both the festive culture of the period and dominant theoretical paradigms with which it has been analyzed. The account of the Lord of Misrule festivities from the *Anatomy*—brief enough to be photocopied onto a one-page handout—describes a tradition that exemplifies festive practices in late medieval and early modern England (146–47). In Stubbes's account, a parodic monarch elected by reveling villagers sets up court in a churchyard and creates a republic marked by dancing, marching, singing, and drinking. When I've asked students to talk about whether this event seems ultimately to challenge or uphold traditional authority, they have launched into a debate that is richly contentious, for indeed the lord's behavior seems both to provide festive release from traditional authority and to reinscribe that authority by reproducing a strictly ruled hierarchy—complete with punishments for nonconformists.

A classroom discussion of Stubbes, then, maneuvers students into using central concepts of carnivalesque theory without (or before) learning its specialized language. The question of festivity's potential to subvert or contain revolutionary impulses has been central to scholarly debates about carnival and theater inspired by the work of Mikhail Bakhtin; the issue is also extremely useful to a class focused on drama as festivity. The extent to which festivity and theater provide a space of license outside the normal laws of the workaday world—a space within which profound challenges to religious, political, and social hierarchies can be launched—is a central concern of Bakhtin's *Rabelais and His World* (see esp. 7–11) and is thoughtfully applied to early modern drama by Bristol's *Carnival and Theater*. Or does festive activity simply provide a contained space where subversive energies can be expended safely, leaving cultural orthodoxies intact? This assumption undergirds C. L. Barber's classic *Shakespeare's Festive Comedy;* it is also the argument (albeit from a very different theoretical perspective) of Stephen Greenblatt's *Shakespearean Negotiations* (see esp. 13–20) and some other works of new historicism. The literary debate about the oppositional possibilities of festivity in early modern England is mirrored in recent historical works that also usefully contextualize the carnivalesque: see Ronald Hutton's *The Rise and Fall of Merry England;* David Underdown's *Revel, Riot and Rebellion;* and David Cressy's *Bonfires and Bells.*

The subversion-containment binary is still helpful to introduce before teaching either a class on festivity or *The Shoemakers' Holiday* and *The Knight of the Burning Pestle,* though exploring the complexities of each play should allow students ultimately to transcend this somewhat limiting paradigm. In teaching *The Shoemakers' Holiday,* I reinforce these ideas—and in the process introduce local traditions associated with the "holy day" mentioned in the play's title—by having students read the account of the London Shrove Tuesday celebrations from John Taylor's pamphlet, *Jack a Lent, His Beginning and Entertainment: With the Many Pranks of His Gentleman-Usher Shrove-Tuesday That Goes before Him.* (Supplementary information about the play's social, economic, and festive context can be found in excellent articles by Paul Seaver and Marta Straznicky.) Shrove Tuesday is, of course, the paradigmatic holiday for carnival, festive misrule, and revelry, especially in its Catholic guise of Mardi Gras or Fat Tuesday. As in Stubbes's account of the Lord of Misrule, Taylor's hilarious description of Shrove Tuesday festivities can elicit a good fifteen-minute discussion about whether this revelry represents a real challenge to the status quo or whether traditional authority is reinscribed by the events of the day. Students familiar with Stubbes can easily see a figure of misrule in Taylor's description of the pancake cooks, those "Monarchs of the Marrow bones, Marquesses of the Mutton, Lords High Regents of the Spit and Kettle, Barons of the Gridiron, and sole Commanders of the frying-pan" (B2v). In Taylor's account of the rioting that follows excessive pancake consumption, the marauding apprentices clearly violate the law, but they also simultaneously enforce traditional, conservative social values by putting "playhouses to the sack, and bawdy-houses to the spoil" (B2v). Moreover, they keep the wheels of commerce greased, since the property they smash on Tuesday must be fixed on Wednesday "to the enrichment of upholsterers, the profit of plasterers and dirtdawbers, the gain of glassiers, joiners, carpenters, tilers and bricklayers"—that is, to the financial benefit of themselves and other members of their guilds. Taylor's account, then, suggests that the Shrove Tuesday riots both subverted and upheld conservative cultural values.

This cultural context allows students to think about *The Shoemakers' Holiday* on two levels: to consider the cultural work being done by the play and to analyze how festivity, class, and commerce are represented within the play. It also provokes a central question around which I structure class discussion: Do festivity and commercialism collide or collude in *The Shoemakers' Holiday*? Simon Eyre provides a useful jumping-off point for this question because, as students primed with Stubbes and Taylor can readily see, in him the values of festivity and the market system converge. Eyre is a lord of misrule, with his madcap and merry ways, linguistic exuberance, and the determination to keep his workers both happy and well liquored; he is also a clever capitalist with an eye always on the bottom line. In Eyre, festive energies seem to have been appropriated to obscure the potential ruthlessness of a market economy. This pattern is repeated in the trajectory of his story, in which an effortless, fairy-tale rise to wealth and power erases the potential moral dubiousness of moneygrubbing. Similarly, the scenes of workers in Eyre's shop are rich in drink, laughter, and singing; the workers even do the morris dance in celebration of Eyre's election as sheriff. Though the real shoemaker's holiday takes place in the play's last scene, it could also be argued that in this shop, every day is a holiday. As with Eyre, the play's representation of the shoemaker's shop seems to romanticize commerce by associating it with older, rural festive traditions.

But the play also allows darker images of the London market economy to surface, particularly in the Rafe and Jane plot. Rafe, unlike Roland Lacy, cannot escape a war that leaves him lame and unable to earn a living; meanwhile his wife, Jane, despite Eyre's promise to watch over her in Rafe's absence, is released to eke out a precarious living in a London shop. Jane's remark to Hammon that she "cannot live by keeping holiday" (12.31) exposes the social fantasy fueling Dekker's representation of Eyre's shop. In this way an oblique criticism of capitalism is launched within the play; festivity both softens that criticism and provides an imaginative solution to the problems caused by a market-driven society. The cultural work done by the play, students can easily be led to see, is partially to palliate the harshness of London's developing market system.

Linking festivity and commercialism also paves the way for an analysis of the actual riots in scene 18. As students familiar with Shrove Tuesday festivities will realize, Dekker significantly revises those traditions in this scene because the riots occur before the pancake feast and the threatened violence is not the result of unfocused festive excess but rather has a clear and conservative social purpose: to rescue Jane from bigamy (and from her foppish upper-class suitor) and restore her to the man who is both her sworn husband and her true love. Yet in making these revisions, Dekker's scene reflects the same social ambiguity surrounding Shrove Tuesday represented in Taylor's later, more historically accurate account of *Jack a Lent*. The play's final scene precludes any need for apprentice riots altogether, as class tensions are magically resolved in a utopian pancake feast that brings together representatives of all classes.

Finally, an initial focus on festivity and commerce provides a structure for thinking about other important themes. The play is everywhere concerned with class hatred, especially in the opening scene and the ongoing tension between Oatley and the Earl of Lincoln. It provides an ambivalent look at social climbing: Margery's social pretensions are held up to ridicule, and an unattractive form of social climbing is represented by the aristocratic hunting of Hammon and Warren; at the same time, Eyre's social rise is represented heroically. This theme impinges on another: the play's celebration of work versus idleness. Work ennobles Lacy and eroticizes Jane, as Hammon's voyeurism in scene 12 suggests: "How prettily she works! O pretty hand! / O happy work!" (12.13–14). All these themes reach a resolution in the play's final scene, which can be seen as a festive solution to the class, economic, and social problems presented elsewhere. Approaching *The Shoemakers' Holiday* through the topic of festivity allows students to see how the play both represents festivity's power to create a sense of community and participates in the definition of the community of London citizens in the 1590s.

The Shoemakers' Holiday celebrates London citizens; it is, in fact, exactly the kind of play that Citizen George of *The Knight of the Burning Pestle* wants the Children of the Revels, a boy company performing at indoor, hall playhouses in the first decade of the seventeenth century, to perform in lieu of their advertised offering, *The London Merchant*. Since *Knight* represents participation in the festive world of early Jacobean London as one way of defining class differences, approaching the play as festivity can help students see how the professional theater took on social functions once performed by traditional pastimes. Also, since *Knight* both sneers at traditional festive customs and appropriates their energies for the professional stage, considering its representation of festivity can help open up the complexities of a play that can sometimes seem to have only one joke, reiterated endlessly at the expense of George and Nell.

Information about the London theater necessary for understanding this joke can be provided through class discussion of the extremely topical first induction; the best resource for teachers here is Andrew Gurr's invaluable *Playgoing in Shakespeare's England,* a book that not only takes a reasonable, evidence-based position on scholarly controversies about the social nature of London audiences but also provides excellent discussions of *Knight* itself (73–74, 102–04). If asked to describe the citizens' theatrical tastes, my students can use *Knight* to produce a list of tastes, which can then be used to typify plays characteristic of the lower-end amphitheaters (discussed in Gurr 72–79). George and Nell like plays that "present something notably in honour of the commons of the city" (lines 25–26; induction); they prefer "huffing part[s]" (line 73; induction); they are so credulous in the face of dramatic illusion that, to give one example among many, Nell offers advice on curing chilblains to Mistress Merrythought in act 3; they relish physical action, particularly sword fighting ("Why, George, shall Rafe beat nobody again?" [2.2.390]); they love mindless spectacle such as the Sophy of Persia episode (a parody of John Day's *Travels of the Three English Brothers,* performed at the Red Bull); and they have a taste for old-fashioned romance, first suggested by their fondness for the old Elizabethan play *Mucedorus* but endlessly elaborated in Rafe's knight-errant adventures. The boy companies established themselves against such vulgar tastes by specializing in satire, irony, urban sophistication, and metatheatricalism—characteristics in tune with both the richer, usually better educated audiences who could afford the higher entrance fees to the hall playhouses, and with the boy companies' reputation for intellectual sophistication and linguistic dexterity (Gurr 73–74 and 158; see also Hattaway's introduction to *Knight,* xi–xii). Although *The London Merchant* cannot quite live up to this ideal, surely *Knight* can because of its rich satire of the citizen class, its verbal heterogeneity, and the laughter it provokes at gulls taken in by theatrical illusion. Seeing *Knight* as part of an attempt on the part of the boy companies to distinguish their theater from the drama of the vulgar masses allows students to consider how festive behavior both reflects and creates communities as it positions audiences at particular points in a socioeconomic system.

One of the primary ways in which different classes are distinguished is by their attitude toward traditional pastimes; George and Nell are branded as plebeian partially because of their fondness for old-fashioned festivals. Bored by *The London Merchant,* George and Nell ask Rafe to perform a May Day pageant and a Mile End March, traditional entertainments that can be introduced through a brief excerpt from John Stow's *A Survey of London* (123–25 and 125–29; see also Dillon 133–35). Stow's accounts are useful in illustrating early modern nostalgia for old festive customs because his tone is elegiac throughout. More important, in describing how these celebrations brought together rich and poor, sick and able-bodied, but brought into conflict citizens and aristocrats, Stow's accounts underline how festive activity defined communities in late medieval England.

An important difference between traditional festivities and the professional stage—a difference students can also see from reading Stow—is that festive celebration was participatory while watching plays was not. Improvisation was identified theatrically with older, communal festivity; as Richard Helgerson has recently argued in *Forms of Nationhood*, purging the stage of the "barbarism" of this tradition was an important development of the theatrical history of the 1590s (195–245). The comedians Richard Tarlton and William Kemp were famous for physical comedy, interactions with the audience, bawdiness, and the kind of improvisation that led Hamlet, in his capacity as playwright, to insist of his players that "those that play your clowns speak no more than is set down for them" (3.2.38–40). The distinction between participating and watching is central to the celebration of professional theater over popular celebrations in *Knight*. George and Nell's disregard of plot and script throughout the play identify them with the old-fashioned, participatory dramatic tradition of Tarlton, Kemp, and medieval marketplaces, a tradition that was derided by the increasingly formalized London stage. When the boy actors worry that George's interference will "utterly spoil our play [. . .] and it cost money" (3.293–94), they show that their goal is not to provide an opportunity for festive play but rather to reproduce and sell a consistent product. Discussing the issue of script versus improvisation, then, can suggest how festivity changed as it was professionalized and commercialized: participatory festivity expresses a community's values in (relatively) spontaneous celebrations; professional theater reproduces a salable commodity guaranteed by the script and ruled over by the playwright, reducing the audience (as Jonson's mock contract at the opening of *Bartholomew Fair* suggests) to passive observers.

Knight takes the side of professionals over amateurs, script or plot over improvisation, the production of consistent merchandise over unpredictable, ever-changing festive play. Script is celebrated over improvisation throughout the play, especially in the opposition between Jaspar, the professional actor, and Rafe, the amateur. Asking students to delineate the parallels between these two apprentices can help them see that Jaspar's besting of Rafe in act 2 expresses this larger theatrical controversy. As Glenn Steinberg points out, Jaspar falters in the play when he fails to follow his own script and improvises the disastrous scene with Luce in the wilderness in act 3 (215). At the same time, by ridiculing the oafish Humphrey and celebrating Jaspar, the plot of *The London Merchant* suggests that theatrical professionalism—the ability to act, script, and direct—enables social mobility and power.

Although *Knight* clearly promotes the theater for which it was first produced, the play in fact takes a more ambiguous attitude toward festivity than a first glance might suggest. For one thing, as Lee Bliss has suggested, George and Nell provide the play's most successful theatrical moments; their dramatic enthusiasm contributes to the play's larger celebration of theatricality (3–4). For another thing, formless festivity is also celebrated within the play in the liminal figure of Merrythought, a Lord of Misrule who happily abjures all thought of the prosaic, workaday world. It is indeed Merrythought who triumphs at the end of the play, when all the characters who represent middle-class respectability and fiscal responsibility are forced to sing and dance and become festive participants at his command (5.216–22 and 230–35). Having precluded the audience's identification with traditional festive entertainments by thoroughly mocking George and Nell, Beaumont ultimately gives his audience a modified—and by the standards of the professional theater, more sophisticated—experience of merriment when they are allowed to *watch* actors celebrate on the stage. As students can readily see, *Knight* wants to have it both ways: to mock traditional festivity as inferior to the formal theater of the boy companies but also to appropriate the energies of festivity to enhance the dramatic and cultural effectiveness of scripted plays.

For teachers interested in focusing more closely on cultural context, Dekker's lord mayor's pageant *Troia-Nova Triumphans* and William Kemp's *Kemps Nine Daies Wonder* can be particularly fruitful companion texts for these two plays. The former provides an account of the unabashed ritual celebration of citizens that is dramatically replicated in *The Shoemakers' Holiday* and mocked in *Knight*; the latter is a rich and entertaining pamphlet that can suggest how traditional pastimes (in this case, morris dancing) were being transformed into salable commodities in the context of the early modern economy. Whether teachers choose to bring festive culture into the classroom by putting such extra texts on the syllabus or through handouts and lectures, they will find that extending the definition of festivity "so as to include both [. . .] theatrical performances and spectacles, and unplanned, contingent outbreaks of misrule and resistance" (Bristol 38) can enrich students' understanding of both the drama and the culture of early modern England.

How Much History Is Enough?
Overcoming the Alienation of
Early Modern Drama

John Hunter

> Putting the text back into history sounds like something
> we might all want to do, but we should be certain we
> know what history means and what the practical conse-
> quences of such a program are.
>
> —Edward Pechter

Most modern undergraduates feel alienation when confronted with the language, situations, and historical references in early modern drama. It is broadly
true today that North American students arrive at the postsecondary level
knowing nothing about even the outlines of British history and having little if
any familiarity with early modern literary language to soften the blow of reading Marlowe, Jonson, and company for the first time. In fact, they will often
be hearing the names of these playwrights for the first time. Moreover, they
frequently come equipped with a vague fear (or, at least, distaste) for anything
written before 1800. This alienation—and its sources and solutions—has been
an ongoing concern for all instructors of early modern literature, and the
purpose of this essay is to offer some suggestions about dispelling it (when
this is desirable) or making it pedagogically productive (when it is not). It may
seem counterintuitive to argue that the defamiliarization created by these plays
might lead to better classroom situations than the confidence instilled by a
smattering of historical knowledge, but this can often be the case. I contend
that many instructors have been wrongfully convinced that the entire problem
of teaching early period texts springs from this lack of historical knowledge in
our students. Instead, we should be examining how the versions of history
that we give them as instructors can actually help create the problems of
historical comprehension that they are intended to solve. Only by reexamining
the relations that we construct between literature and history in the classroom
will we be able to properly address our students' misconceptions and
inhibitions.

I begin by examining some of the extant strategies for overcoming this
problem. If historical distance is a problem for teachers of Renaissance drama,
it is more of a problem for teachers of medieval literature (allegedly even
more alienating to students than its humanist successor). A glance at previous
Approaches to Teaching volumes dealing with medieval literature is revealing
when it comes to proposed solutions. They fall into three broad categories,
all of which speak to the predicaments of teaching the Renaissance as well:

the first approach, which lies beyond the orbit of this essay, is to anchor the study of early drama in the context of performance and to focus on stagecraft, performance history, and theatrical culture. This is, of course, a particular means to immerse students in a carefully demarcated part of history, although it is possible (and, in my experience, necessary) to integrate selected details on stagecraft with more textually based approaches to drama. The second approach suggests ways to teach the specifics of medieval cultural history (either as what we might now call an old historicist context or as a new historicist intertext) alongside literature. As late as 1980, representing the old historicist view, D. W. Robertson, Jr., recommended that all upper-level Chaucer courses should "place Chaucer's work in a cultural tradition that extends from classical antiquity through the early decades of the eighteenth century" by exposing students to an enormous range of material from medieval theology, philosophy, law, and government. In Robertson's view Chaucer's Britain represents a "different and now remote culture," and such a program of study would be an opportunity to engage with this cultural difference and would make reading Chaucer more enjoyable (129). Peggy A. Knapp discusses teaching *Sir Gawain and the Green Knight* in a similar immersion setting and describes a pedagogical technique centered on genre that also proved useful in medieval survey courses: "Using *Gawain* as a frame for other fourteenth-century works allows the class to freeze the flow of historical information for closer inspection and concentrate on the way such an era might have seen itself" (140–41). This approach reverses the polarity of Robertson's method inasmuch as it proceeds from literature to history and not vice versa, but the goal is the same: to work necessary bodies of history into literature courses and to establish some kind of working relation between the two discourses. The third approach to the problem—and it should be stressed that none of these is necessarily opposed to the others—focuses on the problem of historical difference as such. It stresses that the highest pedagogical value of historicizing early modern literature lies in the students' encounter with an alien culture rather than in the particular knowledge that they may acquire. C. Clifford Flanigan, writing about teaching medieval Latin drama, insists that "history must be given its due. We must let the past confront our students in all its alterity—its alien, alienating, and for us irrelevant aspects." For Flanigan this historical difference encourages students' awareness of how postmedieval institutions have appropriated medieval texts and modes of thought and how the interpretive strategies students learn as a result are similar to "the strategies we use with all texts, including the texts of our lives" (56). In the same collection, David Bevington agrees that, for students with no ambitions to go on to graduate school in English, the main value of an encounter with medieval drama lies in "ask[ing] our students to consider a civilization that differs so strikingly from their own"; to do so, Bevington asserts, is "to liberate the mind in a wonderful way" ("Why Teach" 153). Neither of these writers in any way decries teaching the details of medieval history, but their sense of why (and, by extension, how) we might do so is somewhat different from that of Robertson and Knapp.

The pedagogical options suggested by this body of scholarship are thus a detailed investigation of drama with as many other early modern historical discourses as possible and a strategy that approaches the early modern period as a representative type of all forms of alterity; almost inevitably, classroom practice will become some combination of the two. It is at this point, however, that we should recall Edward Pechter's valuable caution, cited in the epigraph to this essay. Although we now teach and write after the dissipation of new historicism as an identifiable movement, the theoretical debates occasioned by it and cultural materialism are still germane to the problems of teaching historically remote plays to undergraduates. Perhaps more than any other issue, these movements kept raising the question of what literature's relation was to its historical moment and what kinds of inquiry could legitimately be termed historical.[1] Unless we imagine that these considerations have no useful application to classroom practice—a difficult hypothesis to defend given the salient changes in the curricula of early modern courses over the past two decades—the question of how much and what kind of history we teach to undergraduate students of drama must inevitably be inflected by them.

Following our two pedagogical options, history's function in literature courses is to dispel the students' feeling of unfamiliarity as much as possible through historical knowledge or to be the means to explore unfamiliarity for its own sake through historical distance. The suggestions that follow can be used with both approaches, but the problem of alienation also highlights a shared limitation: they assume that the relation among an early modern play, its historical period, and the present situation of the student reader is relatively clear. Either clearly understood history will make obscure plays accessible or a clear sense of our own historical position will be brought to bear on a historical period that is by definition alien. But it is in these assumed relations, as much as it is in the plays themselves, that the problems lie for undergraduates. Neither history nor our present situation as readers is so easily defined. What if early modern plays are taught in the context of broad survey courses, where there is neither the time nor the resources to introduce a lot of secondary materials? Or if early modern plays constitute a brief stop in a breakneck tour from Chaucer to Virginia Woolf? And what if, as increasingly happens in an era of shrinking English departments, instructors themselves feel at sea in details and debates of early modern British history that may lie far outside their areas of expertise? How much history is enough—and of what kind must it be—to enable students to understand plays like *The Spanish Tragedy* or *Arden of Faversham*? Do some plays (or entire genres) of early modern drama have to be taught only to specialist upper-level undergraduates or graduate students because of the historical work required?

The answer to this last question is no, and it is pedagogically productive to remember that the problem of alienation is not exclusively historical or particular to early modern literature and to make sure that the students realize it as well. Few students expect that being brought up and immersed in the English-speaking world during the last three decades of the twentieth century will allow them to read or watch the plays of Harold Pinter, Tom Stoppard, or Sam Shepard with complete ease and comprehension, never mind more experimental contemporary drama; any who do expect this are speedily disillusioned. Likewise, teaching David Cronenberg's films or Kathy Acker's fiction will provoke many of the same kinds of difficulties for students that are raised by *Gammer Gurton's Needle* or *The Alchemist*: unfamiliar generic boundaries, dramatic situations outside their normative sense of what film or literature is about, and an artistic use of language (visual or verbal) not readily comprehensible in the terms of ordinary language. Even popular writers like William Gibson and Mark Leyner confront readers with characters who use fully developed fictional dialects of modern demotic English whose decoding requires a significant amount of arcane contemporary cultural knowledge; the process of learning to deal with these dialects is analogous to the process of adjusting to the mannered language found in Marlowe or Middleton, so historical distance is by no means the root of the problem. This is not to minimize or dismiss the problems posed by historical texts or periods; it is to put them in another, equally valid perspective. Simply put, the first step toward dealing with the problem of early modern historical alienation is to point out to the students that they are just as alienated from the artistic products of their own culture.

Far from being debilitating to historical considerations of drama, even a brief class discussion of historical and cultural alienation can be useful, especially if it is done before the students are scheduled to read the early modern plays in question. This discussion forestalls the students' tendency to blame their difficulties reading early drama on the period. A lecture on or (better yet) discussion of the kinds of resistance that most art mounts against easy interpretation reveals how we are all conditioned as readers by our culture and background (any postmodern piece of public art on your campus can be used as an instant reference point for this discussion), which can in turn lead to a discussion of how artistic forms are not merely carriers for troubling language and references but historical entities in their own right. These discussions allow students to read the plays as both bearers and shapers of meaning and enable instructors to begin to suggest that the difficulties of historical drama are not history's fault but simply one manifestation of the dialectical nature of any encounter between an object of interpretation and an interpreter. This point can be an especially valuable part of an introductory-level English course, but it works just as well at advanced levels (when it can be backed up by theoretical secondary readings). Once students realize that their difficulties with early modern texts are a normal part of the interpretive process, they will be much less prone to blame historical distance for any lack of engagement. They are then free to take on early modern dramatic poetry as a historical discourse with which they can grow more comfortable with time and effort. Studying early modern drama can thus be something other than a journey into the unknown that requires the golden bough of a preparatory course in early modern history.

Let me clarify this with an example. Many years ago, in my first stint as a teaching assistant in a Shakespeare course, I tried an experiment when we came to *Richard III*, the first history play in the course. Before the students read the play, I gave half of my section a photocopied excerpt from a standard history of the Wars of the Roses; it explained the factions, personalities, causes, and results of the struggle for war in a lucid and accessible way. I had the other half of the section watch Laurence Olivier's film version of the play (the only one then available). All students then read the play, attended the lecture on it, and met as a tutorial section. I wanted to see if there was a noticeable difference between the two groups, and there was: the students who had watched the film version were much more intellectually agile in the class discussion of the play than were their counterparts who had read the historical material. No matter what issues the discussion generated, even historical ones, the film group was quicker to see what possibilities the play generated for them. It was also easier for this group to accept that drama inevitably inflects history by imposing narrative patterns and personalities that are absent from the historical record. Ironically, some of the students who had done the historical reading found their knowledge erected a barrier between them and the play because they could not get past the fact that Shakespeare had changed history (albeit in small ways). Doubling or tripling the amount of historical reading would not have allayed this response or made any of the dramatic or poetic challenges of the play any clearer because more reading would not have addressed how history could help students engage drama. This is, again, not to say that history inevitably gets in the way of literary analysis; it is only to say that Pechter is right and that history does not necessarily teach its own use. Whatever one's views on the relation between literary and nonliterary texts, students need to be told the specific goals of reading historical material, or it will be wasted labor. In a classroom that acknowledges the difficulties of interpreting history as well as historical literature, students feel empowered to think about what separates them from early modern drama and to link it to their experience of art as a whole. If the instructor wishes, they can also be led to consider the general issue of history's relationship to literature.

I have been performing variations on the theme of this experiment ever since, and the results have mostly reflected this initial result. If nothing else, this result validates the assumption that has always motivated those instructors who teach early drama through performance and its history; a performance of a play can indeed lead to a level of comfort and comprehension that all the lectures in the world cannot match. Beginning a course or course section on early drama with a text for which you do have access to a taped or live performance can give students a sense that there are dramatic possibilities in these texts, and it encourages them to be imaginative about the possibilities of those plays for which no kind of performance is available. But I also would not wish to repress the benefits that a historical text can have on a class discussion of an early modern play. Sometimes in my *Richard III* experiment, I have substituted an account of Tudor gender relations for the history of the Wars of the Roses and asked the students to focus on the role of women in the play. Here, the differences between the play's world and the "real" world of history have led to a productive discussion of how—and why—Shakespeare invests the female characters in the play with attributes and roles that none of the men share. This, in turn, created an opportunity to address the question of how gender roles in an early modern play relate to historical gender roles. Anyone who has taught early period literature can confirm that students often use whatever limited historical knowledge they have as a template for their literary expectations. Any early period text they subsequently read will be forced to conform with those expectations, no matter what distortions result. Complicating the relation between history and literature can encourage them to see that sometimes literary works take a deliberately oppositional stance to the norms of the culture that produced them.

Every early modern play presents its own specific difficulties, of course, and fairness to the real benefits of historicist approaches obliges me to end with two examples of how the results of my *Richard III* experiment have been reversed in other contexts. Once when teaching *Arden of Faversham*, I gave half of the class some material on the Tudor social class structure and the passage from Holinshed on which the play was based; lacking a performance for the others, I arranged for them to have a discussion of the text during the tutorial hour (before the main class meeting) in order to help clear up comprehension difficulties. The students who had done the historical reading were much quicker to realize how thoroughly the play is imbricated in class issues and were able to notice that the playwright has had to invent a nonhistorical character (Franklin) to solve certain dramatic problems that have nothing to do with the historical scenario. In this instance, a historical source created possibilities for discussing the historical formation of social class. It also raised the question of how all representational forms impose structural changes on narratives that have nothing to do with the specifics of the narratives themselves. Another example occurred when I taught *The Duchess of Malfi*. Half of the class read Matteo Bandello's novella containing an earlier version of the same story (3–43), and the other half watched the BBC's televised adaptation of the play. The students who watched the play on videotape were much more at ease with discussing the text in general, but only the readers of Bandello's version could point out how an enormous layer of moralizing about the Duchess's behavior has been added to the original story. This observation, in turn, led to a discussion of how events in drama are framed to create certain interpretive possibilities, what the role of gender is in this process, and, again, how literature is just as liable as history to reshape narratives for ideological purposes that are not inherent in the events of the narratives themselves—an insight that performance alone cannot generate. Only the historical reading made that insight and the subsequent discussion so easily accessible to the students; the text on its own did not.

By now it will be obvious that all of the teaching situations and methods that have been discussed here must be subjected to the contingent situations of different courses, different groups of students, and different early modern texts. But this is surely one of the most important things to remember in teaching any literary text: one must always resign oneself to an approach that leaves ninety percent of the things to be said about a text unsaid. The important corollary of this reminder is that an instructor must have goals in mind for any historicizing readings or lectures to be offered and that the students need to understand the value of these materials for comprehending the play. Whatever one's theoretical approach to teaching early modern drama and its historical issues, the initial alienation that students feel when confronted with these texts will be a constant. The only partial exception to this is Shakespeare, whom students expect to spontaneously enjoy and admire, but teaching *Troilus and Cressida* or *Pericles* soon puts that expectation to the test. It is worse than useless to blame the students for feeling disappointed, and there is no universally applicable remedy. Becoming comfortable with the language of early modern drama can only happen after a lot of reading and hard work. As I have tried to suggest here, however, student alienation can be channeled to form the basis not only for useful discussions of specific texts but also for the larger and more difficult examination of literature, history, and interpretation. Once students realize that difference is a mutable and contingent condition of all reading and not the exclusive property of the past, the act of reading itself can be historicized and analyzed. With this recognition of difference in place, one can investigate the specificities of the early modern period and the ways in which we construct relations between it and the present. The complex interactions between history and literature can thus become the crucial subjects of a course rather than just the unspoken assumptions behind it.

NOTE

[1]For representative examples of this debate, see Belsey, "Richard Levin"; Goldberg, "Making Sense"; Levin, "Unthinkable Thoughts"; and Pechter.

Jonson's *Bartholomew Fair* and Brueghel's *Children's Games*

Judith Weil

At the end of an essay about Pieter Brueghel's painting *Children's Games*, published in *Sports Illustrated*, the art historian Alexander Eliot describes "the most mysterious and graceful figure in the entire composition." Wearing a jester's hood, he perches on a workbench, lower left, and holds a toy known as a *rosmoelen*. This toy, Eliot writes,

> consists of a hollowed-out apple, a wooden spindle, three small horizontal crosses fitted with paper sails and finally some string, which is wrapped tight around the spindle. Whoever yanks that string out through the hole in the apple will make the sails twirl round and lift the spindle straight into the sky, like a helicopter.

For Eliot, the rosmoelen sums up his pleasure in exploring Brueghel's mind and scene, "winged as it is with children" (56). For me, the whirligig and the painting have provided challenging ways to approach Ben Jonson's *Bartholomew Fair* in Renaissance drama courses. Students respond immediately to the appeal of *Children's Games* and speak confidently about it without thinking that they must be art experts. Unlike the rosmoelen, poised to whirl up into the air, they can be drawn into the actions represented by Jonson and Brueghel when asked to compare their works.

These comparisons are both broad and specific. Through *Children's Games*, students who have not read much of Lucian, Erasmus, or Rabelais can explore visually one of the traditions that has shaped *Bartholomew Fair*—Menippean satire, with its social inclusiveness, picaresque energy, and tantalizing significance. Both works employ childhood as a symbol for the paradoxes of wisdom and folly, innocence and ignorance. Both works invite moralistic responses and then test these responses. In my experience, students do not feel liberated by paradox until they have tried out different possible approaches to it. On the way to good debates about which of Jonson's characters, plots, or settings are more important, it is helpful to consider Brueghel's problematic design—an urban crossroad skewed to one side, so that a short branch on the left leads to a few passive, naked swimmers in a mill pond, while a long branch on the right slants past active groups (and a possible execution) toward a cathedral. Like Jonson's dramatic structure, this design may prompt viewers to doubt the pertinence of comprehensive explanations, even as it provokes a desire for them. In a broader sense, both artists use summer festivals on the margins of towns to anatomize social order. They upset distinctions between holiday and everyday and unsettle any confidence that the violence they include is wholly playful.

Pieter Brueghel, *Children's Games* (1560). Oil on wood panel. Kunsthistoriches Museum, Vienna. Image available at <http://www.khm.at>.

More specific comparisons focus on the roles of spectators as opposed to those of participants within each work, on the functions of adults or authority figures, on the gendering of different games and pastimes, and on the kinds of creativity they express. I want students to notice how both painting and play (see Cave 98) gather their populations around diverse centers of interest and explore the dynamics of converging groups. Edward Snow's wonderful study, *Inside Bruegel*, provides a rich source of speculation about latent pictorial narratives, which concern Snow primarily as methods for fashioning individual selves. I am more interested in understanding Jonson's "Littlewit" not as a character but as a motive for the rudimentary imitations presented by Brueghel and Jonson. How Brueghel's children employ the materials with which they play, especially the bricks evoking a deconstructed Tower of Babel, offers a stimulating analogy to how Jonson's characters employ language. If students can recover the childlike pleasures of "littlewit" by plunging into Brueghel, they may find Bartholomew Cokes less idiotic when he plunges so joyously into the fair, losing money, clothes, companions, and a fiancée.

This project seems to work best over a period of two to three weeks, or six hours of class time. I introduce the painting early to define the scope and genre of Jonson's play, then return to it in the next-to-last class as we reach the puppet show. Art books, slides, or a stack of color copies can be used to acquaint students with the picture. The last option is the most satisfactory if students are to investigate the painting carefully, climbing down in effect from the imaginary platform that seems to support an initial perspective detached from and superior to Brueghel's busy scene. In the center of his composition, either spying or calling into a barrel, crouches a small girl whose curiosity may be contagious enough to pull viewers into the painting (Snow 16, 72–73). To encourage self-involvement (and self-criticism about reliable viewpoints), I give students study questions closely related to the more specific similarities mentioned above: Which games are especially interesting or strange? What differences do the age, size, and gender of participants make? How do the children employ materials? one another? What significance do relations among groups or their locations in the picture seem to have? What kinds of make-believe or dramatic activity are involved?

Because this is a somewhat open-ended exercise that cannot finally be pinned down to an exact sequence of reactions or intellectual maneuvers, I also ask students to note any resemblances of the painting to the play that strike their attention. Some of the most illuminating connections have emerged when students have become intrigued with particular features in the painting, such as the large mask in the window lower left or the water wings supporting a swimmer. I stress that a number of the ninety games identified in the painting represent adult work or rituals and that art historians disagree about their meanings. For example, is that a body being burned in the distance toward the center of the town?

To anticipate our comparative explorations, I lecture briefly on the festive contexts of both works. Sandra Hindman has argued that with its bonfire, hanging baskets, swimmers, and mimicries of marriage and baptism, *Children's Games* probably depicts Saint John's Day, which would coincide with the great summer solstice festival, Midsummer's Eve, 24 June. Through his travesties of fairylands and queens (Ursula, with her changeling tapster, Mooncalf), Jonson might have jogged memories of Shakespeare's *A Midsummer Night's Dream* and of the earlier Corpus Christi street pageants staged by artisans. The real Bartholomew Fair took place approximately two months after the feast of Saint John the Baptist and the festival of Midsummer's Eve, on a day once dedicated to the patron saint of butchers. Remarkable for its continuity (1150–1855), this fair sprawled across the liberty of Spitalfields, overlapping Smithfield, the site of Marian martyrdoms and a horse market. In Jonson's play, it seems to sprawl as well across two distinct festival seasons: the rejuvenating revels of midsummer and the more elegiac madness of harvest celebrations. (The play was first staged on Halloween in 1614.) I have drawn on studies by Ronald Hutton, Lawrence Manley, and Susan Wells and on the essays assembled by David Smith and his collaborators in *The Theatrical City* for examples of historical change and social conflict especially pertinent to these two occasions.

But what do students already know about events like these? As they begin to tap their own barrels of experience, they recall concerts, riotous study-break holidays, and an occasional immersion in Mardi Gras or Easter Week. Many, however, have never visited an agricultural fair. Others report being briefly lost when very young in a sanitized amusement park or mall. One student may have gotten thoroughly lost in a Middle Eastern bazaar or a Southeast Asian market and want to tell the story. Another may describe being robbed. Several may be able to confirm Peter Burke's point that "as in the less developed countries today, [fairs] were places for young people to meet away from family supervision" (112).

Such memories can be carried over into a discussion of children as facts and figures within the play itself. Looking for their presence helps alert students to the "central problem" in interpreting *Bartholomew Fair*, "the difficulty of comprehending its unusual mixture of satiric criticism and festive release" (Kay 299). Students find the attitudes implied by dramatic evidence more fertile than Jonson's own oft-cited meditations in his *Timber; or Discoveries*: "I *have* considered, our whole life is like a *Play* [. . .] Wee so insist in imitating others, as wee cannot (when it is necessary) returne to ourselves: like Children, that imitate the vices of *Stammerers* so long, till at last they become such [. . .]" (597). Or: "*What* petty things they are, wee wonder at? like children, that esteeme every trifle; and preferre a *Fairing* before their Fathers: what difference is between us, and them? They are pleas'd with Cockleshels, Whistles, Hobby-horses, and such like: wee with Statues, marble Pillars, Pictures, guilded Roofes, where under-neath is Lath, and Lyme; perhaps Lome" (607).

Such moralizing commonplaces are apt to squelch innocent responses and block discoveries that either "Stammerers" or "Lome" can have creative potential. One might spark a discussion by asking why Win's pregnancy and mock hysteria are such important pretexts for visiting the fair? Why does Cokes attract crowds of "little long-coats" (1.4.105; 5.3.14–15)? What distinguishes the wares he purchases for his wedding and future family ("again I ha' children" [3.4.28]) from the genesis of babies or the fashioning of idols, prostitutes, and puppets? Is Cokes ever truly lost? What makes Overdo's comparison of Wasp's onslaught to "childermass" particularly resonant (2.6.135)? Why does the puppet show attract most of the fair's workers and visitors? And why should Whit, a tough pimp, respond to Cokes's enthusiasm for the puppets with lines so perceptive and "generous" (A. Barton 218) as "Let him alone. He is a child i' faith, la" (5.4.205–06)?

Innocence here might also have toughness, a quality acquired through endurance or practice. When we turn to the painting, students are quick to comment that most faces and several bodies seem older. Brueghel's two hundred and thirty-three children (the count provided by Vienna's Kunsthistorisches [art history] Museum) include several infants but also, near the center, a tall Cokes-like adolescent driving a hoop and, just right of the pond, two long-legged figures sitting with a group that is partly covered by a blue cloth. One or two adults seem to guide the children unobtrusively, offering a decided contrast to patriarchs like Overdo, Wasp, and Busy.

Another set of observations apt to surface before others concerns the obscurities of the painting, which seem to differ in kind from those in the play. Students have found that they can't quite see what's going on at the distant bonfire, upper right, or in the darkened house, lower left. Is that a swing inside its upper level? What is the boy, who is fishing through an open space in the wall, trying to catch? What is the large mask gazing down the right branch of the crossroads outside the picture frame? Students surmise that someone may be hiding in the barrel that greatly fascinates Brueghel's small girl and that is enigmatically marked on top with two all but invisible signs, a tiny hand and a Star of David (A. Eliot 49). We generally decide at this stage that as much as Jonson surprises spectators with sudden entries, escapes, and disguises, he also overexposes his characters. They may miss an important crisis in a corner of his fair, but his audience will see it clearly enacted on stage. A tentative conclusion might be that whereas Brueghel's viewers quickly recognize limits to their comprehension, Jonson's characters do not. I say tentative because more analysis of accidents and surprises can reveal striking similarities between the painting and the play.

Suppose, then, that I have repeated the study questions about games that seem particularly striking or strange and about the gender of participants. Students needn't know that Brueghel painted a similar bride in two other works to guess that a wedding procession, largely female and shepherded by an adult woman, is rounding the corner of the fence near the center of the picture. They also recognize that this group, preceded by two little girls carrying a huge basket of flowers, stands out because of its context—a predominantly male variant of gauntlet running to one side and competitive, all-male riding games to the other. Behind the wedding, a young woman entertains an audience on the steps by bearing a young man on her back. Looking straight ahead, through the eyes of the flower maiden, one sees another small child, whose "parents" seem ready to swing and drop their burden. Brueghel's figures have not yet matured into bawds, criminals, and foolish elders, but the artist has surely illustrated the drives and energies that vex Jonson's marriage plots.

Asked to imagine where the wedding party is going (two steeples are behind them), the students can make even more precise connections with *Bartholomew Fair*. If the procession moves straight ahead, avoiding the dropped baby, it will run into a wooden chamber pot that someone, perhaps the little boy on a hobbyhorse, has managed to miss. If the procession turns slightly, it will head toward a structure that combines several properties of a theater and tiring-house, the most notable of which is the broad aperture in its loft that invites us to see around and behind the mask wearer. In the shadows over a workbench sits an owl—a more promising emblem for wisdom than the pig's head over Ursula's booth but similarly oracular (cf. 3.2.50–66). Another procession nearing this play barn precedes the wedding group and represents either a baptism or a funeral. Baptism would be in keeping with Saint John's Day, but these cloaked walkers look melancholy and slow. In any case, why would Brueghel have placed baby before marriage in the temporal scheme of his picture?

We are now ready to consider two topics that bring out the most significant connections between painting and play: the role of accident and the nature of "littlewit." Snow thinks that the path of the two processions toward an indoor altar is being blocked by a pair of female "fates" playing knucklebones. However, if one of these girls is in the act of making the best possible throw with her last bone, she becomes "an image of imminent good fortune" (156–58). So, I think, does Littlewit when he opens the play by rejoicing at his "luck" in finding that summer day and new client share a name: "Barthol'mew upon Barthol'mew! There's the device! Who would have marked such a leapfrog chance now? A very less than ames-ace [double aces] on two dice!" (1.1.7–9). Fortune seems rampant in both works if we consider how the madman, Trouble-all, influences Jonson's calculating lovers or surmise that many of the children are about to fall or collide in Brueghel's painting. What prevents the player at blindman's buff from dashing into the marchers and riders or the hoop from rolling into the bladder with a bang as flatulent as the explosions of Jonsonian vaporing? (Barish 217–19, 231). "Collision looms," writes Alexander Eliot ("Games" 50), but he also believes that the girls near the doorway are playing an early modern version of jacks with their bones—that is, a game of skill rather than a game of chance (55). We might ask how Quarlous makes his luck work for him. What kind of skill prevents disaster?

An ability to make much from limited material and opportunity, a childlike genius for cramming the large into the small brings about the celebratory ending of *Bartholomew Fair*. Those who regard Jonson's *Fair* as debased and trivial are missing a constructive dimension of his satire. Katharine Maus has suggested that Jonson's comedies emphasize "conservation of matter" (85) as things and people get used, cobbled together, transferred, or even totally consumed. I try to end a comparison of play and painting by showing that they turn such recycling into a creative principle. In effect, we may learn to understand Jonson's "littlewit" by watching Brueghel's children, who seem able to make the most out of the objects and bodies they find. Why ride even a hobbyhorse when you can choose a railing, barrel, child, or log?

Most undergraduates do not feel prepared to discuss Jonson's parodies of Elizabethan epic and romance. But they can stretch their minds and be entertained by unpacking the puns in "what fairest of fairs / Was the fare that thou landedst but now a' Trig Stairs?" (5.4.136–37). Puns crowd multiple meanings into small vessels. They are like the bricks that Brueghel's children seem to have taken from a nascent Tower of Babel (on the right). A girl who pretends to keep shop as she works on a beam with her scales is turning a brick into food (bottom right). Mounted tugging warriors use a bit of brick for a boundary marker (center). Another child has treated his brick as a pet and tied it to his workbench (bottom left). The "vice" of "Stammerers" criticized by Jonson in *Timber; or, Discoveries* becomes a virtue when a babble of puns pours from wooden puppets, "a tiny, concentrated image of the coarse energy that informs the whole Fair" (Leggatt, *Ben Jonson* 16–17). "In a state of necessity, place should give place," quips Littlewit, countering Busy's sense of the fair as a "high place" (1.6.53–54). By punning on "give," he snatches plenitude from absence in order to justify escape-hatch substitutions and a generous expansion of tight little words, booths, and stomachs.

Students with theatrical training have played a major role in mapping our path back to a final class on the puppet show. Although everyone seems to have thought about the large adult mask, it takes actors to realize how unusual this mask is. Except for its eyes, its features are not particularly exaggerated or stylized, and it has a sheen like that of living skin. This insight has led to another: throughout the painting, children revel in rather than disguise their capacity to change. The innocence of Brueghel's children and Jonson's Cokes lies in their ability to enjoy artifice without being deceived by it. The puppets can replace Cokes's lost "fairings" (5.3.123–26) because he would be right at home in *Children's Games* where the redistribution of matter—the Adamic stuff of "Lome," bricks, barrel hoops, and bladders—goes on apace. For a "child i' faith" engaged in this kind of make-believe, the antitheatrical issue of delusion simply does not arise. Cokes's question to Leatherhead after the puppet master brains himself with the fierce blows of Damon and Pythias, "How is't friend, ha' they hurt thee?" (5.4.252), is one that participants ask when games get rough, and Leatherhead echoes both its rhythm and spirit by replying in the unbroken meter of a ballad or puppet show: "O no! / Between you and I sir, we do but make show" (5.4.252–53).

Students generally argue about whether young people should be allowed to play rough, dirty games or to face the dangers on city streets. One final value of approaching Jonson through Brueghel is that the lack of malice in the painting makes the potential for damage in the play much more evident. With its criminals, hypocrites, and many allusions to martyrdom, *Bartholomew Fair* has a darker vision than does *Children's Games*. As late as 1611, heretics were still being burned in the neighborhood of the fair (Haynes 122). From the perspective described above, Brueghel's children would be unlikely to burn a human being in their bonfire; they would get more pleasure from a broomstick. It is also likely, however, that Brueghel wanted his viewers to decide such questions for themselves. The design of his crossroads stimulates ethical imagination and choice; the set of scales sitting on a beam suggests that, like Jonson, he shows us a day of judgment. By exercising our minds in their serious playgrounds, Jonson and Brueghel help us understand the violence ever present in their worlds and in our own.

Pleasure Reconciled to Virtue: Introducing Undergraduates to Stuart Masques and Enjoying It

Randall Ingram

Stuart masques were thoroughly entangled in contemporary politics and were often recorded with special care both by authors, who might display masques in print, and by spectators, who have left a rich archive of eyewitness accounts of specific performances. Despite their importance for scholarship, however, Stuart masques are not always an important part of undergraduate courses on Renaissance drama. As teachers of *The Tempest* and *Women Beware Women* will attest, the masques within Renaissance plays can be the most confusing aspect of those plays for undergraduates. Even teachers who appreciate the value of introducing masques to undergraduates might be understandably reluctant to devote class time to a potentially baffling form; teaching masques can seem all virtue, no pleasure.

This article does not attempt to minimize the challenges of teaching masques, but it suggests that those challenges offer opportunities for considering aspects of Renaissance drama easily slighted in a survey of plays. Recent publications, such as David Lindley's excellent anthology *Court Masques: Jacobean and Caroline Entertainments, 1605–1640*, make previously hard-to-find works available in affordable, thoughtfully prepared editions, but I emphasize the virtues and pleasures of including a single masque in a survey of Renaissance drama or literature. In particular, teaching masques foregrounds the politics of performances at court and the transition from a specific, often unique performance to a printed, widely reproducible text. Moreover, masques allow teachers, in the tradition of masquers, to reflect on their teaching as a performance that invites ordered participation from spectators. In the two sections that follow, I outline two possible steps for teaching masques: at the first step, teachers can in one class meeting introduce students to some of the political questions raised by masques and by teaching masques; at the second step, teachers can in subsequent class periods use masques to broaden discussions of text and performance.

Teaching, Masques, Politics

Teaching masques can be especially challenging for teachers of discussion-based courses. Many undergraduates come to class equipped to discuss, say, character in Renaissance plays, but that familiar approach to character can be frustrated by figures with names such as Pleasure and First Pygmy. Alongside (and sometimes embedded within) Renaissance plays, masques can also seem short on plot; for the uninitiated, masques on printed pages can read as series of loosely stitched-together lyrics. Often undergraduates will have seen a Renaissance play in performance and so can see some possibilities for performing even unfamiliar plays. Students will not have seen a masque performed, however, and will understandably have difficulty comprehending the form as it appears in anthologies. As a result, teaching masques often requires lecturing, assigning critical articles, or both. But I have found that this necessity allows me to link the politics of the masque to classroom politics, to explore parallels between an intensely hierarchical form and a hierarchical pedagogy.

My teaching of masques roughly follows the sequence often found in masques: an antimasque, when forces of confusion threaten to overwhelm order; a masque proper, when order is restored; and revels, when masquers and spectators interact. The classroom version of the antimasque takes place in the first few moments of class time after students have read a masque. Ben Jonson's often anthologized *Pleasure Reconciled to Virtue* (1618) provides a solid introduction to masques and usually provokes a suitably confused response, despite headnotes and footnotes. Told that the masque stages Hercules's choice between virtue and pleasure, students tend to expect climactic scenes of choosing—something like Milton's masque, where Comus is a real threat rather than a comic figure to be quickly dismissed. Having read *Pleasure Reconciled to Virtue*, however, students are often unable to summarize its limited plot, but they do recognize the centrality of Mercury's first speech for understanding the masque's events. They also recognize that this long speech dispels rather than heightens the possible tensions of the second antimasque. Mercury begins, after all, by encouraging Hercules to keep sleeping and to ignore the pygmies who have sneaked up on him:

> Rest still, thou active friend of Virtue; these
> Should not disturb the peace of Hercules.
> Earth's worms and honour's dwarfs, at too great odds,
> Prove, or provoke the issue of the gods.   (142–45)

Clearly the sleeping hero can keep resting because the forces of the antimasque are "at too great odds" to generate suspense. Students who have read at least one of Jonson's plays may wonder why a playwright capable of creating individuated characters and suspenseful plots failed to create either in this masque. Left to the apparatuses of anthologies, students struggle to understand how *Pleasure Reconciled to Virtue* relates to the other plays they have encountered during the semester, but I have found that asking students to articulate their confusion can be an effective beginning to a class on the masque. Students' questions can begin to define the masque (e.g., Why is there so much rhyme? We have been talking about family relationships in plays, but do these characters even have families? Why is there more song than speech near the end of the work? Why is the stage described in such detail throughout?). By interrogating how Jonson's masque departs from plays they have read, students, like Jonson himself, begin to differentiate "play" from "masque."

Of course, students need teachers to answer their questions, just as Hercules needs Mercury. So after the very brief antimasque in which confused students have noted how the masque differs from previous readings, I deliver a lecture on the Stuart masque as a form and on Jonson's important role in shaping that form. This lecture first emphasizes the elements of Stuart masques that *Pleasure Reconciled to Virtue* exemplifies particularly well: the masque's dependence on highly specific staging; the movement in masques from disorder to finely crafted order; and the importance of music for embodying and expanding order, since spectators join masquers in dance. The lecture then addresses the politics of Stuart masques, taking *Pleasure Reconciled to Virtue* as an especially fascinating case. Scholars regularly read the first antimasque as criticism of the lavish feasts and heavy drinking at the court of James I. For example, in his essay "The Politics of the Jacobean Masque," Graham Parry suggests that the first antimasque of *Pleasure Reconciled to Virtue* may have been a frank affront to the court and to James, grossly embodied in the comic figure of Comus: "Commentators made much of the growth of extravagant and wasteful feasting at court in the year or so preceding this masque [*Pleasure Reconciled to Virtue*], and of the king's excessive drinking" (117n27). Defined against this dissolution, Prince Charles makes his first appearance in a masque as part of a "younger generation of courtiers who seemed to promise reformation in court morals" (110). That James famously disapproved of *Pleasure Reconciled to Virtue* may indicate that he recognized the antimasque as a pointed criticism of his court and his conduct, and with that displeasure in mind, I ask a student to read from the opening hymn:

> Hail, hail, plump paunch, O founder of taste
> For fresh meats, or powdered, or pickle, or paste;
> Devourer of broiled, baked, roasted, or sod,
> And emptier of cups, be they even, or odd;
> All which have now made thee, so wide i' the waist
> As scarce with no pudding thou art to be laced;
> But eating and drinking, until thou dost nod,
> Thou break'st all thy girdles, and break'st forth a god.
> (26–33)

Other masques enact the monarch's deification, but not by way of gourmandizing. After students have reconsidered this hymn in the context of its first performance, they understand why Jonson felt it necessary to eliminate this first antimasque when a version of *Pleasure Reconciled to Virtue* was staged six weeks later for Queen Anne, who had been too ill to attend the first performance. By the end of the lecture, I hope that students can appreciate the masque as a distinct form capable of generating considerable tension, even if printed texts of masques do not always reflect that tension.

As "masques could serve as a prism for refracting the white light of authority" in the Stuart court (Parry 110), they can also expose the workings of classroom politics. Like many who attended graduate school in the early 1990s, I was trained primarily to lead productive discussions—although, at the time, I may have been uncomfortable even with the verb "lead," having embraced the ideal of the decentered classroom. Teaching masques taught me the necessity of lecture, the need for occasional intervention from above. But because the class period on *Pleasure Reconciled to Virtue* roughly follows the masque's structure, I can draw attention to my intervention as a part of a prescribed, formal performance, and, in the time remaining, I can engage the class in discussion of the possible links between the centralized politics of the masque and lecture. I ask, "Does the masque transmit its politics into our classroom?" and we ponder how Jonson or James I might have responded to the late-twentieth-century verb *decenter*. As we discuss, I point out how our class period has ended in revels, a period of interaction, but ordered, directed interaction.

Text, Masques, Performance

The pleasures of this class period's virtuous work extend beyond a single period because this discussion helps students become savvy readers of masques in Renaissance plays and of masquelike entertainments in their own culture. From reading and discussing a masque, students can also gain a critical awareness that a dramatic text reproduced in a twentieth-century anthology cannot fully re-present a seventeenth-century theatrical event. After spending one class meeting on an exemplary masque, teachers can later use the masque as a special case for discussing questions about the relation between printed drama and performed drama—a special case because, as students will know after only one class period, the circumstances of performing masques often differed profoundly from the circumstances of performing plays in theaters, but special too because studying masques can provide a wealth of information about at least one kind of Renaissance theatrical performance.

Masques, unlike most Renaissance plays, were typically designed to be performed on a specific occasion. Perhaps as a result of the uniqueness of this performance or the social and cultural importance of the occasions when masques were performed or the memorably elaborate costumes and machinery used for staging masques, a number of contemporary spectators recorded what they saw when they attended masques. Students can find a collection of contemporary responses to Stuart entertainments in Stephen Orgel and Roy Strong's edition *Inigo Jones: The Theatre of the Stuart Court*. Because many spectators observed and remarked on Prince Charles's first appearance in a masque, *Pleasure Reconciled to Virtue* once again provides a good example. Certainly the fullest and, according to Orgel and Strong, "the most important" contemporary description of *Pleasure Reconciled to Virtue* was written by Orazio Busino, chaplain to the Venetian embassy (279). Busino describes who attended the masque, how spectators behaved and misbehaved, and how the masque was staged with "wonderful cunning." Busino pays greater attention to spectacle than to plot or characterization; for instance, his discussion of Hercules's actions is quick and impatient ("Then came a huge man in the shape of Hercules with his club, who wrestled with Antaeus, etc."), but his discussion of stagecraft is characterized by detail and admiration: "The mountain then opened by the turning of two doors, and from behind the low hills of a distant landscape one saw day break, some gilded columns being placed along the sides to make the distance seem greater" (qtd. in Orgel and Strong 283). From Busino's account students can begin to appreciate how the performance of a masque appeared to one spectator, and they can also begin to appreciate how some spectators might have come to see Jones's spectacle as much as to hear Jonson's verse, a fact that printed texts (Jonson's format of choice) can obscure.

Busino's description of the one and only performance of *Pleasure Reconciled to Virtue* can also help introduce students to the necessary flexibility of the masque in performance, how a masque might change in midperformance to accommodate a monarch's wishes or other contingencies. Busino narrates the story of James's outburst during the masque, but he also tells the less famous story of the king's eventual mollification:

> Finally they [the masquers] danced the Spanish dance once more with their ladies, and because they were tired began to lag; and the King, who is by nature choleric, grew impatient and shouted loudly, "Why don't they dance? What did you make me come here for? Devil take all of you, dance!" At once the Marquis of Buckingham, his majesty's favourite minion, sprang forward, and danced a number of high and very tiny capers with such grace and lightness that he made everyone admire and love him, and also managed to calm the rage of his angry lord.
>
> (Orgel and Strong 283)

This politically, erotically, theatrically charged moment can lead class discussion in a number of exciting directions, but students consistently recognize that (to use Jerzy Limon's term) the masque in performance responds to the pressures of its audience as literary texts—circulated in seventeenth-century manuscripts, published in Jonson's monumental folios, or encased in the apparatuses of late-twentieth-century anthologies—cannot. Once students have read Busino's description, they can reflect on *Pleasure Reconciled to Virtue* as a narrative of a theatrical event that may have never happened as described: where Jonson's 1640 folio and later editions present a fixed set of speeches, poems, and songs that pleased his king so much it was repeated with additions, Busino tells of a spectacle that was improvised to placate an annoyed monarch.

Faced with these competing narratives, students might wonder what to make of the masque printed in their anthologies. Is that printed literary text, as Limon would have it, clearly separate from theatrical performance (7–51), or, as Orgel argues, are text and performance simply "two aspects of the same thing" (*Jonsonian Masque* 62)? If masques especially provoke such questions, the questions themselves might apply to a wide range of dramatic texts: for instance, the relation of printed versions of *The Alchemist* to early modern performance perhaps should be considered similarly vexed, even though no spectator's account has survived to contest the massive authority of Jonson's books. Because studying masques can help students think critically about the uses and limitations of printed dramatic texts, teachers who include masques in their surveys of Renaissance drama may find that the rewards of their virtue last at least as long as their courses.

Contextualizing the Demonic:
Marlowe's *Doctor Faustus* in the Classroom

Thomas Akstens

John Madden's film *Shakespeare in Love* raised Christopher Marlowe's recognition factor among the community of students we are likely to encounter
in undergraduate classes in literature and drama. Students who previously had
no knowledge of Marlowe—or may have known him only as the writer of the
frequently anthologized "The Passionate Shepherd to His Love"—were introduced to him as a working theatrical contemporary of Shakespeare. For all
the liberties the director Madden and the screenwriters Marc Norman and
Tom Stoppard took with the chronology of Marlowe's career and the circumstances of his death, their film nevertheless raised the consciousness of its
spectators on an essential point—that the writing of the playscript for *Doctor
Faustus* and its production on the stage were products of a thriving commercial theatrical enterprise. Even while it perpetuates an idealized notion of
Shakespeare as an autonomous authorial genius, Madden's film contextualizes
Doctor Faustus and its writer within a dynamic and complex cultural milieu.

The representation of Marlowe in *Shakespeare in Love* is of particular interest to me, since I first saw the film while drafting this essay, which is
directed at teaching *Doctor Faustus* in the dual contexts of its cultural moment
and our own. But in fact, this discussion had earlier origins, in questions that
were raised by my Elizabethan and Jacobean drama class at Siena College in
1995. The class was considering the Clown and Wagner's encounters with the
devils in scene 4 of the 1604 A-text, when one student asked, "Why would
the audience laugh at something that's as frightening as the appearance of a
devil? Didn't they believe in devils?" Good questions breed other questions,
and some of the questions that arose as our discussion developed helped to
redefine our approach to the play: What did the original spectators feel when
Faustus conjured the devil and when the demons appeared on the stage? Why
did they feel that way? What did the devils look like? How was the experience
of those spectators different from what our own would be?

I have discovered in my subsequent experience teaching *Doctor Faustus* in
period, genre, and survey courses that questions such as these can provide a
specific, manageable focus for the consideration of the continuities and discontinuities between our culture and the culture that produced the play. Ultimately, they have additional value because they make it essential for us to
engage the broader issue of the extent to which we can understand the experience of any theatrical audience four hundred years ago.

Accordingly, my recent classroom approach has been to encourage students
to consider *Doctor Faustus* as the product of a culture with a reality system
somewhat different from our own—specifically, a reality system in which dev-

ils and demons had an ontological status different from the status they have now. I offer this notion to students not as a categorical statement but as a working premise that needs testing in the process of classroom inquiry—and the testing of this premise has yielded some complex and rather surprising results. This inquiry has generally involved three stages: the representation of the devils on Marlowe's stage, the original audience's culturally informed experience of these representations, and our experience of the play (as readers and hypothetical spectators) in our present cultural moment. I have found that by the end of this process of inquiry students have at least begun to consider the relations among cultural context, modes of representation, and the experience of spectatorship.

I like to begin the first stage of this inquiry by focusing on episodes such as 3.24–27, 4.44–53, and 5.144–47. These are brief, theatrically rich episodes in which the costuming of the devils is a counterpoint to the comic action. I want my students to try to visualize and describe the devils as they might have appeared in early performances—and the physical appearance of the devils must have been quite horrific. We have a bit of internal evidence for this: the Clown calls attention to their "vile long nails" and the "horns" of the he-devils and the "clefts and cloven feet" of the she-devils (4.50–53).[1] Surely the devils are "ugly" as Faustus declares (3.25), and we can surmise that Lucifer's entrance in scene 5 is enhanced by his "terrible" appearance (5.261). Students may get a somewhat more vivid image of the appearance of the devils from this description of a 1620 performance: "[. . .] shag-haired devils run roaming over the stage with squibs in their mouths, while drummers make thunder in the Tiring-house and twelve-penny hirelings make artificial lightening in their Heavens" (Cohen 118).

There are also clues to the devils' appearance in representations of devils in roughly contemporaneous pictorial art. The examples are virtually endless, but I have chosen a few images for use in class for which there are readily available reproductions. Most valuable, of course, is the woodcut that appeared on the title page of the 1616 B-text and other early quartos of *Doctor Faustus*. It showed a reptilian devil emerging from an opening in the floor (see Gill's edition 110; Schoenbaum 91)—a detail that further suggests that the devil's initial entrance was probably through a trapdoor in the floor of the stage. The mural from the Guild Chapel at Stratford (which survives only in a watercolor copy [Schoenbaum 41]) showed bestial devils tormenting the damned at the Last Judgment in images that correspond closely to two sixteenth-century European representations of devils that have been reproduced by the theater historian Phyllis Hartnoll (43; 47). Another theater historian, Meg Twycross, has reproduced an early sixteenth-century German illustration that "incidentally shows what devils looked like on [the medieval] stage" (51). I have also shown classes Luca Signorelli's fresco *The Damned in Hell*, which was painted for the Orvieto Cathedral around 1500 (Morgan and Morgan 72). Signorelli's demons are mostly horned but have human feet and are relatively humanoid in appearance. The inherent theatricality of the demons—at least to our eye—is reinforced by the arch that frames the action as the demons torture the damned, as if Signorelli had anticipated the effect of the proscenium. Whatever the specific physical representation of Marlowe's devils may have been, they undoubtedly relied on the conventions of representation that are evident in these visual images—conventions that our own culture has inherited to a significant degree: horns, cloven hooves, bat's wings, and other animal body parts; pitchforks and other torture devices.

Given such a strong and relatively consistent set of representational conventions, spanning more than a hundred years of visual art and stage practice, how might the audience have responded to the devils when they burst onto Marlowe's stage? To begin this second stage of inquiry, I stress to students that the audience's response must have been complex, since it was informed by the traditions of the medieval cycle plays, which sometimes featured both the slapstick comedy of the devils and the nightmare of the gaping hellmouth. It's important to note that, within the established representational conventions, the devil may be seen as both a clown and a menace. What is even more significant is that the devil (as signified by the devil on the stage) was widely perceived to be real. To provide context for this essential point, I have used the 1587 report of the trial and condemnation of the German woman Walpurga for witchcraft and demonality (Ross and McLaughlin 258–62). The text provides a graphic summary of a court proceeding, during which Walpurga was condemned to a brutal dismemberment and execution; the point again is that the devil himself and the devil's intercourse with a human being were treated in this proceeding as unquestionably factual. With all this in mind, it should not surprise students to encounter the following conclusion: "Many of those who attended the first performances of the plays in this volume [*Three Jacobean Witchcraft Plays*] would have accepted the notion of the devil's direct intervention in the affairs of men and the attempt by individuals to invoke his assistance" (Corbin and Sedge 1).

I've gone a step further in upper-level courses and used these issues as an opportunity for students to become familiar with some of the methods of materialist cultural criticism. The text I use is "Shakespeare and the Exorcists," from Stephen Greenblatt's *Shakespearean Negotiations* (94–128). Greenblatt's discussion of the learned controversy about demonic possession and exorcism in the 1580s and 1590s would be pertinent, if only because it demonstrates that possession was taken seriously enough to be a subject of controversy in the first place. The skeptical Samuel Harsnett argued in 1603 that exorcisms were only conduced when "a great assembly [was] gathered together" (Greenblatt 101). Harsnett's entire argument against the validity of exorcism is, in fact, driven by his fear of the credulity of the audience—that they believed the contrived signs of demonic possession. Two years later, that same credulity was satirized in Ben Jonson's *Volpone* (5.12.22–33), in an episode that has provoked some of my students to question again the role of comedy in the treatment of devils: "If something is so threatening, why laugh about it?" I've asked the students to consider whether Jonson's satire implies that at least some of his audience held a certain skepticism about the ontological status of devils and the possibility of demonic possession that allowed them to laugh— or did they need to laugh as a way to manage their anxiety about some very frightening realities? My students' willingness to engage these questions indicates that they are seeking the inherent complexity in the audience's response—and perhaps anticipating some complexity in their own.

The final stage of our inquiry asks the students to examine their own responses in the light of the preceding discussion. Recently, I have initiated this stage by assigning students to search several key words on the Internet: "Faustus," "Faust," "devil," and "Satan." My goal is to help students realize the extent to which their responses are culturally informed. The results of this Internet search can be chilling—or funny ("The Ten Top Reasons Why Santa Is Really Satan"). Most of these sites occupy a marginal position in our culture, but the sheer volume of material that comes up in these searches is impressive. My search of "Satan" on *Yahoo* in March 1999 referred me to more than 66,000 Web pages. It is evident that our culture devotes considerable energy and attention to the demonic. We are left to wonder what would have appeared in searches if there had been an Elizabethan Internet.

In this final stage of inquiry, I readily admit to students that when I first undertook this cultural approach to *Doctor Faustus* I was wedded to the hypothesis that our culture tended to trivialize the demonic. Evidence of this seemed to be everywhere: cable reruns of *Bewitched*, the New Jersey Devils hockey team, the cover photograph of the Rolling Stones' *Their Satanic Majesties* album, silly Halloween greeting cards and costumes, Underwood deviled ham labels, and comic films such as *Bedazzled* and *Damn Yankees* that treat the Faustian bargain as a joke. A somewhat more contemporary example is provided by the film *Spawn*, which features John Leguziamo as a wise-cracking devil and includes a graveyard scene that burlesques the demonic cults that are presumed by the media to be popular among the suburban, teenage, male population that was (in fact) the target audience for the film.

However, I'm equally candid that my hypothesis was shaken one evening when I was exploring our cultural response to the demonic with a class and asked them (somewhat facetiously) what their reaction would be if I were to draw the conjurer's circle on the floor with the blackboard chalk and recite Faustus's invocation (3.16–23). One student blurted out, "If you do that, I'm leaving! And I mean it!" After some discussion, it became clear that about a quarter of the class were genuinely uneasy with the idea of conjuration. Another student explained, "I'm just afraid we'd get into some kind of *Exorcist* thing." This prompted a discussion about *The Exorcist* and the anxiety about the demonic that evidently persists beneath the rationalist, secular facade of our culture. I suggested that the realistic mise-en-scène of *The Exorcist* provides credibility to the story and heightens our anxiety; the horrors of possession seem to be happening to ordinary middle-class people. Siena is a Franciscan college, and two other members of the class began an animated discussion in response, speculating on whether the friars conducted exorcisms in the local community, as if the students assumed that exorcism is a common event. Another student called our attention to the film *Devil's Advocate*, in which Al Pacino portrays Satan. The film includes an episode of forced demonality; Pacino's character (incongruously named "John Milton") violently rapes the wife of his young legal associate. The student contended, "If we weren't frightened somewhere deep inside that the devil could come into our world and hurt us or do something like this, the idea of the devil raping someone would just seem stupid. We wouldn't care as much about what happened to her, unless we were afraid that it could happen to us."

On the basis of this and subsequent classroom discussions, I have come to believe that our culture's response to the demonic is considerably more complex than I had anticipated. And while it is certainly important to understand that many in Marlowe's audience "accepted the notion of the devil's direct intervention" in human affairs (Corbin and Sedge 1), it seems just as important to note that our cultural context has prepared us to appreciate the irony of Faustus's surly "Come, I think Hell's a fable" (5.127)—spoken, after all, to a devil—as fully as Marlowe's audience did. And while it may be productive to consider whether we experience the horror of Faustus's damnation as intensely as Marlowe's audience did, I have become wary of the temptation to employ generalized formulations such as "Marlowe's audience believed in the devil, but we don't" to fully account for either audience's experience of meaning in the play.

What now seems more important to me is the question of whether our pluralistic, postindustrial society can entertain any belief system in sufficient commonality to allow for the kind of theatrical experience that seems so basic to *Doctor Faustus*—the dramatization of a crisis of faith. In response to this question, one of my students referred to the end of Tony Kushner's *Angels in America: Millennium Approaches*, which a touring company had recently performed at Proctor's Theater, the grand old vaudeville house a few miles away in Schenectady, New York. She said, "When the angel comes down at the end, you don't actually have to believe in angels yourself; you just have to believe in what's happening to the character. What's important is to accept the character's belief in the angel at that moment. That's a belief that the audience can share." This elegantly simple distinction—between our belief in the character's experience and our belief in angels or devils—has so far been the most useful product of our inquiry. It has reaffirmed for me the value of reading *Doctor Faustus* with the generation of students for whom Marlowe is a secondary character in an Oscar-winning film.

NOTE

[1]Quotations of *Doctor Faustus* are from Roma Gill's edition.

Tamburlaine to Tarantino

Paul Budra

It is always useful to poll a class of undergraduate students taking a Renaissance drama course about their theater attendance. If my classes are any indication, very few undergraduate students see any professional theater at all. Certainly, some students are theater buffs and attend everything. And, certainly, some will have seen the monster musicals of Andrew Lloyd Webber fame. A small number may have seen a professional production of a Shakespeare play, possibly as part of a high school field trip. But all these students, no matter how much I may cherish their enthusiasm, represent a statistically insignificant portion of my class populations. The vast majority of my students have never seen any theater outside the productions put on by their high school drama clubs, and sometimes not even those. No student I have had has ever seen a professional, or even an amateur, production of a non-Shakespearean Renaissance play although most of my students live in a major urban center.

So before we begin to teach our students Renaissance drama and theater history, we should admit to ourselves the most essential, and apparently overlooked, fact: the greatest impediment to teaching Renaissance drama is that many students have no experience of drama and therefore do not think dramatically. For these students, the vocabulary of theatrical gesture, the possibilities of theatrical spectacle, the very nature of theatrical acting are things that have to be imagined from the start. The conventions of contemporary theater may be as foreign to these students as the culture of sixteenth-century England is.

What this means in practical, pedagogical terms is that we have yet another thing to teach our students in courses that are becoming increasingly weighed down with the information that the current critical trend toward historical and cultural studies requires us to supply. Not only must we teach the history and nuances of the drama before us, the historical and cultural background that informs that drama, and the conventions of Renaissance theatrical performance and theater construction, but, it turns out, we must also teach how drama and theater—any drama and theater—work.

If this were not enough, the students are not tabulae rasae on which we can easily inscribe this material, even if we had the time. Although the students may be unfamiliar with the conventions of drama and theater, they are very knowledgeable about another form of representative narrative art: film. Students see movies, lots of them. Film-buff students are much more common than theater-buff students if only because film, thanks to video technology, is accessible and cheap, two things that theater is not. It is hardly surprising, then, that our students, unthinkingly familiar with the visual rhetoric, narrative conventions, acting styles, and even history of film, automatically translate play texts into movie screenplays as they read, imagining the camera angles and soundtrack music and casting Hollywood actors in their minds. I have spent years fighting students' inclination to think of drama in film terms, trying to get them to imagine the play text as it would have been performed on the largely empty Elizabethan stage, but I am beginning to wonder if the battle is worth the cost. Increasingly, in short school terms and crowded classes, I wonder if the students' predisposition to think cinematically can be used as a tool in teaching Renaissance drama, at least at the undergraduate level. I am not here referring to the popular pedagogical gambit employed by Shakespeare instructors of showing students two or three, and sometimes more, film versions of a single play or scene. There are very few easily accessible film versions of non-Shakespearean Renaissance plays (see Philippa Sheppard's filmography in this volume for a list of those that are available), so film cannot be readily used as a tool to explore performative possibilities. Rather, I mean calling on our students' general film knowledge to offer a series of accessible analogies and exercises that can help the students imagine the conditions that defined, and the conventions that developed in, the production of Renaissance drama.

One area in which film experience can be helpful is in the social situation of the theater enterprise itself. For example, when I ask my students to imagine contemporary theatergoing and the demographics of the theater audience, they immediately describe a homogeneously well-heeled audience at an expensive, and often ponderously solemn, gathering. They are not far wrong. But as theater historians such as Andrew Gurr have shown, the demographics of the English Renaissance public theater were not like this at all; the theaters attracted a much more eclectic audience and offered one of the few settings in which the various social classes mixed, mixed to the point that social authorities saw the breakdown of class lines as threatening (*Playgoing* 191–204). The theater audiences were, in fact, much more like contemporary film audiences than they were like contemporary theater audiences. Contemporary movies, especially high-profile movies, have radically heterogeneous audiences, and these audiences, like those of the Elizabethan theater, can relate to the spectacle on a variety of levels: some members are there for violence, sex, and cheap thrills; some are there because they are indiscriminate; some are there to scrutinize specific techniques; some are pedants.

The role of the Renaissance playwright in theater production bears an analogy to the screenwriter in movie production that students can understand. Asked to name a Hollywood star, students will do so without hesitation. Asked to name a director, they will certainly conjure up one or two. But when asked to name a Hollywood screenwriter, most will not be able to do so. Asked how many screenplays for major films they have read, they will answer none. Asked where they would go if they wanted to find a screenplay to read, most will not be able to answer. This analogy can be used to illustrate the marginal literary status of the play text, and perhaps the playwright, in Renaissance theatrical production. It can also serve as a useful illustration of the contingent nature of scripts. As can be demonstrated to students with one or two examples, most Hollywood film scripts go through multiple authors, sometimes committees of authors, before reaching production, where they are often simply ignored by directors and actors. Something similar happened in the committee-written plays of the Renaissance and, undoubtedly, in the theaters once the scripts were delivered (see the article on collaboratively written Renaissance plays by Jayson B. Brown, William W. E. Slights, and Reta Terry in this volume).

An analogy to film production also promotes an understanding of the economic priorities of Renaissance theater. Students have some idea of the financial costs and pressures involved in moviemaking. These can, with a film like *Titanic*, make the front pages of the newspapers. But students can have a surprisingly nonmaterialist view of historically distant cultural production, brought about, no doubt, by the teaching of Shakespeare as a transcendent, and therefore it is assumed nonentrepreneurial, figure. If the two periods are aligned, students can compare the money that Philip Henslowe spent on costumes with what he spent paying writers. It seems disproportionate and eccentric. They can then compare the percentage of film budgets spent on special effects with the percentage spent on writers, and the discrepancy does not seem so strange.

These sorts of analogies can also help our students understand the evolution of drama and its cultural impact on the Renaissance. Film, whatever its early history in kinescope, seems to have come out of nowhere and, in a remarkably short period of time, has become not only a major cultural force but also a remarkably sophisticated narrative form. The innovations in technique and narrative construction—from *The Great Train Robbery* (1903) to *Citizen Kane* (1941) in just under forty years—can be paralleled with the explosion of English professional drama, which, whatever its long and complex roots in native and classical traditions, became a cultural and economic force in an amazingly short period of time as it too evolved in narrative complexity: from *Gorboduc* (1561) to *Hamlet* (1601).

The rapid progress of professional drama, like the rapid progress of film, meant that audience sophistication increased at an exponential rate. So, while the first generations of filmgoers were entertained by a series of technical innovations (sound, color, cinemascope), later generations, generations that grew up with all the major innovations already in place, had a sophistication that the filmmakers had to take into account. We see something roughly analogous happen in the Renaissance drama of the professional public theaters in London. Later plays—say, those staged after 1600—could be written with the assumption that the audience grew up with professional theater, knew its conventions, and was conversant enough with those conventions that they could be invoked, parodied, or frustrated in interesting ways. This was not true in 1560.

The best example of this sophistication that I have encountered is the variously attributed *The Revenger's Tragedy*. My students regularly compare it with the films of Quentin Tarantino, especially *Reservoir Dogs* and *Pulp Fiction*. Those films, with their black humor, sly references to other movies, complicated timelines that assume audience sophistication with film narrative, tongue-in-cheek visual references, and surprises, exhibit a deep self-consciousness. So, for example, the second scene of *Reservoir Dogs* is a slow-motion shot of a group of criminals walking across a parking lot: their matching black suits and thin ties mark them as not only criminals but movie criminals. The opening of *The Revenger's Tragedy* has Vindice, carrying a skull, commenting on the passing spectacle of the court, in an ironic tribute to *Hamlet* and other plays of the revenger and malcontent, a cliché that is acknowledged in the first dialogue of the play when Vindice's brother comments, "Still sighing o'er Death's vizard?" (1.1.49).

Something similar happened with representations of violence. As the violence in both traditions became more complex and realistic, it was at the same time undercut with grim humor: the audience was sophisticated enough, had seen enough stage or film violence, that the later representations had to be either gruesomely innovative or amusing. The scene in *Reservoir Dogs* in which an ear is severed to the soundtrack of "Stuck in the Middle with You" bears a stylistic resemblance to the scene in *The Revenger's Tragedy* in which Vindice kills the Duke by having him kiss the poisoned skull of his lover (3.5).

And film analogies can offer a shortcut to the profound effects of popular narrative on human subjectivity itself. I ask students whether or not they have ever stopped in an action and thought "this is just like being in a movie." Most have experienced such a moment. I point out to them that before movies existed, consciousness of the moment was simply not possible. Narrative representation, then, has changed consciousness. And this self-awareness is reflected back in the medium: characters in movies talk and act in imitation of what they have seen in movies. In *The Last Boy Scout* the character played by Bruce Willis meets a bad guy and says, "You're the bad guy, right?" In *Repo Man* thugs commit a robbery and then flee the scene singing the "Ride of the Valkyries" in imitation of *Apocalypse Now*. Students can be invited to look for moments in Renaissance drama that reach for a similar effect—say, the dying Bosola explaining the death of Antonio in *The Duchess of Malfi*: "Such a mistake as I have often seen / In a play" (5.5.95–96).[1]

Other areas of class discussion that can be facilitated by drawing on students' film knowledge include the use of stock or allegorical characters (English drama's evil Italians versus American film's Middle Eastern terrorists), or the comic Vice figure (who resurfaces in Dr. Evil of *Austin Powers: International Man of Mystery*); the problems of sequelization (compare *Speed 2: Cruise Control* with *Tamburlaine, Part 2*); and the star system (Edward Alleyn versus Harrison Ford).

Practical classroom exercises emerge from our students' proclivity for thinking cinematically. I always ask students to imagine that they have to cast the characters of the plays that we are studying with well-known actors. Many have already silently done so while reading the play: Sigourney Weaver is often cast as the Duchess of Malfi; Christopher Walken is regularly suggested as a natural De Flores. I then call upon the students to justify their choices. Heated discussions often follow, which can be directed back to the details of the text: how do you know the character looks and sounds like that?

Another useful exercise—a creative one—is to have the students do film treatments of a play, updating the material as much as possible. From the treatment (which need be only four or five pages long) they can take one scene and write a page of screenplay: they have to use all the original dialogue but write in the intonations as well as the camera shots. This exercise forces the students to think about what is important in the scene: blocking, detail, facial expression, vocal expression, composition.

Is all this as good as teaching Renaissance drama as, well, drama? No, but for many of us it is a practical alternative. And while analogies in themselves prove nothing, they are evocative aids to imagination. If nothing else, drawing on our students' cinematic imaginations forces them to acknowledge that they do think cinematically, that they are unthinkingly caught in the rhetoric of film. Once they understand that the conventions of representation through which they filter the plays are, in fact, only conventions, then they can begin to think historically and to imagine other traditions of representation. In other words, they must articulate the drama as film so they can rediscover drama.

NOTE

[1]Quotation of *The Duchess of Malfi* is from Elizabeth M. Brennan's edition.

SURVEY PARTICIPANTS

Thomas Akstens, *Empire State College, State University of New York*
Peter Ayers, *Memorial University*, Newfoundland
Michael Best, *University of Victoria*
David Bevington, *University of Chicago*
Lee Bliss, *University of California, Santa Barbara*
Rick Bowers, *University of Alberta*
A. R. Braunmuller, *University of California, Los Angeles*
Paul Budra, *Simon Fraser University*
Joseph Candido, *University of Arkansas, Fayetteville*
Jeffrey Cass, *Texas A&M International University*
Mario DiGangi, *Lehman College, City University of New York*
Frances E. Dolan, *Miami University, Oxford*
Steven Downing, *University of Georgia*
Charles R. Forker, *Indiana University*
Lori Schroeder Haslem, *Knox College*
James Hirsh, *Georgia State University*
Brian R. Holloway, *College of West Virginia*
Jean E. Howard, *Columbia University*
John Hunter, *University of Toronto*
Randall Ingram, *Davidson College*
Phebe Jensen, *Utah State University*
Nely Keinanen, *University of Helsinki*
Arthur F. Kinney, *University of Massachusetts, Amherst*
Anne Lancashire, *University of Toronto*
Leanore Lieblein, *McGill University*
Naomi C. Liebler, *Montclair State University*
Christina Luckyj, *Dalhousie University*
Laurie Maguire, *Magdelen College, University of Oxford*
Irena Makaryk, *University of Ottawa*
Randall Martin, *University of New Brunswick*
C. E. McGee, *Saint Jerome's University, Waterloo*, Ontario
Karen Newman, *Brown University*
Helen Ostovich, *McMaster University*
Francesca Royster, *University of California, Berkeley*
Anne Russell, *Wilfrid Laurier University, Waterloo*, Ontario
G. B. Shand, *York University, Glendon College*, Toronto
James Shapiro, *Columbia University*
William E. Sheidley, *University of Southern Colorado*
Philippa Sheppard, *University of Toronto*
William W. E. Slights, *University of Saskatchewan*
Goran Stanivukovic, *St. Mary's University*
Karoline Szatk, *Iona College*
Frances Teague, *University of Georgia*

Bente Videbaek, *State University of New York, Stony Brook*
Judith Weil, *University of Manitoba*
Paul Werstine, *University of Western Ontario, King's College*
Suzanne Westfall, *Lafayette College*
Daniel L. Wright, *Concordia University*

NOTES ON CONTRIBUTORS

Thomas Akstens is visiting assistant professor at Siena College and Empire State College, State University of New York. He has published articles in *Journal of Dramatic Theory and Criticism, Shakespeare Bulletin, New England Theatre Journal*, and *Philological Quarterly*. His research and teaching interests include the representation of gender in theater and film and the adaptation of drama to film.

Rebecca Ann Bach, associate professor at the University of Alabama, Birmingham, is the author of *Colonial Transformations: The Cultural Production of the New Atlantic World: 1580–1640* (Palgrave, 2000) and articles on various aspects of early modern culture, including bearbaiting, masques, and maps, as well as essays on Shakespeare, Jonson, and Heywood. She is at work on a second book, "Early Modern England without Heterosexuality."

Karen Bamford is associate professor at Mount Allison University and the author of *Sexual Violence on the Jacobean Stage* (St. Martin's, 2000).

A. R. Braunmuller is professor of English at the University of California, Los Angeles. Recent publications include the New Cambridge Shakespeare edition of *Macbeth* and a critical book on Chapman's tragedies. He is the editor of the New Penguin editions of *The Merchant of Venice* (2000) and *Hamlet* (2001). Current projects include the Arden 3 edition of *Measure for Measure* and a critical essay on *Henry IV, Part 2* forthcoming in *Shakespeare Quarterly*.

Jayson B. Brown, a doctoral candidate at McMaster University, is the author of two articles on witchcraft in Renaissance drama. His research interests include collaborative authorship in the Renaissance, queer theory, and gothic literature and film.

Paul Budra is associate professor of English, Simon Fraser University, author of *A Mirror for Magistrates and the De Casibus Tradition* (U of Toronto P, 2000) and coeditor of *Part Two: Reflections on the Sequel* (U of Toronto P, 1998). He has published articles on Renaissance dramatic and nondramatic literature and on twentieth-century popular culture.

Joseph Candido is professor of English at the University of Arkansas. He is the author of *Shakespeare: The Critical Tradition: King John* (Athlone P, 1996) and numerous articles on Shakespeare and Renaissance drama in, among others, *Philological Quarterly, Shakespeare Studies, Shakespeare Quarterly, Anglia, Studies in Philology*, and *SEL*. He is currently editing *King John* in the New Variorum series.

Mario DiGangi is assistant professor of English at the Graduate Center and Lehman College, City University of New York. He is the author of *The Homoerotics of Early Modern Drama* (Cambridge UP, 1997) and of articles on Shakespeare, Marlowe, Barnfield, Middleton, Jonson, and Ford. He has contributed to *Approaches to Teaching Shorter Elizabethan Poetry* (MLA, 2000) and *Lesbian and Gay Studies and the Teaching of English* (NCTE, 2000).

Lori Schroeder Haslem is associate professor of English at Knox College. She has published articles on Renaissance drama in *Shakespeare Studies, Modern Philology,* and *English Language Notes*; an article on pedagogy and the Western canon in *Profession 1998*; and reviews in *Renaissance Quarterly* and *Theater Journal*. She is working on a project that considers connections in Shakespeare's plays among riddles, oracles, and prophecies; representations of the female body and speech; and dramatic closure.

James Hirsh is professor of English at Georgia State University. He is the author of *The Structure of Shakespearean Scenes* (Yale UP, 1981) as well as articles in *Shakespeare Quarterly, Modern Language Quarterly, Essays in Theatre,* and elsewhere. He is the editor of *English Renaissance Drama and Audience Response*, the Spring 1993 issue of *Studies in the Literary Imagination,* and *New Perspectives on Ben Jonson* (Fairleigh Dickinson UP, 1997).

John Hunter is assistant professor of English at Bucknell University. He is the author of "The Euphuistic Memory: Humanist Culture and Bacon's *Advancement of Learning*," in *Renaissance Papers* (1995) and is coediting "Renaissance Literature: An Anthology" for Blackwell. His research interests include early modern theories of memory and knowledge.

Randall Ingram is associate professor of English at Davidson College. He has published articles on Cavendish, Herrick, and Milton, among others. He is at work on a book-length project entitled "The Makings of Seventeenth-Century Books: Authors, Readers, Materials." The project examines how some famous seventeenth-century books of poems (by Milton, Herrick, Cavendish, and Cowley) negotiated the changing material conditions of authorship and readership during the 1640s and 1650s.

Phebe Jensen is associate professor of English at Utah State University. She has published articles on Renaissance literature and culture in *Shakespeare Quarterly, Renaissance and Reformation, Criticism, Literature and History* and *Reformation*. She is currently working on a book-length study of Catholicism and festivity in early modern England.

Arthur F. Kinney is Thomas W. Copeland Professor of Literary History and director, Massachusetts Center for Renaissance Studies, at the University of Massachusetts, Amherst. He has edited *The Witch of Edmonton* for the New Mermaids series and *Arden of Faversham* and other plays in *Renaissance Drama: An Anthology of Plays and Entertainments* (Blackwell, 1999). He has written widely on drama, including essays on teaching *Romeo and Juliet, Hamlet,* and *The Tempest* for the ML A series Approaches to Teaching World Literature. He is the author of *Lies like Truth: Shakespeare, Macbeth, and the Cultural Moment* (Wayne State UP, 2001), editor of *Hamlet: New Critical Essays* (Routledge, 2001), *The Cambridge Companion to English Literature 1500–1600* (Cambridge UP, 2000), and coeditor of *Tudor England: An Encyclopedia* (Garland, 2000).

Ric Knowles is professor of drama at the University of Guelph. He has written articles and chapters in books and periodicals on Shakespeare in performance, Canadian theater, and pedagogy. He is the author of *The Theatre of Form and the Production of Meaning: Contemporary Canadian Dramaturgies* (ECW, 1999). Current projects include "Reading the Material Theatre" for the Theatre and Performance Theory Series of Cambridge UP. He is editor of *Modern Drama* and coeditor of *Canadian Theatre Review*.

Alexander Leggatt is professor of English at University College, University of Toronto. He has written many books and articles on Renaissance drama. His most recent titles include *Introduction to English Renaissance Comedy* (Manchester UP, 1999), *English Stage Comedy, 1490–1990* (Routledge, 1998), and *Jacobean Public Theatre* (Routledge, 1992).

Theodore B. Leinwand is professor of English at University of Maryland, College Park. His publications include *The City Staged: Jacobean Comedy 1603–1613* (U of Wisconsin P, 1986), *Theatre, Finance and Society in Early Modern England* (Cambridge UP, 1999), and an edition of Middleton's *Michaelmas Term* in *The Collected Works of Thomas Middleton* (forthcoming, Oxford UP). A portion of his current project, "Reading Shakespeare," has recently apeared in *Kenyon Review*.

Christina Luckyj is associate professor of early modern literature and culture in the English department at Dalhousie University. She is the author of *"A Winter's Snake": Dramatic Form in the Tragedies of John Webster* (U of Georgia P, 1989), *"A Moving Rhetoricke": Gender and Silence in Early Modern England* (Manchester UP, 2002), as well as articles on gender in Shakespeare and Webster. She edited John Webster's *The White Devil* in the New Mermaids series (1996). She is planning a book-length study of early women writers and the canon.

Laurie Maguire is tutorial fellow in English at Magdalen College and University Lecturer, Oxford. In addition to numerous articles on Renaissance drama, she is the author of *Shakespearean Suspect Texts* (Cambridge UP, 1996) and, with Thomas L. Berger, coeditor of *Textual Formations and Reformations* (U of Delaware P, 1998). She is currently completing a cultural history of Helen of Troy and a book on onomastic theory in Renaissance drama.

Leah S. Marcus is Edwin Mims Professor of English, Vanderbilt University. Her publications on Renaissance literature include *Childhood and Cultural Despair: A Theme and Variations in Seventeenth-Century Literature* (U of Pittsburgh P, 1978), *The Politics of Mirth: Jonson, Herrick, Milton, Marvell, and the Defense of Old Holiday Pastimes* (U of Chicago P, 1986), *Puzzling Shakespeare: Local Reading and Its Discontents* (U of California P, 1988), and *Unediting the Renaissance: Shakespeare, Marlowe, Milton* (Routledge, 1996). She has coedited *Elizabeth I: Collected Works* (Chicago, 2000) with Janel Mueller and Mary Beth Rose.

C. E. McGee is associate professor in the English department at St. Jerome's College, University of Waterloo. With Rosalind Conklyn Hays, he is the coeditor of *Dorset Records of Early English Drama* (U of Toronto P, 1999). He developed a course on literary studies in electronic forms for the University of Waterloo and served for seven years on the Education Committee of the Stratford Festival (Stratford, Ontario).

Helen Ostovich is professor of English at McMaster University and has published numerous articles on Jonson and Shakespeare. She has edited *Jonson: Four Comedies* (Longman Annotated Texts, 1997), *Ben Jonson: Every Man out of His Humour* (Revels Plays, 2001) and is currently editing *The Magnetic Lady* for the Cambridge Ben Jonson.

She is the founding editor of the journal *Early Theatre* and editor of the Ashgate series Studies in Performance and Early Modern Drama.

Philippa Sheppard is a lecturer in English at University College, Dublin. She has taught Renaissance drama at Memorial University and at the University of Toronto. Since completing her D.Phil at Oxford, she has published articles and reviews on Shakespeare in scholarly and nonscholarly journals. Her teaching and research interests are performance and military aspects of Renaissance plays and the art of rhetoric. She is currently working on a book about Shakespeare on the screen.

William W. E. Slights is professor of English at the University of Saskatchewan. He is the author of *Ben Jonson and the Art of Secrecy* (U of Toronto P, 1994) and *Managing Readers: Printed Marginalia in English Renaissance Books* (U of Michigan P, 2001), as well as several articles on Renaissance drama. His current projects include a study of the image and icon of the heart in the Renaissance.

Jan Stirm is assistant professor of English at the University of Wisconsin, Eau Claire. She is author of " 'For Solace a Twinne-like Sister': Teaching Themes of Sisterhood in *As You Like It* and Beyond" (*Shakespeare Quarterly*, 1996) and a book-length study of early modern women's relationships. Her research interests include theories of embodiment and virtual reality.

Frances Teague is professor of English at the University of Georgia. Her research focuses on Renaissance drama and early women writers. She has published a number of books, which include *The Curious History of* Bartholomew Fair (Bucknell UP, 1985), *Shakespeare's Speaking Properties* (Bucknell UP, 1991), *Acting Funny* (Fairleigh Dickinson UP, 1993), and *Bathsua Makin, Learned Woman* (Bucknell UP, 1998).

Reta Terry has recently completed her PhD at the University of Saskatchewan. She is the author of " 'Vows to the Blackest Devil': *Hamlet* and the Evolving Honor Code in Early Modern England" (*Renaissance Quarterly*, 1999) and "National Unity and English (Dis)Honour: *A Game at Chess* and the Spanish Match" (*English Studies in Canada*, 2002). Her dissertation was on representations of honor in the seventeenth century.

Judith Weil is professor of English at the University of Manitoba. She is author of *Christopher Marlowe: Merlin's Prophet*, as well as various essays on Peele, Shakespeare, Marlowe, Webster, and Herbert. With Herbert Weil, she is coeditor of the New Cambridge *King Henry IV, Part 1*. Her current projects include a book on service and dependency in Shakespeare's plays.

WORKS CITED

Abbott, Mary. *Life Cycles in England, 1560–1720: Cradle to Grave*. London: Routledge, 1996.

Acheson, Katherine Osler. "The Modernity of the Early Modern: Anne Clifford." *Discontinuities: New Essays on Renaissance Literature and Criticism*. Ed. Paul Stevens and Viviana Comensoli. Toronto: U of Toronto P, 1998. 27–51.

Albanese, Denise. *New Science, New World*. Durham: Duke UP, 1996.

Altman, Joel B. *The Tudor Play of Mind: Rhetorical Inquiry and the Development of Elizabethan Drama*. Berkeley: U of California P, 1978.

Anglo, Sydney. *Images of Tudor Kingship*. London: Seaby, 1992.

Apocalypse Now. Dir. F. F. Coppola. United Artists, 1979.

Arden of Faversham: The Tragedy of Master Arden of Faversham. Ed. Martin L. Wine. The Revels Plays. London: Methuen, 1973.

Aughterson, Kate, ed. *Renaissance Woman: A Sourcebook: Constructions of Femininity in England*. Routledge: London, 1995.

Austin Powers: International Man of Mystery. Dir. Jay Roach. Capella, 1997.

Bach, Rebecca Ann. "The Homosocial Imaginary of *A Woman Killed with Kindness*." *Textual Practice* 12 (1998): 503–24.

Bakhtin, Mikhail. *Rabelais and His World*. Trans. Helene Iswolsky. Cambridge: MIT P, 1968.

Bandello, Matteo. "The Duchess of Malfi." *The Palace of Pleasure*. Trans. William Painter. Ed. Joseph Jacobs. Vol 3. New York: Dover, 1966.

Barber, C. L. *Shakespeare's Festive Comedy: A Study of Dramatic Form and Its Relation to Social Custom*. Princeton: Princeton UP, 1959.

Barclay, Michael. "*Woman Killed with Kindness* Saved by Solid Performances." *Ontarion* 3 Mar. 1992: 16.

Barish, Jonas A. *Ben Jonson and the Language of Prose Comedy*. New York: Norton, 1970.

Barton, Anne. *Ben Jonson, Dramatist*. Cambridge: Cambridge UP, 1984.

Barton, John. *Playing Shakespeare*. London: Methuen, in assoc. with Channel 4 Television Co., 1984.

Bate, Jonathan, and Russell Jackson. *Shakespeare: An Illustrated Stage History*. Oxford: Oxford UP, 1996.

Beaumont, Francis. *The Knight of the Burning Pestle*. Ed. Michael Hattaway. New Mermaids. New York: Norton, 1996.

Beaumont, Francis, and John Fletcher. *The Maid's Tragedy*. Ed. Howard B. Norland. Regents Renaissance Drama. Lincoln: U of Nebraska P, 1968.

Bedazzled. Dir. Stanley Donen. Twentieth Century Fox, 1967.

Bedazzled. Dir. Harold Ramis. Twentieth Century Fox, 2000.

Bella, Valeria, and Piero Bella. *Cartografia rara: Antiche carte geografiche, topografiche e storiche dalla collezione Franco Novacco*. Milan: Cromorama, 1991.

———. "Emblem and Antithesis in *The Duchess of Malfi*." *John Webster's* The Duchess of Malfi. Ed. Harold Bloom. Modern Critical Interpretations. New York: Chelsea, 1987. 97–113.

———. "Richard Levin and In-different Reading." *New Literary History* 21 (1990): 449–56.

———. *The Subject of Tragedy: Identity and Difference in Renaissance Drama*. London: Methuen, 1985.

Bennett, Alan. *Talking Heads*. London: BBC, 1988.

Bentley, G. E. *The Profession of Dramatist in Shakespeare's Time, 1590–1642*. Princeton: Princeton UP, 1986.

Berger, Harry, Jr. "The Early Scenes of *Macbeth*: Preface to a New Interpretation." *ELH* 47 (1980): 1–31.

———. *Making Trifles of Terrors: Redistributing Complicities in Shakespeare*. Ed. Peter Erickson. Stanford: Stanford UP, 1997.

Bevington, David. *From* Mankind *to* Marlowe: *Growth of Structure in the Popular Drama of Tudor England*. Cambridge: Harvard UP, 1962.

———. "Why Teach Medieval Drama?" Emmerson 151–56.

Biganzoli, Lisa. *Shakespeare's Britain*. Map. Washington: Natl. Geographic Soc., May 1964.

Binda, Hilary. "Hell and Hypertext Hath No Limits: Electronic Texts and the Crises in Criticism." *Early Modern Literary Studies* 5.3. Spec. issue 4 (Jan. 2000). 1 May 2001 <http://www.shu.ac.uk/emls/05-3/bindmarl.html>.

Blaeu, Joan. *Blaeu's the Grand Atlas of the Seventeenth Century World*. New York: Rizzoli, 1991.

Blatherwick, Simon. "The Archaeological Evaluation of the Globe Playhouse." *Shakespeare's Globe Rebuilt*. Ed. J. R. Mulryne and Margaret Shewring. Cambridge: Cambridge UP, 1997. 67–80.

Bliss, Lee. " 'Plot Mee No Plots': The Life of Drama and the Drama of Life in *The Knight of the Burning Pestle*." *Modern Language Quarterly* 45 (1984): 3–21.

Bluestone, Max, and Norman Rabkin, eds. *Shakespeare's Contemporaries*. Introd. Alfred Harbage. 1962. 2nd ed. Englewood Cliffs: Prentice, 1968.

The Book of Common Prayer. 27 Nov. 1998. Anglican Resource Collection. Soc. of Archbishop Justus. 20 Mar. 2002 <http:justus.anglican.org/resources/bcp/>.

Boureanu, Radu. *Holbein*. Trans. Florin Ionescu. London: Abbey Lib., 1977.

Bowers, Fredson. *Elizabethan Revenge Tragedy, 1587–1642*. Princeton: Princeton UP, 1940.

Boyd, Morrison Comegys. *Elizabethan Music and Musical Criticism*. Philadelphia: U of Pennsylvania P, 1940.

Bradbrook, M. C. *The Growth and Structure of Elizabethan Comedy*. New ed. London: Chatto, 1973.

———. *Themes and Conventions of Elizabethan Tragedy*. 2nd ed. Cambridge: Cambridge UP, 1980.

Braunmuller, A. R. " 'To the Globe I Rowed': John Holles Sees *A Game at Chess.*" *English Literary Renaissance* 20 (1990): 340–55.

Braunmuller, A. R., and Michael Hattaway, eds. *The Cambridge Companion to English Renaissance Drama*. Cambridge: Cambridge UP, 1990.

Bray, Alan. "Homosexuality and the Signs of Male Friendship in Elizabethan England." Goldberg, *Queering* 40–61.

Bristol, Michael. *Carnival and Theater: Plebian Culture and the Structure of Authority in Renaissance England*. New York: Methuen, 1985.

Bromley, Laura. "Domestic Conduct in *A Woman Killed with Kindness.*" *Studies in English Literature 1500–1900* 26 (1986): 259–76.

Brooke, C. F. Tucker, and Nathaniel Burton Paradise, eds. *English Drama, 1580–1642*. Lexington: Heath, 1961.

Brough, Neil. *New Perspectives on Faust: Studies in the Origins and Philosophy of the Faust Theme in the Dramas of Marlowe and Goethe*. Frankfurt: Lang, 1994.

Brown, John Howard. *Elizabethan Schooldays: An Account of the English Grammar Schools in the Second Half of the Sixteenth Century*. Oxford: Blackwell, 1933.

Brown, John Russell. Introduction. *The Duchess of Malfi*. By John Webster. London: Methuen, 1964. xvii–lxxii.

Bryan, Margaret B. "Food Symbolism in *A Woman Killed with Kindness.*" *Renaissance Papers*. Durham: Duke UP, 1974. 9–17.

Burgess, Antony. *Shakespeare*. Harmondsworth: Penguin, 1970.

Burke, Peter. *Popular Culture in Early Modern Europe*. London: Temple, 1983.

Burton, Robert. *The Anatomy of Melancholy*. Ed. Floyd Dell and Paul Jordan-Smith. New York: Tudor, 1929.

Caldwell, Ellen M. "John Lyly's *Gallathea*: A New Rhetoric of Love for the Virgin Queen." *Women in the Renaissance: Selections from* English Literary Renaissance. Ed. Kirby Farrell, Elizabeth H. Hageman, and Arthur F. Kinney. Amherst: U of Massachusetts P, 1990.

Canuteson, John. "The Theme of Forgiveness in the Plot and Subplot of *A Woman Killed with Kindness.*" *Renaissance Drama* ns 2 (1969): 123–47.

Carson, Neil. *A Companion to Henslowe's Diary*. Cambridge: Cambridge UP, 1988.

Cary, Elizabeth. *The Tragedy of Mariam*. Ed. A. C. Dunstan and W. W. Greg. Malone Society Reprints. London: Malone Soc., 1914.

———. *The Tragedy of Mariam, the Fair Queen of Jewry*. Ed. Stephanie Hodgson-Wright. Peterborough: Broadview, 2000.

———. *The Tragedy of Mariam, the Fair Queen of Jewry*. Ed. Barry Weller and Margaret W. Ferguson. Berkeley: U of California P, 1994.

Cave, Richard Allen. *Ben Jonson*. New York: St. Martin's, 1991.

Cerasano, S. P., and Marion Wynne-Davies, eds. *Renaissance Drama by Women: Texts and Documents*. London: Routledge, 1996.

Chamberlain, John. *The Letters of John Chamberlain*. Ed. N. E. McClure. 2 vols. Philadelphia: APS, 1939.

Chambers, E. K. *The Elizabethan Stage*. 4 vols. Oxford: Oxford UP, 1923.

Chapman, George. *The Plays of George Chapman: The Comedies, a Critical Edition*. Ed. Alan Holaday. Urbana: U of Illinois P, 1970.

———. *The Widow's Tears*. Ed. Ethel M. Smeak. Regents Renaissance Drama. Lincoln: U of Nebraska P, 1966.

Chartier, Roger. *The Order of Books: Readers, Authors, and Libraries in Europe between the Fourteenth and Eighteenth Centuries*. Trans. Lydia G. Cochrane. Stanford: Stanford UP, 1994.

Church of England. "The Sermon against Idleness." *Certain Sermons Appointed by the Queen's Majesty to be . . . Read . . . in . . . Churches* [. . .]. 1574. Ed. G. E. Corrie. Cambridge, 1850. 516–24.

Citizen Kane. Dir. Orson Welles. RKO, 1941.

Clark, James M. *The Dance of Death in the Middle Ages and the Renaissance*. Glasgow: Jackson, 1950.

Cleaver, Robert. *A Godly Form of Householde Governement*. London, 1598.

Clifford, Lady Anne. *The Diary of Lady Anne Clifford*. Martin 245–75.

Cogswell, Thomas. *The Blessed Revolution: English Politics and the Coming of War, 1621–1624*. Cambridge: Cambridge UP, 1989.

Cohen, Helen Louise. *Milestones of the Drama*. New York: Harcourt, 1940.

Comensoli, Viviana. *Household Business: Domestic Plays of Early Modern England*. Toronto: U of Toronto P, 1996.

Cook, Ann Jennalie. *Making a Match: Courtship in Shakespeare and His Society*. Princeton: Princeton UP, 1991.

Cook, David. "*A Woman Killed with Kindness*: An Unshakespeariean Tragedy." *English Studies* 45 (1964): 353–72.

Corbin, Peter, and Douglas Sedge, eds. *Three Jacobean Witchcraft Plays*. Manchester: Manchester UP, 1986.

Coryate, Thomas. *Coryat's Crudities*. 1611. 2 vols. Glasgow: James MacLehose, 1905.

Cox, John D., and David Scott Kastan, eds. *A New History of Early English Drama*. New York: Columbia UP, 1997.

Craven, Wesley Frank. *The Virginia Company of London, 1606–1624*. Williamsburg: Virginia 350th Anniversary Celebration, 1957.

Cressy, David. *Bonfires and Bells: National Memory and the Protestant Calendar in Elizabethan and Stuart England*. Berkeley: U of California P, 1989.

Cunningham, J. V., ed. *In Shakespeare's Day*. Greenwich: Fawcett, 1970.

Cust, Lionel. *Notes on the Authentic Portraits of Mary Queen of Scots*. London: Murray, 1903.

Damn Yankees. Dir. George Abbott and Stanley Donen. Warner Bros., 1958.

Davenport, Hugh. Rev. of *Edward II*, dir. Derek Jarman. *Weekly Telegraph* 27 Oct. 1991: 27.

Day, John. *Travels of the Three English Brothers*. *Three Renaissance Travel Plays*. Ed. Anthony Parr. Manchester: Manchester UP, 1995.

Dekker, Thomas. *The Shoemaker's Holiday*. Ed. Anthony Parr. New Mermaids. 2nd ed. New York: Norton, 1990.

———. *Troia-Nova Triumphans. The Dramatic Works of Thomas Dekker*. Ed. F. T. Bowers. Vol. 3. Cambridge: Cambridge UP, 1958. 229–46.

Dessen, Alan C. *Elizabethan Stage Conventions and Modern Interpreters*. Cambridge: Cambridge UP, 1984

Dessen, Alan C., and Leslie Thomson. *A Dictionary of Stage Directions in English Drama, 1580–1642*. Cambridge: Cambridge UP, 1999.

Devil's Advocate. Dir. Taylor Hackford. Warner Bros., 1997.

DiGangi, Mario. *The Homoerotics of Early Modern Drama*. Cambridge: Cambridge UP, 1997.

Dillon, Janette. " 'Is Not All the World Mile End, Mother?': The Blackfriar's Theater, the City of London, and *The Knight of the Burning Pestle*." *Medieval and Renaissance Drama in England: An Annual Gathering of Research, Criticism, and Reviews* 9 (1997): 127–48.

Dolan, Frances E. "Household Chastisements: Gender, Authority, and 'Domestic Violence.' " Fumerton and Hunt 204–25.

Dollimore, Jonathan. *Radical Tragedy: Religion, Ideology, and Power in the Drama of Shakespeare*. 2nd ed. New York: Harvester, 1989.

———. *Sexual Dissidence: Augustine to Wilde, Freud to Foucault*. Oxford: Clarendon-Oxford UP, 1991.

Dollimore, Jonathan, and Alan Sinfield, eds. *Political Shakespeare: New Essays in Cultural Materialism*. Ithaca: Cornell UP, 1985.

Doran, Madeline. *Endeavors of Art: A Study of Form in Elizabethan Drama*. Madison: U of Wisconsin P, 1954.

Douglas, Mary. *Purity and Danger: An Analysis of Concepts of Pollution and Taboo*. Harmondsworth: Penguin, 1970.

Dovey, Zillah. *An Elizabethan Progress*. Herndon, Eng.: Sutton, 1996.

Drew-Bear, Annette. "Face-Painting in Renaissance Tragedy." *Renaissance Drama* ns 12 (1981): 71–93.

Duffy, Eamon. *The Stripping of the Altars: Traditional Religion in England, c. 1400-c. 1580*. New Haven: Yale UP, 1992.

Dyer, Richard. *White*. New York: Routledge, 1997.

Eccles, Audrey. *Obstetrics and Gynaecology in Tudor and Stuart England*. Kent: Kent State UP, 1982.

Edward II. Dir. Derek Jarman. Sales Co., 1991.

Elbow, Peter. "Teaching Thinking by Teaching Writing." *Change* 15 (1983): 37–40.

———. *Writing without Teachers*. 2nd ed. New York: Oxford UP, 1998.

Eliot, Alexander. "Games Children Play." *Sports Illustrated* 11 Jan. 1971: 46–56.

Eliot, T. S. *Elizabethan Dramatists*. London: Faber, 1963.

"Elizabethan Homilies." *Renaissance Electronic Texts*. Ed. Ian Lancashire. 1997. U of Toronto. 15 Feb. 1999 <http://library.utoronto.ca/www/utel/ret/ret.html>.

Emig, Janet. "Writing as a Mode of Learning." *College Composition and Communication* 28 (1977): 122–28.

Emmerson, Richard K., ed. *Approaches to Teaching Medieval English Drama*. New York: MLA, 1990.

The English Faust Book. Trans. P. F. Gent. London: 1592.

Enterline, Lynn. " 'Hairy on the In-side': *The Duchess of Malfi* and the Body of Lycanthropy." *Yale Journal of Criticism* 7.2 (1994): 85–129.

Evans, Christopher. Rev. of *Edward II*, dir. Derek Jarman. *Spectator* 19 Oct. 1991: 48–49.

Everyman. Gassner 207–30.

Ferguson, Margaret W., Maureen Quilligan, and Nancy J. Vickers, eds. *Rewriting the Renaissance: The Discourses of Sexual Difference in Early Modern Europe*. Women in Culture and Society. Chicago: U of Chicago P, 1986.

Flanigan, C. Clifford. "Teaching the Medieval Latin 'Drama': Reflections Historical and Theoretical." Emmerson 50–56.

Flower, Linda, and John R. Hayes. "A Cognitive Process Theory of Writing." *College Composition and Communication* 32 (1981): 365–87.

Foakes, R. A. *Illustrations of the English Stage, 1580–1642*. London: Scolar, 1985.

Foister, Susan, Robin Gibson, and Jacob Simson. *The National Portrait Gallery Collection*. London: Natl. Portrait Gallery, 1988.

Ford, Boris, ed. *The Age of Shakespeare*. Rev. ed. Harmondsworth: Penguin, 1982. Vol. 2 of *The New Pelican Guide to English Literature*.

Ford, John. *The Lover's Melancholy*. Ed. R. F. Hill. The Revels Plays. Manchester: Manchester UP, 1985.

———. *Perkin Warbeck*. Ed. Donald K. Anderson, Jr. Regents Renaissance Drama. Lincoln: U of Nebraska P, 1965.

———. *Three Plays*. Ed. Keith Sturgess. Harmondsworth: Penguin, 1970.

Foucault, Michel. "What Is an Author?" *The Foucault Reader*. Ed. Paul Rabinow. New York: Pantheon, 1984. 101–20.

Fraser, Russell A., and Norman Rabkin, eds. *Drama of the English Renaissance*. 2 vols. New York: Macmillan, 1976.

Freytag, Gustav. *Die Technik des Dramas*. Darmstadt: Wissenschaftliche Buchgesellschaft, 1969.

Fumerton, Patricia, and Simon Hunt. *Renaissance Culture and the Everyday*. Philadelphia: U of Pennsylvania P, 1999.

Garber, Marjorie. "Shakespeare as Fetish." *Shakespeare Quarterly* 41 (1990): 242–50.

Gassner, John. *Medieval and Tudor Drama*. New York: Applause, 1987.

Gassner, John, and William Green, eds. *Elizabethan Drama: Eight Plays*. New ed. New York: Applause, 1990.

Gent, Lucy, and Nigel Llewellyn. *Renaissance Bodies: The Human Figure in English Culture, c. 1540–1660*. London: Reaktion, 1990.

Gibbons, Brian. *Jacobean City Comedy*. 2nd ed. London: Methuen, 1980.

Gilbert, Miriam. "Teaching Shakespeare through Performance." *Shakespeare Quarterly* 35 (1984): 601–08.

Goldberg, Jonathan. "Making Sense." *New Literary History* 21 (1990): 457–62.

————, ed. *Queering the Renaissance*. Durham: Duke UP, 1994.

————. *Sodometries: Renaissance Texts, Modern Sexualities*. Stanford: Stanford UP, 1992.

Goodison, Jack Weatherburn. *Catalogue of Cambridge Portraits: The University Collection*. Cambridge: Cambridge UP, 1955.

Gosson, Stephen. *Plays Confuted in Five Actions*. New York: Garland, 1972.

Gouge, William. *Of Domesticall Duties, Eight Treatises* [. . .]. London, 1622.

Gramsci, Antonio. *An Antonio Gramsci Reader*. Ed. David Forgacs. New York: Schocken, 1988.

Graves, R. B. *Lighting the Shakespearean Stage, 1567–1642*. Carbondale: Southern Illinois UP, 1999.

The Great Train Robbery. Dir. Edwin S. Porter. T. A. Edison, 1903.

Greenblatt, Stephen. *Renaissance Self-Fashioning: From More to Shakespeare*. Chicago: U of Chicago P, 1980.

————. *Shakespearean Negotiations: The Circulation of Social Energy in Renaissance England*. Berkeley: U of California P, 1988.

Gunther, R. T. *Early Science in Oxford*. Oxford: Oxford UP, 1921.

Gurr, Andrew. *Playgoing in Shakespeare's London*. Cambridge: Cambridge UP, 1987.

————. *The Shakespearean Stage, 1574–1642*. 3rd ed. Cambridge: Cambridge UP, 1992.

Gurr, Andrew, and John Orrell. *Rebuilding Shakespeare's Globe*. New York: Routledge, 1989.

Gutierrez, Nancy. "The Irresolution of Melodrama: The Meaning of Adultery in *A Woman Killed with Kindness*." *Exemplaria* 1 (1989): 265–91.

Guy, John. *Tudor England*. Oxford: Oxford UP, 1988.

"Haec Vir." Henderson and McManus 277–89.

Hale, John R. *The Art of War and Renaissance England*. Washington: Folger Shakespeare Lib., 1961.

Hall, Kim F. *Things of Darkness: Economies of Race and Gender in Early Modern England*. Ithaca: Cornell UP, 1995.

Halperin, David M. "Is There a History of Sexuality?" *The Lesbian and Gay Studies Reader*. Ed. Henry Abelove, Michele Aina Barale, and Halperin. New York: Routledge, 1993. 416–31.

Halpern, Richard. *Shakespeare among the Moderns*. Ithaca: Cornell UP, 1997.

Hartley, L. P. *The Go-Between*. Harmondsworth: Penguin, 1961.

Hartnoll, Phyllis. *The Theatre: A Concise History*. Rev. ed. New York: Thames, 1985.

Hartt, Frederick. *History of Italian Renaissance Art: Painting, Sculpture, Architecture*. Englewood Cliffs: Prentice, 1987.

Harvey, P. D. A. *Maps of Tudor England*. London: British Lib., 1993.

Hattaway, Michael. *Elizabethan Popular Theatre: Plays in Performance*. Theatre Production Studies. London: Routledge, 1982.

Hawkes, Lory. *A Guide to the World Wide Web*. Upper Saddle River: Prentice, 1999.

Haynes, Jonathan. *The Social Relations of Jonson's Theater*. Cambridge: Cambridge UP, 1992.

Headlam, Cecil. *The Inns of Court, Painted by Gordone Home, Described by Cecil Headlam*. London: Black, 1909.

Helgerson, Richard. *Forms of Nationhood: The Elizabethan Writing of England*. Chicago: U of Chicago P, 1992.

Hellinga, Robert R. "Elizabethan Dramatic Conventions and Elizabethan Reality." *Renaissance Drama* ns 12 (1981): 27–49.

Henderson, Katherine Usher, and Barbara F. McManus, eds. *Half Humankind: Contexts and Texts of the Controversy about Women in England, 1540–1640*. Urbana: U of Illinois P, 1985.

Henslowe, Philip. *Henslowe's Diary*. Ed. R. A. Foakes and C. T. Rickert. Cambridge: Cambridge UP, 1961.

———. *The Henslowe Papers*. Ed. R. A. Foakes. 2 vols. London: Scolar, 1977.

Hewitt, Bernard, ed. *The Renaissance Stage: Documents of Serlio, Sabbattini, and Furttenbach*. Trans. Allardyce Nicoll, John H. McDowell, and George R. Kernodle. Coral Gables: U of Miami P, 1958.

Heywood, Thomas. *Gunaikeion; or, Nine Books of Various History Concerning Women*. London, 1624.

———. *A Woman Killed with Kindness*. Ed. Brian Scobie. New Mermaids. London: Black, 1985.

———. *A Woman Killed with Kindness*. Ed. R. W. Van Fossen. The Revels Plays. London: Methuen, 1961.

Hic Mulier. Henderson and McManus 264–76.

Hindman, Sandra. "Pieter Brueghel's *Children's Games*, Folly, and Chance." *Art Bulletin* 63 (1981): 447–75.

Hirschfeld, Heather A., and A. Leigh DeNeef. "Collaborative Pedagogy: An Experiment in Team-Teaching Shakespeare." *Renaissance Papers 1997*. Ed. T. H. Howard-Hill and Philip Rollinson. New York: Camden, 1997. 75–85.

Hoby, Margaret. *Diary of Lady Margaret Hoby, 1599–1605*. Ed. Dorothy M. Meads. London: Routledge, 1930.

Hoffman, Ann. *Lives of the Tudor Age, 1485–1603*. London: Osprey, 1977.

Holbein, Hans. *The Dance of Death*. London: Phaidon, 1947.

Holderness, Graham, ed. *The Shakespeare Myth*. Manchester: Manchester UP, 1988.

Holinshed, Raphael. *Chronicles of England, Scotland, and Ireland*. Excerpt. *Arden of Faversham* 148–59.

Holles, John. *Letters of John Holles, 1587–1637*. Ed. P. R. Seddon. 3 vols. Nottingham: Derry, 1975.

Hope, Annette. *Londoner's Larder: English Cuisine from Chaucer to Present*. Edinburgh: Mainstream, 1990.

Horger, J. "Derek Jarman's Film Adaptation of Marlowe's *Edward II*." *Shakespeare Bulletin: A Journal of Performance, Criticism, and Scholarship* 11.4 (1993): 37–40.

Howard, Jean E. "Power and Eros." *The Stage and Social Struggle in Early Modern England*. London: Routledge, 1994. 93–128.

————. "Women as Spectators, Spectacles, and Paying Customers." Kastan and Stallybrass 68–74.

Howard-Hill, Trevor. "The Author as Scribe or Reviser? Middleton's Intentions in *A Game at Chess*." *Text: Transactions of the Society for Textual Scholarship* 3 (1987): 305–18.

Hoy, Cyrus. "Critical and Aesthetic Problems of Collaboration in Renaissance Drama." *Research Opportunities in Renaissance Drama* 19 (1976): 3–6.

Hunt, Maurice. "Webster and Jacobean Medicine: The Case of *The Duchess of Malfi*." *Essays in Literature* 16 (1989): 33–49.

Hunter, G. K. "Five-Act Structure in *Doctor Faustus*." *Tulane Drama Review* 8.4 (1964): 77–91.

Hutton, Ronald. *The Rise and Fall of Merry England: The Ritual Year, 1400–1700.* Oxford: Oxford UP, 1994.

Hyde, Patricia. *Thomas Arden in Faversham: The Man behind the Myth.* Faversham: Faversham Historical Soc., 1996.

Ingpen, Elizabeth, and A. N. Court. *Oxford in Colour.* Norwich, Eng.: Jarrold, 1981.

Ingram, Martin. *Church Courts, Sex and Marriage in England, 1570–1640.* Cambridge: Cambridge UP, 1987.

The Internet Shakespeare Editions. Ed. Michael Best. 1996. U of Victoria. 6 June 2001 <http://web.UVic.CA/shakespeare/index.html>.

Jardine, Lisa. *Still Harping on Daughters: Women and Drama in the Age of Shakespeare.* 2nd ed. New York: Columbia UP, 1989.

Jarman, Derek. *Queer Edward II.* London: British Film Inst., 1991.

Joel, Billy. "Only the Good Die Young." *Streetlife Serenader.* Sony, 1974.

Jonson, Ben. *The Alchemist.* Brooke and Paradise 573–623.

————. *The Alchemist.* Ed. J. B. Steane. London: Cambridge UP, 1967.

————. *Bartholomew Fair.* Ed. Eugene M. Waith. New Haven: Yale UP, 1963.

————. *Epicoene. Ben Jonson's Plays and Masques: Texts of the Plays and Masques, Jonson on his Work, Contemporary Readers on Jonson, Criticism.* Ed. Robert M. Adams. New York: Norton, 1979. 98–175.

————. *Epicoene, or The Silent Woman. Ben Jonson: Four Comedies.* Ed. Helen Ostovich. London: Longman, 1997.

————. *Pleasure Reconciled to Virtue.* Lindley 117–25.

————. *Timber; or, Discoveries. Ben Jonson.* Vol. 8. Ed. C. H. Herford, Percy Simpson, and Evelyn Simpson. Oxford: Clarendon, 1947. 561–649.

————. *Volpone.* Ed. R. B. Parker and David Bevington. The Revels Student Editions. Manchester: Manchester UP, 1999.

Josselin, Ralph. *The Diary of Ralph Josselin, 1616–1683.* Ed. Alan Macfarlane. London: Oxford UP, 1976.

Kareda, Urjo. Rev. of *The Duchess of Malfi*, by John Webster. *Toronto Daily Star* 9 June 1971: 78.

Kastan, David Scott. "Is There a Class in This (Shakespearean) Text?" *Renaissance Drama* ns 24 (1993): 101–21.

Kastan, David Scott, and Peter Stallybrass, eds. *Staging the Renaissance: Reinterpretations of Elizabethan and Jacobean Drama.* New York: Routledge, 1991.

Kaufman, Ralph James. *Elizabethan Drama: Modern Essays in Criticism.* New York: Oxford UP, 1961.

Katz, Jonathan Ned. *The Invention of Heterosexuality.* New York: Dutton, 1995.

Kay, W. David. "*Bartholomew Fair*: Ben Jonson in Praise of Folly." *English Literary Renaissance* 6 (1976): 299–316.

Kemp, Peter. *The Campaign of the Spanish Armada.* Oxford: Phaidon, 1988.

Kemp, William. *Kemps Nine Daies Wonder.* Ed. Alexander Dyce. New York: AMS, 1968.

Keyishian, Harry. "Checklist of Medieval and Renaissance Plays (Excluding Shakespeare) on Film, Tape, and Recording." *Research Opportunities in Renaissance Drama* 17 (1974): 45–58.

Kinney, Arthur F., ed. *Renaissance Drama: An Anthology of Plays and Entertainments.* Oxford: Blackwell, 1999.

Klein, Joan Larsen, ed. *Daughters, Wives, and Widows: Writings by Men about Women and Marriage in England, 1500–1640.* Urbana: U of Illinois P, 1992.

Knapp, Peggy A. "Gawain and the Middle Ages: Teaching History, Teaching Genre." *Approaches to Teaching* Sir Gawain and the Green Knight. Ed. Miriam Youngerman Miller and Jane Chance. New York: MLA, 1986. 138–43.

Knights, L. C. *Drama and Society in the Age of Jonson.* London: Chatto, 1937.

Kussmaul, Ann. *Servants in Husbandry in Early Modern England.* Cambridge: Cambridge UP, 1981.

Kyd, Thomas. *The Spanish Tragedy.* Brooke and Paradise 98–135.

———. *The Spanish Tragedy.* Ed. Philip Edwards. London: Methuen UP, 1959.

———. *The Spanish Tragedy.* Ed. J. R. Mulryne. New Mermaids. New York: Norton, 1990.

Laroque, François. *Shakespeare's Festive World: Elizabethan Seasonal Entertainment and the Professional Stage.* Trans. Janet Lloyd. Cambridge: Cambridge UP, 1991.

The Last Boy Scout. Dir. Tony Scott. Warner Bros., 1991.

Leedham-Green, Elisabeth. *A Concise History of the University of Cambridge.* Cambridge: Cambridge UP, 1996.

Leggatt, Alexander. *Ben Jonson: His Vision and His Art.* London: Methuen, 1981.

———. *Citizen Comedy in the Age of Shakespeare.* Toronto: U of Toronto P, 1973.

———. *English Drama: Shakespeare to the Restoration, 1590–1660.* London: Longman, 1988.

Leinwand, Theodore B. *Theatre, Finance and Society in Early Modern England.* Cambridge: Cambridge UP, 1999.

Levenson, Jill. "Comedy." Braunmuller and Hattaway 263–300.

Levin, Richard. *The Multiple Plot in English Renaissance Drama.* Chicago: U of Chicago P, 1971.

———. "Unthinkable Thoughts in the New Historicizing of English Renaissance Drama." *New Literary History* 21 (1990): 433–47.

Lewis, Cynthia. "Heywood's *Gunaikeion* and Woman-kind in *A Woman Killed with Kindness.*" *English Language Notes* 32.1 (1994): 24–37.

Limon, Jerzy. *The Masque of Stuart Culture.* Newark: U of Delaware P, 1990.

Lindley, David, ed. *Court Masques: Jacobean and Caroline Entertainments, 1605–1640.* Oxford: Oxford UP, 1995.

Linthicum, Marie Channing. *Costume in the Drama of Shakespeare and His Contemporaries.* Oxford: Clarendon, 1936.

Literary Resources on the Net. Ed. Jack Lynch. 1998. Rutgers U. 6 June 2001 <http://andromeda.rutgers.edu/jlynch/Lit/>.

Macfarlane, Alan. *Marriage and Love in England: Modes of Reproduction, 1300–1840.* Oxford: Blackwell, 1986.

Maclean, Ian. *The Renaissance Notion of Women: A Study in the Fortunes of Scholasticism and Medical Science in European Intellectual Life.* Cambridge: Cambridge UP, 1980.

Manley, Lawrence. "From Matron to Monster: Tudor-Stuart London and the Languages of Urban Description." *The Historical Renaissance: New Essays on Tudor and Stuart Literature and Culture.* Ed. Heather Dubrow and Richard Strier. Chicago: U of Chicago P, 1988. 347–74.

Marcus, Leah S. *Unediting the Renaissance: Shakespeare, Marlowe, Milton.* London: Routledge, 1996.

Marini, Paola, Paolo Rigoli, and Aldo Dell'Igna. *Cucine, cibi, e vini nell'eta di Andrea Palladio.* Vicenza: Neri Pozza, 1981.

Marlowe, Christopher. Doctor Faustus A- *and B- texts (1604, 1616): Christopher Marlowe and His Collaborator and Revisers.* Ed. David Bevington and Eric Rasmussen. The Revels Plays. Manchester: Manchester UP, 1993.

———. *The Tragedie of Doctor Faustus (B text). The Tragicall History of D. Faustus (A text).* Ed. Hilary Binda. Sept. 1999. *Perseus Project.* Ed. Gregory Crane. Tufts U. 22 Aug. 2002. <http://www.perseus.tufts/edu/Texts/faustus.html>.

———. *Doctor Faustus.* Ed. Roma Gill. New Mermaids. 2nd ed. London: Black, 1989. Excerpted in *Norton Anthology of English Literature.* 6th ed. 1: 768–800.

———. *Edward II.* Ed. W. Moelwyn Merchant. New Mermaids. New York: Norton, 1987.

———. *The Jew of Malta.* Ed. N. W. Bawcutt. Manchester: Manchester UP, 1978.

———. *The Tragical History of Doctor Faustus.* Ed. Frederick S. Boas. Vol. 5 of *The Works and Life of Christopher Marlowe.* Ed. R. H. Case. London: Methuen, 1932.

Marston, John. *The Dutch Courtesan.* Ed. M. L. Wine. Regents Renaissance Drama. Lincoln: U of Nebraska P, 1965.

Martin, Randall, ed. *Women Writers in Renaissance England.* London: Longman, 1997.

Massinger, Philip. *A New Way to Pay Old Debts.* Fraser and Rabkin 2: 681–713.

———. *A New Way to Pay Old Debts.* Ed. T. W. Craik. New Mermaids. New York: Norton, 1993.

Masten, Jeffrey. *Textual Intercourse: Collaboration, Authorship, and Sexualities in Renaissance Drama*. Cambridge: Cambridge UP, 1997.

Maus, Katharine Eisaman. "Facts of the Matter: Satiric and Ideal Economies in the Jonsonian Imagination." *Ben Jonson's 1616 Folio*. Ed. Jennifer Brady and W. H. Herendeen. Newark: U of Delaware P, 1991. 64–89.

McCullough, Christopher J. "The Cambridge Connection: Towards a Materialist Theatrical Practice." Holderness 112–21.

McDonald, Russ. *The Bedford Companion to Shakespeare: An Introduction with Documents*. New York: St. Martin's, 1996.

McGann, Jerome J. "The Rationale of Hypertext." *Electronic Text: Investigations in Method and Theory*. Ed. Kathryn Sutherland. Oxford: Clarendon, 1997. 19–46.

McLuskie, Kathleen E. *Dekker and Heywood: Professional Dramatists*. New York: St. Martin's, 1994.

———. *Renaissance Dramatists*. Atlantic Highlands: Humanities Internatl., 1989.

McQueen, William A., ed. *A Selection of Emblems, from Herman Hugo:* Pia Desideria; *Francis Quarles:* Emblemes; *Edmund Arwaler:* Pia Desideria. Los Angeles: William Andrews Clark Memorial Lib., 1972.

Melville, Herman. *Moby Dick, or, The Whale*. 1851. New York: Modern Lib., 1992.

Mendelson, Sara, and Patricia Crawford. *Women in Early Modern England, 1550–1720*. Oxford: Clarendon, 1998.

Merian, Matthaus. *1300 Real and Fanciful Animals from Seventeenth-Century Engravings*. Toronto: Dover, 1998.

Middleton, Thomas. *A Game at Chess*. Ed. Trevor Howard-Hill. The Revels Plays. Manchester: Manchester UP, 1993.

———. *Michaelmas Term*. A Mad World, My Masters *and Other Plays*. Ed. Michael Taylor. Oxford: Oxford UP, 1995.

———. *The Roaring Girl*. Ed. Paul A. Mulholland. The Revels Plays. Manchester: Manchester UP, 1987.

Middleton, Thomas, and Thomas Dekker. *The Roaring Girl*. *The Longman Anthology of British Literature*. Vol 1. Ed. David Damrosch. New York: Longman, 1999. 1358–424.

Middleton, Thomas, and William Rowley. *The Changeling*. Ed. George Walton Williams. Regents Renaissance Drama. Lincoln: U of Nebraska P, 1966.

Mildmay, Lady Grace. *Autobiography*. *Women Writers in Renaissance England*. Ed. Randall Martin. London: Longman, 1997. 208–27.

Milton, John. *Comus*. 1634. *The Riverside Milton*. Ed. Roy Flannagan. Boston: Houghton, 1998. 109–71.

Morgan, Genevieve, and Tom Morgan. *The Devil: A Visual Guide to the Demonic, Evil, Scurrilous, and Bad*. San Francisco: Chronicle, 1996.

Morse, H. K. *Elizabethan Pageantry: A Pictorial Survey of Costume and Its Commentators from c. 1560–1620*. New York: Blom, 1934.

Mountfield, David. *Everyday Life in Elizabethan England*. Geneva: Minerva, 1978.

Mr. William Shakespeare and the Internet. Ed. Terry Gray. 1995. Palomar Coll. 6 June 2001 <http://shakespeare.palomar.edu/>.

Mullaney, Steven. *The Place of the Stage: License, Play, and Power in Renaissance England*. Chicago: U of Chicago P, 1988.

Munday, Anthony, et al. *Sir Thomas More: A Play*. Ed. Vittorio Gabrieli and Giorgio Melchiori. The Revels Plays. Manchester: Manchester UP, 1990.

Nash, Johnny. "I Can See Clearly Now." *I Can See Clearly Now*. Columbia, 1972.

Newman, Karen. *Fashioning Femininity and English Renaissance Drama*. Chicago: U of Chicago P, 1991.

The Norton Anthology of English Literature. Ed. M. H. Abrams et al. 2 vols. 4th ed. New York: Norton, 1979. 6th ed. New York: Norton, 1993.

Nungezer, Edwin. *A Dictionary of Actors and Other Persons Associated with the Public Representation of Plays in England before 1642*. New Haven: Yale UP, 1929.

O'Brien, Peggy, et al., eds. *Shakespeare Set Free: Teaching* Hamlet, Henry IV, Part One. New York: Washington Square, 1994.

———. *Shakespeare Set Free: Teaching* Romeo and Juliet, Macbeth, A Midsummer Night's Dream. New York: Washington Square, 1993.

———. *Shakespeare Set Free: Teaching* Twelfth Night, Othello. New York: Washington Square, 1995.

On-line Books Page. Ed. John Mark Ockerbloom. 1993. U of Pennsylvania. 1 May 2001 <http://onlinebooks.library.upenn.edu/>.

Orgel, Stephen. *Impersonations: The Performance of Gender in Shakespeare's England*. Cambridge: Cambridge UP, 1996.

———. *The Jonsonian Masque*. 1965. New York: Columbia UP, 1981.

Orgel, Stephen, and Roy Strong, eds. *Inigo Jones: The Theatre of the Stuart Court, Including the Complete Designs for Productions at Court, for the Most Part in the Collection of the Duke of Devonshire, Together with Their Texts and Historical Documentation*. 2 vols. London: Sotheby Parke Bennet; Berkeley: U of California P, 1973.

Orlin, Lena Cowen. *Elizabethan Households: An Anthology*. Washington: Folger Shakespeare Lib., 1995.

———. "Three Ways to Be Invisible in the Renaissance: Sex, Reputation, and Stichery." Fumerton and Hunt 183–203.

Orme, Nicholas. *Education and Society in Medieval and Renaissance England*. London: Hambledon, 1989.

Osborne, June. *Entertaining Elizabeth I: The Progresses and Great Houses of Her Time*. London: Bishopsgate, 1989.

Palmer, Alan, and Veronica Palmer. *Who's Who in Shakespeare's England*. Brighton: Harvester, 1981.

Panek, Jennifer. "Punishing Adultery in *A Woman Killed with Kindness*." *Studies in English Literature* 34 (1994): 357–78.

Parker, Patricia. *Shakespeare from the Margins: Language, Culture, Context*. Chicago: U of Chicago P, 1996.

Parry, Graham. "The Politics of the Jacobean Masque." *Theatre and Government under the Early Stuarts*. Ed. J. R. Mulryne and Margaret Shewring. Cambridge: Cambridge UP, 1993. 87–117.

Paster, Gail Kern. *The Body Embarrassed: Drama and the Disciplines of Shame in Early Modern England*. Ithaca: Cornell UP, 1993.

Patterson, Annabel. *Censorship and Interpretation: The Conditions of Writing and Reading in Early Modern England*. Madison: U of Wisconsin P, 1984.

Pechter, Edward. "The New Historicism and Its Discontents: Politicizing Renaissance Drama." *PMLA* 102 (1987): 292–303.

Perry, Maria. *The Word of a Prince: A Life of Elizabeth I from Contemporary Documents*. Woodbridge, Eng.: Boydell, 1990.

Peterson, Joyce E. *Curs'd Example: The Duchess of Malfi and Commonweal Tragedy*. Columbia: U of Missouri P, 1978.

Platter, Thomas. *Thomas Platter's Travels in England 1599*. Trans. Clare Williams. London: Cape, 1937.

Pomeroy, Elizabeth W. *Reading the Portraits of Queen Elizabeth I*. Hamden: Archon, 1989.

Prest, John. *The Illustrated History of Oxford University*. Oxford: Oxford UP, 1993.

Price, David C. *Patrons and Musicians of the English Renaissance*. Cambridge: Cambridge UP, 1981.

Prockter, Adrian, and Robert Taylor, comp. *The A to Z of Elizabethan London*. Publication 122. London: London Topographical Soc., 1979.

Pulp Fiction. Dir. Quentin Tarantino. Miramax, 1994.

The Puritan. Disputed Plays of William Shakespeare. Ed. William Kozlenko. New York: Hawthorn, 1974. 224–61.

Quinn, David B., and A. N. Ryan. *England's Sea Empire, 1550–1642*. London: Allen, 1983.

"Race." *The Oxford English Dictionary*. 2nd ed. 1989.

Rackin, Phyllis. *The Stages of History: Shakespeare's English Chronicles*. Ithaca: Cornell UP, 1990.

Records of Early English Drama. Ed. Abigail Ann Young. 1998. Victoria U, U of Toronto. 1 May 2001 <http://www.chass.utoronto.ca/~reed/reed.html>.

Repo Man. Dir. Alex Cox. Universal, 1983.

Reservoir Dogs. Dir. Quentin Tarantino. Miramax, 1992.

The Revels *History of Drama in English*. Vol. 3: 1576–1613. Ed. J. Leeds Barroll et al. London: Methuen, 1976. Vol. 4: 1613–1660. Ed. Philip Edwards et al. London: Methuen, 1981.

Ribner, Irving. *The English History Play in the Age of Shakespeare*. Rev. ed. London: Methuen, 1965.

Richard III. Dir. Laurence Olivier. London Films Voyager Co., 1955.

Riggio, Milla Cozart, ed. *Teaching Shakespeare through Performance*. New York: MLA, 1999.

Roberts, Josephine A. "Editing the Women Writers of Early Modern England." *Shakespeare Studies* 24 (1996): 63–70.

Robertson, D. W., Jr. "The Intellectual, Artistic, and Historical Context." *Approaches to Teaching Chaucer's* Canterbury Tales. Ed. Joseph Gibaldi. New York: MLA, 1980. 129–35.

Rose, Mary Beth. *The Expense of Spirit: Love and Sexuality in English Renaissance Drama*. Ithaca: Cornell UP, 1988.

————, ed. *Women in the Middle Ages and the Renaissance: Literary and Historical Perspectives*. Syracuse: Syracuse UP, 1986.

Rosen, Barbara. *Witchcraft in England, 1558–1618*. Amherst: U of Massachusetts P, 1991.

Ross, James Bruce, and Mary Martin McLaughlin, eds. *The Portable Renaissance Reader*. Rev. ed. New York: Penguin, 1968.

Rothwell, Kenneth Sprague, and Annabelle Henkin Melzer. *Shakespeare on Screen: An International Filmography and Videography*. New York: Neal-Schuman, 1990.

Rowley, William, Thomas Dekker, John Ford, et al. *The Witch of Edmonton*. Corbin and Sedge 143–209.

Rowse, A. L. *The Illustrated History of Britain*. New York: Crescent, 1979.

Rutter, Carol Chillington. *Documents of the Rose Playhouse*. Manchester: Manchester UP, 1984.

Sadie, Stanley, ed. *The New Grove Dictionary of Musical Instruments*. 3 vols. New York: Grove, 1984.

Salgado, Gamini, ed. *Eyewitnesses of Shakespeare: First Hand Accounts of Performances, 1590–1890*. London: Sussex UP, 1975.

Salingar, Leo, Gerald Harrison, and Bruce Cochrane. "Les comédiens et leur public en Angleterre de 1520 à 1640." *Dramaturgie et société: Rapports entre l'oeuvre théâtrale, son interprétation et son public aux XVIe et XVIIe siècles. Nancy, 14–21 avril 1967*. 2 vols. Paris: CNRS, 1967. 525–76.

Sargeaunt, Joan Margaret. *John Ford*. New York: Russell, 1966.

Sawday, Jonathan. *The Body Emblazoned: Dissection and the Human Body in Renaissance Culture*. London: Routledge, 1995.

Schilder, Gunter, Bernard Aikema, and Oeter van der Krogt, eds. *The Atlas Blaeu-Van Der Hem of the Austrian National Library*. 8 vols. Goy-Houten, Neth.: H&S, 1996.

Schoenbaum, Samuel. *Shakespeare: The Globe and the World*. New York: Oxford UP, 1979.

Seaver, Paul S. "Thomas Dekker's *The Shoemaker's Holiday*: The Artisanal World." Smith, Strier, and Bevington 87–100.

The Second Maiden's Tragedy. Ed. Anne Lancashire. The Revels Plays. Manchester: Manchester UP, 1978.

The Second Shepherd's Play. Gassner 102–27.

Sedgwick, Eve Kosofsky. *Epistemology of the Closet*. Berkeley: U of California P, 1990.

Serlio, Sebastiano. *The Five Books of Architecture: An Unabridged Reprint of the English Edition of 1616*. New York: Dover, 1982.

Sex, Lies, and Videotape. Dir. Steven Soderbergh. CLM, 1989.

Shakespeare, William. *All's Well That Ends Well*. Ed. G. K. Hunter. Arden Edition. London: Methuen, 1967.

————. *The Merchant of Venice*. Ed. John Russell Brown. Arden Edition. Surrey: Nelson, 1997.

————. *The Riverside Shakespeare*. Ed. G. Blakemore Evans et al. 2nd ed. Boston: Houghton, 1997.

Shakespeare in Love. Dir. John Madden. Miramax/Universal, 1998.

Shand, G. B. "Classroom as Theatre: A Technique for Shakespeare Teachers." *English Quarterly* 8 (1975): 13–19.

————. "Reading Power: Classroom Acting as Close Reading." Riggio 244–55.

Shapiro, James. *Shakespeare and the Jews*. New York: Columbia UP, 1996.

Sinfield, Alan. "Royal Shakespeare." Dollimore and Sinfield 158–81.

Sleep, Derrick. "*A Woman Killed with Kindness*: Crystal, Brass and Class." *Argosy Weekly* 9 Feb. 1989: 13+.

Slights, William W. E. "*Oberon, the Faery Prince: A Masque of Prince Henries*, 1611." *Shakespeare Bulletin* 12.1 (1994): 46.

Smith, Bruce R. *Homosexual Desire in Shakespeare's England: A Cultural Poetics*. Chicago: U of Chicago P, 1991.

Smith, David L., Richard Strier, and David Bevington, eds. *The Theatrical City: Culture, Theatre, and Politics in London, 1576–1649*. Cambridge: Cambridge UP, 1995.

Smith, Logan Pearsall. *Life and Letters of Henry Wotton*. 2 vols. Oxford: Oxford UP, 1907.

Snow, Edward A. *Inside Bruegel: The Play of Images in* Children's Games. New York: North Point, 1997.

Spawn. Dir. Mark. A. Z. Dippe. New Line Cinema, 1997.

Speed, John. *The Counties of Britain: A Tudor Atlas*. London: Pavilion, 1988.

Speed 2: Cruise Control. Dir. Jan de Bont. Twentieth Century Fox, 1997.

Stallybrass, Peter. "Patriarchal Territories: The Body Enclosed." Ferguson, Quilligan, and Vickers 123–42.

Steinberg, Glenn A. " 'You Know the Plot / We Both Agreed On?' Plot, Self-Consciousness, and the London Merchant in Beaumont's *The Knight of the Burning Pestle*." *Medieval and Renaissance Drama in England* 5 (1991): 211–24.

Stone, Lawrence. *The Family, Sex, and Marriage in England: 1500–1800*. Abr. ed. New York: Harper, 1979.

Stone, Lilly C. *English Sports and Recreations*. Washington: Folger Shakespeare Lib., 1960.

Stow, John. "The History of a Most Horrible Murder Committed at Faversham in Kent." Kinney 719–24.

————. *A Survey of London*. Ed. Henry Morley. London: Sutton, 1994.

Straznicky, Marta. "The End(s) of Discord in *The Shoemaker's Holiday*." *Studies in English Literature, 1500–1900* 36 (1996): 257–372.

Strong, Roy C. *The Cult of Elizabeth: Elizabethan Portraiture and Pageantry*. London: Thames, 1977.

Stubbes, Phillip. *The Anatomy of Abuses*. Amsterdam: Theatrum, 1972.

———. *A Crystal Glass for Christian Women*. London, 1591. Rpt. in Aughterson 237–44.

———. *Phillip Stubbes' Anatomy of the Abuses in England in Shakspere's Youth, A.D. 1583*. Ed. Frederick J. Furnivall. London, 1877–82.

Taylor, John. *Jack a Lent, His Beginning and Entertainment* [. . .]. London, 1620.

Tennenhouse, Leonard. *Power on Display: The Politics of Shakespeare's Genres*. New York: Methuen, 1986.

Thompson, Ann. "*King Lear* and the Politics of Teaching Shakespeare." *Shakespeare Quarterly* 41 (1990): 139–46.

Thomson, Peter. *Shakespeare's Theatre*. London: Routledge, 1992.

Titanic. Dir. James Cameron. Twentieth Century Fox, 1997.

To Die For. Dir. Gus Van Sant. Columbia, 1995.

Todd, Margo. *Christian Humanism and the Puritan Social Order*. Cambridge: Cambridge UP, 1987.

Tourneur, Cyril. *The Revenger's Tragedy*. Ed. R. A. Foakes. Manchester: Manchester UP, 1996.

Townsend, Geo Fyler, trans. *Aesop's Fables*. Chicago, 1882.

Traub, Valerie. "The (In)Signficance of 'Lesbian' Desire in Early Modern England." Goldberg, *Queering* 62–83.

Twycross, Meg. "The Theatricality of Medieval English Plays." *The Cambridge Companion to Medieval English Theatre*. Ed. Richard Beadle. Cambridge: Cambridge UP, 1994. 37–84.

Underdown, David. *Revel, Riot and Rebellion: Popular Politics and Culture in England, 1603–1660*. Oxford: Oxford UP, 1985.

Vandereycken, Walter, and Ron Van Deth. *From Fasting Saints to Anorexic Girls: The History of Self-Starvation*. New York: New York UP, 1994.

———. "Miraculous Maids? Self-Starvation and Fasting Girls." *History Today* 43 (1993): 37–42.

Varty, Kenneth. *Reynard the Fox: A Study of the Fox in Medieval English Art*. Leicester: Leicester UP, 1967.

Vecellio, Cesare. *Vecellio's Renaissance Costume Book: All 500 Woodcut Illustrations from the Famous Sixteenth-Century Compendium of World Costume*. New York: Dover, 1977.

Vinycomb, John. *Fictitious and Symbolic Creatures in Art, with Special Reference to Their Use in British Heraldry*. London: Chapman, 1951.

Warren, Michael J. "*Doctor Faustus*: The Old Man and the Text." *English Literary Renaissance* 11 (1981): 111–47.

Webster, John. *The Devil's Law-Case*. Ed. Frances A. Shirley. Regents Renaissance Drama. Lincoln: U of Nebraska P, 1972.

———. *The Duchess of Malfi*. Ed. Elizabeth M. Brennan. New Mermaids. 3rd ed. London: Black, 1993.

———. *The Duchess of Malfi*. Brooke and Paradise 645–86.

————. *The Duchess of Malfi*. Ed. Fred B. Millet. Crofts Classics. Arlington Heights: AHM, 1953.

————. *The White Devil*. Ed. John Russell Brown. Cambridge: Harvard UP, 1960.

————. *The White Devil*. Ed. Christina Luckyj. New Mermaids. 2nd ed. London: Black, 1996.

Wells, Susan. "Jacobean City Comedy and the Ideology of the City." *English Literary History* 48 (1981): 37–60.

Whately, William. *A Care-Cloth; or a Treatise of the Cumbers and Troubles of Marriage* [. . .]. London, 1624.

Williams, Neville. *Reform and Revolt*. New York: Newsweek, 1974.

Wilson, C. Anne. *Food and Drink in Britain from the Stone Age to Recent Times*. Harmondsworth: Penguin, 1973.

Wine, Martin L. *Drama of the English Renaissance*. New York: Modern Lib., 1969.

Winton, John. *Sir Walter Ralegh*. London: Joseph, 1975.

Woolf, Virginia. *A Room of One's Own*. London: Harper, 1994.

Worthen, W. B. *Shakespeare and the Authority of Performance*. Cambridge: Cambridge UP, 1997.

Wrightson, Keith. *English Society, 1580–1680*. London: Hutchinson, 1982.

Yarwood, Doreen. *The Architecture of England, from Prehistoric Times to the Present Day*. London: Batsford, 1963.

INDEX OF PLAYWRIGHTS

INDEX OF DRAMAS

INDEX OF NAMES

Modern Language Association of America

Approaches to Teaching World Literature

Joseph Gibaldi, series editor

Gilman's "The Yellow Wall-Paper" and Herland. Ed. Denise D. Knight and
    Cynthia J. Davis
Goethe's Faust. Ed. Douglas J. McMillan. 1987.
Hebrew Bible as Literature in Translation. Ed. Barry N. Olshen and
    Yael S. Feldman. 1989.
Homer's Iliad *and* Odyssey. Ed. Kostas Myrsiades. 1987.
Ibsen's A Doll House. Ed. Yvonne Shafer. 1985.
Works of Samuel Johnson. Ed. David R. Anderson and Gwin J. Kolb. 1993.
Joyce's Ulysses. Ed. Kathleen McCormick and Erwin R. Steinberg. 1993.
Kafka's Short Fiction. Ed. Richard T. Gray. 1995.
Keats's Poetry. Ed. Walter H. Evert and Jack W. Rhodes. 1991.
Kingston's The Woman Warrior. Ed. Shirley Geok-lin Lim. 1991.
Lafayette's The Princess of Clèves. Ed. Faith E. Beasley and Katharine Ann
    Jensen. 1998.
Works of D. H. Lawrence. Ed. M. Elizabeth Sargent and Garry Watson. 2001.
Lessing's The Golden Notebook. Ed. Carey Kaplan and Ellen Cronan Rose. 1989.
Mann's Death in Venice *and Other Short Fiction.* Ed. Jeffrey B. Berlin. 1992.
Medieval English Drama. Ed. Richard K. Emmerson. 1990.
Melville's Moby-Dick. Ed. Martin Bickman. 1985.
Metaphysical Poets. Ed. Sidney Gottlieb. 1990.
Miller's Death of a Salesman. Ed. Matthew C. Roudané. 1995.
Milton's Paradise Lost. Ed. Galbraith M. Crump. 1986.
Molière's Tartuffe *and Other Plays.* Ed. James F. Gaines and
    Michael S. Koppisch. 1995.
Momaday's The Way to Rainy Mountain. Ed. Kenneth M. Roemer. 1988.
Montaigne's Essays. Ed. Patrick Henry. 1994.
Novels of Toni Morrison. Ed. Nellie Y. McKay and Kathryn Earle. 1997.
Murasaki Shikibu's The Tale of Genji. Ed. Edward Kamens. 1993.
Pope's Poetry. Ed. Wallace Jackson and R. Paul Yoder. 1993.
Shakespeare's Hamlet. Ed. Bernice W. Kliman. 2001.
Shakespeare's King Lear. Ed. Robert H. Ray. 1986.
Shakespeare's Romeo and Juliet. Ed. Maurice Hunt. 2000.
Shakespeare's The Tempest *and Other Late Romances.* Ed. Maurice Hunt. 1992.
Shelley's Frankenstein. Ed. Stephen C. Behrendt. 1990.
Shelley's Poetry. Ed. Spencer Hall. 1990.
Sir Gawain and the Green Knight. Ed. Miriam Youngerman Miller and
    Jane Chance. 1986.
Spenser's Faerie Queene. Ed. David Lee Miller and Alexander Dunlop. 1994.
Stendhal's The Red and the Black. Ed. Dean de la Motte and Stirling Haig. 1999.
Sterne's Tristram Shandy. Ed. Melvyn New. 1989.
Stowe's Uncle Tom's Cabin. Ed. Elizabeth Ammons and Susan Belasco. 2000.
Swift's Gulliver's Travels. Ed. Edward J. Rielly. 1988.
Thoreau's Walden *and Other Works.* Ed. Richard J. Schneider. 1996.

Vergil's Aeneid. Ed. William S. Anderson and Lorina N. Quartarone. 2002.
Voltaire's Candide. Ed. Renée Waldinger. 1987.
Whitman's Leaves of Grass. Ed. Donald D. Kummings. 1990.
Woolf's To the Lighthouse. Ed. Beth Rigel Daugherty and Mary Beth Pringle. 2001.
Wordsworth's Poetry. Ed. Spencer Hall, with Jonathan Ramsey. 1986.
Wright's Native Son. Ed. James A. Miller. 1997.